Daughter of Fire

Daughter of Fire
A Portrait of Iceland

by Katharine Scherman

Little, Brown and Company
Boston – Toronto

FIRST EDITION

T 03/76

THE PHOTOGRAPHS ARE BY THE AUTHOR AND HER HUSBAND.

Library of Congress Cataloging in Publication Data

Scherman, Katharine.
  Daughter of fire.

  Includes index.
  1. Iceland. I. Title.
DL305.S26   949.1'2   75-30731
ISBN 0-316-77325-5

The author is grateful to the following publishers for permission to quote from previously copyrighted materials:

THE AMERICAN-SCANDINAVIAN FOUNDATION, for *The Skalds*, translated by Lee M. Hollander, Princeton University Press, 1945. Copyright 1945, © 1973 by The American-Scandinavian Foundation.

THE UNIVERSITY OF NEBRASKA PRESS, for *Eyrbyggja Saga*, translated by Paul Schach and Lee M. Hollander. Copyright © 1959 by the University of Nebraska Press.

PENGUIN BOOKS LTD., for *Njal's Saga*, translated by Magnus Magnusson and Hermann Pálsson. Copyright © 1965 by Magnus Magnusson and Hermann Pálsson.

UNIVERSITY OF MANITOBA PRESS, for *Landnamabok (The Book of Settlements)*, translated with Introduction and Notes by Hermann Pálsson and Paul Edwards. Copyright © 1972 by University of Manitoba Press. Volume I in the University of Manitoba Icelandic Studies, General Editors—Haraldur Bessason and Robert J. Glendinning.

Published simultaneously in Canada
by Little, Brown & Company (Canada) Limited

PRINTED IN THE UNITED STATES OF AMERICA

Contents

List of Illustrations and Maps

Preface

ICELAND HAS A homogeneity that few modern countries possess. Not only does it seem that everyone in the nation knows almost everyone else, but the Icelanders' present is clearly connected with a living past. As they speak of their history one has the sense that they are personally remembering: things that happened to ancestors many hundreds of years ago are related with immediacy, as if they had happened yesterday to relatives in the next county.

When one travels in the country the sense of the blending of past and present becomes even stronger. It is not that monuments of history are strewn over the countryside; on the contrary, most of Iceland is as grandly lonesome today as it was when the first Norsemen found it, fresh to humans, its only occupants a handful of Irish monks living in frugal tranquillity on the harsh shores. But the look of the country is young and clean and ever-changing. Its very loneliness is evocative. It invites things to happen. Uncomplicated as the landscape is by the clutter of modern civilization, it is easy to see the drama of history rolling across it. The things that occurred then could easily occur now.

The following account has arranged itself around the compelling blend of past and present. After each encounter with history I have turned to look at the locale of the events, to see what things look like now. As Iceland is still so wild and pure, the glance of the present day inevitably falls on its natural history as well as its historical connotations. Flora and fauna are much in evidence everywhere: the flora the small bright enduring growth of the far north, the fauna the multitudes of birds that find the ocean-secluded country as attractive as did its human settlers, and for much the same reasons.

Iceland began with a volcano. The forces under the earth's crust have determined all her history, human and natural, and for good or ill they will continue to rule her future. So my story starts and ends with Iceland's most inescapable fact of life. Our earth, after all, is our Norn. There is no escaping her.

Daughter of Fire

ONE

In the Beginning . . .

IN THE HALF-LIGHT of the November morning the ocean is dark gray and white, roughened by the wind that nearly always blows over the North Atlantic. Puffins beat directly across its wave tops, never touching the whitecaps. Fulmars soar out of the swells, bank and swoop without moving a wing down into the valleys. Gray shading to white, they look like sea waves that have taken flight.

Below the surface a multitude of capelins swirl, mouths open, consuming quantities of the transparent floating animals that live in the ocean's fertile upper layer. A school of cod comes up, following the early morning light, and the capelins surface in a nearly solid mass that flickers as if light were playing on silk. While the cod range through the glimmering flood, devouring from below, the puffins gather at the surface to pluck the little fish out of the water and depart shoreward, half a dozen heads and tails sticking out of each triangular red-orange beak.

All at once there is a sound, a muffled rumble that reverberates and increases, pulsing through the water, seeming to come from everywhere at once. A warm sluice courses up from the bottom and the familiar currents turn on themselves, roiled with eddies and strange-smelling bubbles. Alarm sets all the animals fleeing and within a few minutes the ocean is deserted. No fish breaks the surface, no bird flies. The wind has dropped and there is silence. But the water is not still. Smooth-sided waves surge high and slide

3

into their own valleys. The reflection of the lightening sky is like circles of oil. One wave subsides into a whirlpool as the water is sucked downward, leaving a sudden hole. A great black bubble fills the hole, wells outward and bursts in a towering fountain of ash. The long battle between earth and water is under way.

It began far under the bottom of the ocean, at the roots of a mountain, part of a vast undersea range lying along a split in the earth's crust. Magma — liquid rock — seamed through with hot gases slowly revolved under the mountain, expanding with its own heat and motion but kept down by the combined weight of the mountain and three thousand feet of water above it. At last the pressure could be withstood no longer, the ocean floor tilted, the mountain swelled and water flowed violently in contrary directions. Held under the earth too long, the liquid rock and overheated gases burst forth in an excessive surge, cooling instantly and exploding into tephra — ash, pumice and lava bombs.

One after another black bubbles break in the same place, and a steady column of steam and ash rises into the air, interspersed with lumps of molten rock. The clear morning light is darkened as sulphur fumes roll over a brown-green sea that no longer reflects. A circle of bubbles forms around the first column, smoke from them billowing into one mammoth cloud tower lightened by flashes of fire. The only sound is the hissing of the water as the hot stones fall back in. Around the tower, waves heave in giant eddies but do not break. Fingers of cloud made of black ash stretch over the sea, more and more as the day passes until they join in a ceiling of darkness. Late afternoon passes imperceptibly into night, and there is a new sound — the breaking of waves. At the base of the smoke pillar the head of a steep wave curls over into surf. Another follows it in the same place, its top breaking high. Through the night the waves break, one after the other, always in the same place.

It is not quite light. A breaking wave falls back and in its trough a rounded body is visible for an instant before a second wave covers it. The third wave does not cover it. The body swells, black and long and fat above the surf, like a slow live animal. Along its outcurving side the sea breaks sharply. Within the body's

4

arc smoke and fire erupt with fresh violence. Where yesterday there was only ocean, this morning there is an island.

It has a tenuous hold on existence. Its hills are of pumice, its beaches of ash. As long as the explosive eruption produces only tephra the ocean dissipates the young island as it is forming. But it keeps coming out of the sea. In the first four months it changes shape several times as new explosive vents open and the waves break over their rims, washing away the tentative land. It is a fierce conflict. The silence of the island's birth has given way to the sounds of explosions as red-hot boulders crash into the sea, of thunder as the smoke columns are hit by lightning from the clouds above, of the roaring of waves beaten into storms by heat-generated whirlwinds. At night the sky is dull pink and the eruption is a pillar of fire. The vents, low above the ocean, pulse with seeming life as glowing stones roll from their red throats, to blast with fire and steam as they sink back into the sea. In the daytime dense white and black smoke billows far over the ocean and a mile high in the air. A veil of woolly vapor hangs continuously just above the surface.

The material spewed out with such force would make an island many times the size of this one. But it is dust. If the eruptions ceased even for a short time the little island would die. A sister, to be stillborn a month after it, would never breach the ocean's surface, and another a year and a half later would be entirely blown into the sea within five months. But new life comes to this one from under the ocean floor. With repeated eruptions the pressure has lessened and the material from within the earth can cool at a slower rate. The magma, instead of exploding into ash and pumice, rises in a deliberate thick stream of lava. Up through the volcanic throat comes the hot flow, and spreads into a red lake in the crater. It overflows the edge and pours massively down the side, to offer new resistance to the ocean. At first there is only one stream. When it reaches the shore it spreads into spidery rivulets and hardens, its stone net holding the powder of the beach against the attack of the waves. The eruption gains force and fountains of liquid rock fly high in the air, showering brightly into the sea or crashing on the shore. Inside the hot lake viscid waves break heavily. The lava boils up to the rim and spills over. The new rivers roll against the waves and harden as they roll, with clouds of steam and the sound of gunfire. Soon there is a barrier of red and yellow and green rock all around the island, protecting its soft cliffs and ashy beaches. Ocean water, trapped behind the rock barrier, turns brackish with rain and becomes a calm lagoon. The volcanic throat grows into a cone, lava congealing on its sides in an ever broader, higher collar, until at last it is tall enough so that the waves can no longer breach its rim.

After five months of war between earth and water, earth has won. It is the spring of the year, and now it is life's turn.

The first to look into the possibilities of the new land were gulls. The island was only two weeks old when the black-backs started to alight on the warm sand. Each paroxysm of eruption drove them off and they wheeled, crying, through the smoke, watching the tephra whirl out of the crater and waiting for the dust to settle. Sometimes they dove downward, several birds at a time, as a stone fell into the ocean from the smoke column. There was a flurry of wings at the surface as the gulls nearly collided in the sudden flash of steam. For a few seconds they quarreled sharply, then they separated to hunt for the food that had unaccountably vanished in the water. As the weeks passed the gulls were not discouraged. Where there was so much motion there was bound to be something alive, and they were always there, hunting and keening through the hot dust.

The droppings of the gulls included undigested seeds. In the beginning the seeds were washed out to sea or blown away with the weightless sands, but the coming of the lava brought stability to the island. Not many of the seeds were fertile. Of those that were few were able to find nourishment on the barren ground. Out of the hundreds that fell only a handful found life. As rain and sun followed one another in the slow northern spring, thread-like roots spread through the fine sand and leaf buds appeared, swelling pale green against the black ground. They were *Cakile edentula*, sea rocket, tenacious weeds undaunted by wind and sand and salt. They sent long taproots down through the sand to find whatever moisture was held below the dry surface. Rubbery stems, fleshy and water-retaining, lay flexibly along the beach, impervious to wind, and narrow-toothed leaves offered little surface to rasping sand or burning sun. Salt water held no dangers for these tough plants, which originally found their way from North America by ocean currents. But well-equipped as they were to colonize the sea-drenched, windswept new island, the sea rockets could not compete with the volcano. Poisonous smoke and ash from the vents wounded their leaves, and long before the time of their purple flowering all the little plants were dead.

Mosses were slower to come but more successful. Spores light as the dust of the volcano floated on the wind over the island and into the vent itself. Several kinds found the still-warm rocks habitable, *Bryum argentium*, silvery moss, *Funaria hygrometrica*, *Rhacomitrium lanuginosum* and *R. canescens*, all of them rock-loving mosses common over the northern world. As long as lava was pouring out they could not survive, but as soon as it cooled the spores, each of which was both male and female, began to develop. As the sea rockets thrived on sand, the mosses were best adapted to the firm porous rock of the cone. Once the lava had stopped erupting they came to life on the rim, even inside the crater. The rock was warm and moist from the steam that still came from the vent, ideal for moss. Fine hairs on the undersides of the plants sought crevices to cling to and began extracting minerals and chemicals. The leafy shoots were grayish or dull yellow-green, and fine-branched. Less than a quarter of an inch higher than their rock base, they resembled outgrowths of lava, and the crater began to take on a fuzzy look. Four years after the liquid rock had come up out of the depths of the earth it was already being reduced to soil by these hardy settlers.

When lava brought stability to the island, other birds besides gulls found it a temporary refuge. Lying far out in a lonely ocean, it was a haven for small birds flying north over the water. That first spring saw redwings, phalaropes, ringed plovers, dunlins and snow buntings alight briefly to rest on their way to northern nesting grounds. They could not stay long for there was nothing to eat. But the lagoon offered water, and summer latecomers found a new, small source of food — flies. A few midges blown out to sea from a not-far-distant mainland had survived the journey and blown against the high rocks. Some of these in turn survived. They

7

Langjökull

Faxafloi

Hvalfjord

Reflavik

★Reykjavik

REYKJANES PENINSULA

†Thingvellir

Geysir

River

BURFELL

Hveragerdi

Selfoss

Thjorsa

RANGAR

HEKLA VELLIR

Oddi †

□†Keldur

Hlidarendi
†□

Markarfljot River

Myr

K

Bergthorshvoll□

Atlantic Ocean

Heimaey

Surtsey

Westmann Islands

Dyrh

V

SBank 1975

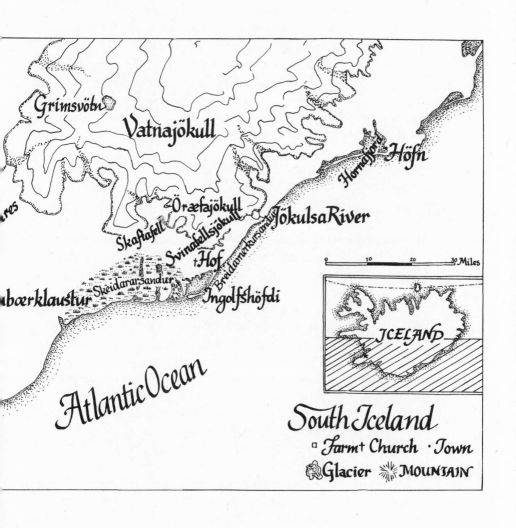

Grimsvötn

Vatnajökull

...res

Öræfajökull

Skaftafell

Svínafellsjökull

†Hof

Breidamerkursandur

Jökulsa River

Hornafjord

·Höfn

Skeidararsandur

...bærklaustur

Ingolfshöfdi

Atlantic Ocean

0   10   20   30 Miles

ICELAND

South Iceland

▫ Farm † Church · Town

🏠 Glacier ☀ MOUNTAIN

found the bleak island a source of life. The lagoon water and the fine black sand of the beach warmed in the long days of June when the sun hardly set, providing water and heat, all they needed to live their short lives and reproduce. Where three or four midges had blown to the edge of the lagoon one windy night, the next damp warm day found eighty to one hundred hatched and swarming over the calm water.

It took a long time for the water around the island to get back to normal. During the tephra explosions the ocean for hundreds of feet around was colored and thickened by volcanic debris. Sulphur from the open fissures below poisoned it and steam heated it. When the lava began flowing, the water was further disturbed and its temperature rose. Fish stayed away, as did the birds whose diet was fish, with the exception of the gulls — daring, greedy and ever hopeful. It was well into summer before the ocean settled and cooled to a healthy climate for ocean creatures. The first marine life on the island were diatoms, single-celled plants enclosed in sculptured glassy shells. These light plants float all over the oceans and form the main part of the phytoplankton, pasture of the sea, on which all marine animal life finally subsists. As soon as the rock had hardened and cooled, the diatoms settled between the tide lines in a glowing golden-brown film that represented millions of plants.

The lava offered a riddled surface good for holdfasts, and larger plants soon joined the diatoms: *Ectocarpus confervoides*, a yellow-brown seaweed with lacy, twisted filaments a few inches high, and *Porphyra umbilicalis*, purple laver, a round, ruffled leaf. Below the tide line grew a kelp, *Alaria esculenta*, dabberlocks, with a single long frond and a holdfast like a hawk's talon to secure it in the backwash of waves on offshore rocks. *Desmarrestia viridis*, sea sorrel, another brown seaweed, grew alongside it, its fronds finely divided to the texture of coarse hair (it is also known as "landlady's wig") so the tug of currents would not tear it.

With the coming of the seaweeds the ocean's cycle of life started around the island. The smallest animals ate diatoms. These were euphausids, two-inch-long bright red translucent crustaceans, luminescent at night, with numerous legs, some for swimming, some for walking, some for jumping. They lived near the surface of the water, barely below tide line, where their food dwelt, and

8

ocean waves sometimes brought masses of them up on the rocks and beaches. Gulls found them first, later shore birds came to feast on the moving tomato-colored tide. For the oyster catchers they were a particular delicacy. The big shore birds plodded on long three-toed feet over the beach, darting their heavy red beaks through the leaping flood. The euphausids that escaped, hopping back into the sea on the next wave, were no better off, for herrings and capelins found them. The small fish, hunting in schools in shallow water just offshore, were in turn hunted, as cod came up from their preferred deeper waters to ravage among the silver hordes. Once in a while a shark sliced through the water, interrupting the entire chain from diatom to cod.

Though gulls had been the first to come and shore birds the first to find food, the first to nest were birds of the open ocean. As the fish returned, so did the fulmars, flying low over the waves, banking, turning, rising, diving, with hardly a motion of long dark wings. Their nests were on mainland cliffs, and they scoured the ocean for many miles around to feed their large feeble chicks. The waters around the new island were a fruitful source. All through the long days the fulmars quartered the waves, soaring back and forth around the lava cliffs. Black guillemots winged straight across wind and wave, unmindful of either, to land in the shallow water between offshore rocks. There they floated, looking for fish. When they dove they swam underwater, using their wings, red legs trailing behind. Coming up with a beakful of capelins, they rose from the water with extreme difficulty, running along its surface and beating their short water-adapted wings against the waves until they were airborne. Though they lacked the felicity of the fulmars in the air they also were cliff-dwellers, nesting in rock crevices. The new island's plentitude of fish, its craggy lava cliffs, above all its remoteness, away from the predatory populations of the mainland, made it a friendly shore for the fulmar and the black guillemot, nine-tenths of whose lives were spent far from land, roaming the sea or resting on the waves. Many of them landed on the still-warm rocks, exploring ledges and crevices, although it would be years before the island was stable enough for nesting. While lava still seeped out of the crater and gases escaped from new vents in the side of the cone there was no safety

9

for chicks, helpless on a rock ledge. But the birds kept coming back, fishing in the rich waters and roosting on the cliffs, until one summer, seven years after the island's birth, came the birth of its first warm-blooded inhabitants, two black guillemots and one fulmar.

By this time the 1.08 square miles of ash and rock had become a genuine island, with the varied scenery of a countryside that had existed far longer than seven years. Quickly come, it was evidently here to stay. Some plants had taken root long enough to flower. Moss softened the raw rock of the crater, barnacles encrusted the rocks at the edge of the sea and flies multiplied freely on the warm, damp sand. A few butterflies, blown from the mainland, fed on the flowering plants, cross-fertilizing them, so the newest plant growth was island-native. Rain had eroded the lava cliffs, and the pieces that broke off were smoothed by wave action into cobbles that looked hundreds of years old. The sand cliffs above the beaches were wind-shaped and water-carved into high curving escarpments. The beaches themselves, of fine black volcanic ash, lined the shore in wide sloping arcs. The volcanic cone, from repeated flows of lava, was a rounded dome, and inside the crater, where the molten lake had heaved and splashed, the coils of still warm lava were deep red and yellow.

The island had taken its place in the world. The Icelanders, of its mother island, named it Surtsey for the Norse precursor of the gods, Surtur, the Fire Giant, invisible, unintelligible being who was at the same time First Cause and World Destroyer. "Surtur rides first," it is written in *Ragnarök, World Doom*, "and both before and behind him flames burning fire. His sword outshines the sun itself."[1]

The birth of Surtsey was in 1963, but it could as well have occurred fifty million years earlier. In the Eocene epoch, when the world was already old and the first primates crept through the trees of an African jungle, fissures opened under the sea in the same earth cleft that was to spawn Surtsey. Floods of liquid basalt burst forth in a series of titanic eruptions that brought a subcontinent out of the ocean, the Thulean Province. It encompassed

[1] *The Prose Edda* of Snorri Sturleson

more than 620,000 square miles from the 60th to the 67th parallels
and from the west coast of Greenland to Scotland, including what
are today southern Greenland, northern Ireland, the Hebrides, the
Faeroes and Iceland. After the great lava floods came to an end
the Thulean Province, weathered and eroded, slowly sank back into
the sea, becoming the North Atlantic basin as cold water from the
Arctic inundated its drowned mountains.

A few elevated islands were left, among them a scattering of
basalt hills that outlined modern Iceland. Between these hills was a
shallow underwater trough that, in the beginning of the Pleistocene epoch about three million years ago, began to rise once more
in a surge of new volcanic upheavals. At the same time the polar
ice cap started to expand, its ice sheets advancing to cover the
northern hemisphere, and Iceland's latest mountains were born
under many thousand feet of glacier.[2] About 12,000 years ago
the ice began to recede and the island of Iceland at last emerged, a
40,000-square-mile expanse of crumpled, sharply angled land
deeply scarred by the forces that formed it, ice and fire, wind and
water and sand.

Iceland lies within the latitudes 63'40" and 66'30" in the middle of the North Atlantic on an intensely volcanic submarine
mountain range, the Mid-Atlantic Ridge, part of a 47,000-mile belt
of ocean mountains that meanders all around the globe. Most of
the peaks of the 13,200-mile Atlantic range, though higher than
the Alps, lie many fathoms underwater. The fluid rock that underlies this line of violence has surfaced in only three other places:
Tristan da Cunha, 37'15" south, Ascension, 7'57" south, and the
Azores, 38'30" north. The mountain chain winds from Arctic to
Antarctic, following the contours of the European, African and
American continents, and it marks the line where once they joined.
The force that brought it into existence is the same that two hundred million years ago began the separation of the continents and
the creation of the Atlantic Ocean. The earth's rigid crust, resting
on a hot, plastic and ever-moving mantle, is cracked into at least
six major plates and four or more smaller ones. With the motion of

[2] It is thought that increase in volcanic activity all over the world, with
the consequent pollution of the air and dimming of the sun, may have in
great part caused the climate to cool and the ice sheets to form.

11

the soft rock beneath them these plates move, in some places colliding, in others moving apart, and they carry the continents with them. The Mid-Atlantic Ridge is the line of divergence of two sets of plates, the Eurasian and African, from those of the Americas. The welling up of hot rock all along the crack has been forcing the plates apart over the millennia, separating the land into four continents and creating an ever-wider basin, the Atlantic, into which the earth's surface water could flow.

The focus of this motion is a "plume," of which there are probably twenty around the earth, each about sixty miles in diameter. Through these hot spots, vents whose origins lie deep within the earth, wellings of plastic rock, heated by radioactivity, rise from the mantle up to the crust. The liquid rock spreads immediately under the crust, forcing the plates asunder. As the plates are dragged apart, all along the boundary of separation molten material rises from beneath, in a series of volcanoes, to fill the gap, and the earth's crust is broadened along that line. The Mid-Atlantic Ridge is such a boundary and its action, perennially volcanic, continues to spread the floor of the Atlantic Ocean.

But the surface of the earth is not growing any larger. The plates that meet in the Atlantic — Eurasian, African and American — ever being forced apart at the Mid-Atlantic Ridge, are crumpling up against other plates on the far sides of their continents and being thrust underneath them. All along the west coasts of the Americas, for instance, the turbulent impact of Atlantic and Pacific plates produces fierce seismic disturbances as the edges of the eastern plates are forced by those of the west to dip back into the earth's interior. California's San Andreas Fault is a notorious result of the collision of these two plates.

The plume on which the northern sector of the Mid-Atlantic Ridge depends is in the middle of Iceland. There, through a vast well whose source is over a thousand miles deep in the earth's mantle, seeps upward continuously the slow liquid rock that is widening the ocean floor and changing the shapes of the continents. This crucial hot spot is centered on a volcano, Kverkfjöll, The Throat, at the northern end of the ice sheet Vatnajökull, a remnant of the Pleistocene ice. It is a collection of ice-shrouded peaks and craters deformed by glacial action, surrounded by a freakish complex of hot springs, seething mud pots and simmering lakes, with steam shooting through holes in old ice and cauldrons of boiling water under a frozen cover.

From this theatrical display of fire and ice radiate the forces that keep Iceland in a continuing cycle of creation and destruction. The present volcanic belt runs diagonally through the island from northeast to southwest, and contains 150 live volcanoes, more than any other place in the world of comparable size. Not only is Iceland the most volcanic place on earth, it too, like the floor of the Atlantic Ocean, is spreading. Every year the island grows four-tenths of an inch wider, and in some places its rifting is dramatically visible.

Though its roots are a thousand miles below the ocean floor, Iceland appears a child of the North Atlantic. From its low coast-lines, raggedly indented by fjords, ranges of crooked hills climb away to the savage central heights, a region of old ice and young mountains untamed by time and weather. From a distance its gnarled outlines could be unruly waves under a sky of storm clouds. Winds and rains of open ocean scour its peaks and the snow of the chill Atlantic winter, swept from its rocky summits, lies deep in its cols and valleys. Its weather is oceanic. The prevailing south-westerlies bring moist warm air which, hitting the hills and cliffs that rise immediately behind the coastal flats, precipitate into rain, while on the rare days when the north wind blows the air is clearer and the sun brighter than they can ever be on a mainland. Winter brings thunderstorms and gales but seldom Arctic temperatures. Though Iceland is on a level with such chilly landmarks as Frobisher Bay and Mount McKinley, much of it is embraced by a branch of the North Atlantic drift, a continuation of the Gulf Stream called the Irminger Current. This warm stream is deflected westward because of submarine heights between Iceland and Scotland, and flows clockwise, washing the south and west coasts. In the north, because of its higher salinity, the Irminger Current is submerged under the East Greenland Polar Current, and along the north and east coasts the breath of tropical climate gives way to frigid air off the Arctic water. In the south and west the winter temperatures rarely fall below freezing, while summer weather is like our April, capricious and teasing. In a sudden gusty rainstorm smelling of the sea the temperature will drop to forty, to rise again into the sixties or higher as the wind blows the clouds away in a flurry of rainbows and the sun burns with extra clarity through air fresh as the world's first springtime. You can almost watch the flowers open. The north and east coasts, though colder, are subject to the same ocean weather that envelops Iceland as if the island were a ship at sea. Only in the central highlands does the near-Arctic latitude show itself. There the flora is Arctic and alpine and the birds are the ground nesters of the tundra. But nowhere on the island is the climate steadfast from year to year. The clash of polar and temperate air gives rise to occasional devastating freakishness. One year snowstorms lasting into the middle of June will destroy the crops; the next year the grass will stay green all winter and flowers bloom in January.

Young and changeable, subject to the winds and waves above and the eternal ferment below, Iceland has all the freshness of her latest island.

TWO

Surtur's Children

SEVENTEEN MILES SOUTH of the mainland, Surtsey is the last of a group of islands, the Westmanns, at the southern end of Iceland's active volcanic belt. Though easily accessible by boat and small plane, this newest land on earth has been declared a sanctuary, to remain relatively unsullied. Scientists have here a singular opportunity to study existence in its very beginnings, to see what comes first, what is destroyed, what survives; to chart the entire history, animal, vegetable and mineral, of a fresh land. To avoid unnecessary contamination very few can gain permission to visit, and the alien must stay close to the island custodian. Even extra footprints are discouraged. We were among the fortunate few allowed to land.

It is a ten-minute flight to Surtsey from Heimaey, Home Island, the only one of the Westmann chain that is inhabited. Our plane is a one-engined Super Cub with three-foot propeller blades and a top speed of ninety-five miles per hour. Nothing larger can land on the island. Only one of us can go at a time, seated behind the pilot in a sort of inside rumble seat. The pilot takes off with me first, at eight o'clock in the evening. In early summer it doesn't matter what time it is. The sun sets around eleven-thirty and rises around two o'clock. In the midnight hours the twilight never deepens enough to dim the earth. Sleep is when you can get it; every-

15

thing else comes first. That day the weather report for the morrow was bad, so the young pilot decided to go after supper.

The sun is low in the northwest and shines through a gold haze, harbinger of rain. We fly south over a flat gray ocean along which the tall islands of the Westmann group throw long shadows. They look like giant rocks thrown haphazardly into the sea. Except for their thatching of green grass they might have been, like their sister, born yesterday. In fact they are about 10,000 years older. There are fifteen large enough to be dignified by the appellation of island, with a scattering of single crags, and they all came out of the sea as she did.

In a few minutes Surtsey's mountain reaches toward us. We circle its torn craters and straighten out alongside a brown cliff which falls straight into the ocean. Beyond the cliff, on the island's north side, a stretch of level beach appears, narrow and only about three hundred feet long. There we descend, nearly scrape the dark sand, then rise again. Three times the pilot closes in, only to swoop upward at the last minute. He is trying to observe the sand to determine which way the wind is blowing. Though the landing area is marked with oil drums the wind sock has been blown off its pole. The fourth time the wheels set down. We roll a short distance and stop, the plane sagging to one side. The wheels have dug into the fine volcanic ash which forms the beach.

The stillness of the beginning of the world is around us. The haze has swallowed the sun. Under a white sky there are no shadows, and colors are monotoned to degrees of brown and gray. Nothing exists but water and sand and rock. No bird calls and even the ocean is quiet, as if the world were yet too new for wind. Surtsey's cone looms over the beach. On its side is a swelling of black cinders; from it a thin column of smoke rises straight in the air.

In a corner of the mountain is a strange vision: a severe A-frame wooden house. A figure leaves it and approaches us across the beach, a tall young man with shoulder-length blond hair. He is Jon Eldon, a graduate student in biology from Reykjavik, who has been assigned to watch over Surtsey for the summer. He and the pilot pull the plane out of the deep ruts it has made, the pilot climbs aboard, Jon and I give a push and the little machine is off the

Water erodes its brittle lava cliffs and wind blows its sandy hills into the ocean but Surtsey, the new volcanic island, is still growing. It has the stillness of the beginning of the world, its only sign of life the caretaker's hut.

ground in a few seconds. It circles, dips a wing in salute, then disappears into the mist toward Heimaey.

We go back to the house to await Axel. Inside it is roomy and civilized. Butane gas, a generator for electric light and radiotelephone, built-in wall bunks, a wide, open loft that can sleep fifteen, a separate laboratory and library, all is designed for comfortable living on this island that has barely finished coming out of the sea. On the vaulted ceiling are intricate designs in white rope, religious in character, executed by a predecessor of Jon who had evidently been both bored and inspired by the emptiness of the first days of Creation that surrounded him.

Jon is mostly alone on the island. On fine days he is not lonely because there is a lot to do. Every good day he walks all over the island looking for changes in its shape, either of growth or diminution; ascends the mountain to look into its two craters and note any new developments from beneath the earth; observes the plants and empties his insect traps; climbs the cliffs to check the birds' nests. He knows the birds, one from another. He knows when each egg was laid and when it will probably hatch, and he hates the familiar black-backed gull that has eaten one. He knows each young plant, worries over a drooping leaf and rejoices over a flower. As he walks along the beach, seals follow him in the ocean, curious, heads high, and he knows which is which. On rainy days, however, he finds the island tiresome; and the Westmann Islands have more rain than sun. Then there is nothing to do but keep records, a task soon finished. He is wearily alone on those long days. A companion is supposed to join him, but illness keeps the other student in Reykjavik. In mid-July fifteen scientists will come for two weeks, as they do every summer, each to make his own specialized study for the annual analysis. Jon's day-by-day recordings are essential for the scientists' reports, and loneliness, he knows, is a small price to pay.

We hear the plane and go out to meet it. The clouds have descended almost to the ocean and a captious wind blows the waves into white curls. The pilot comes running. Axel is not with him, and I am to return to Heimaey at once as a big storm is coming. The pilot should not have come back at all, but he wanted to save

21

me from spending a day or more — maybe a week — on Surtsey. I am ordered off, and go with extreme reluctance. A day or a week seems little to devote to contemplation of the creation of the world. A scant three-quarters of an hour is cruel.

After three days the north wind blows the storm away and the pilot comes back with his little plane. This bright day even the black-gray rocks of Surtsey are vivid, and every crevice of the scoriaceous lava is sharply shadowed. After the storm's confinement Jon is ready to stretch his long legs, and he strides over the island at such an eager pace that we have to run to keep up.

A brown cloud of dust hangs over the cliffs that guard the lower slopes of the cone. They look as if they are of smooth rock, deeply carved in sweeping curves. Jon kicks an overhang and it startlingly disintegrates. The entire line of cliffs is made of volcanic ash. Someday it will be rock, what remains of it. Slowly the percolation of ground water and the heat which still lies barely under Surtsey's surface is stiffening it into a clayey soil which will finally harden into a layered rock called palagonite tuff. In the meantime the weather is dangerously hollowing out its sculpture. Every day Surtsey is a little smaller. The wind is blowing its cliffs into the sea, the rain is flattening its profile and the waves are nibbling at its coastline. There were two mild earthquakes, Jon said, on the two previous nights, possibly heralding an eruption which would add new land to make up for that lost. The fight between fire and water for Surtsey's existence is still going on.

An insect trap on the beach holds a few midges. The trap consists of a vertical sheet of opaque glass underlaid by a metal basin with formaldehyde in it. Midges are the only insects which reproduce, though Jon has caught many others including butterflies. The lagoon which formed in Surtsey's early months has long since dried up, and all the little flies have is dew. Still they continue to colonize the sand, multiplying by hundreds on warm sunny days.

Near the trap is a circle of *Honkenya peploides*, seaside sandwort, the hardy succulent that has replaced Surtsey's first flowering plants, sea rockets. From its creeping rootstock, barely underground, issue thick fleshy stems that sprawl across the sand, and

22

branches lift their fat leaves, shining green, only a few inches above the ground. The whole assemblage looks limp and loose. But its flaccidity is an asset; the pliant succulent is the only land plant that has survived during Surtsey's first years. The shine of the leaves is another asset: it comes from a thin coating of wax, which repels water as well as protecting them against drying winds. Scattered over the beach are other clumps of the same plant, some with small blunt green and white blossoms. Jon kneels beside one whose leaves are browning. Wind has blown the sand so that the long thick roots are exposed, and the plant is dying. He stretches out a hand as if to cover the drying root, then withdraws it.

"We are not allowed to help them," he says.

We ascend through blowing sand to the wrinkled lava of the cone's summit. The first sight, as we come out of the dusty fog, is a round hole in the rock, about a foot in diameter. Around it are ripples of lava that look liquid and are in fact warm to the touch. A wave of heat comes from the hole, a black well whose invisible source is the throat of the still-active volcano. The crater's edge, a few yards above it, is a cracked, potholed ruin of scorched lava. Under the attacks of wind and rain the wall is coming apart, some of it sliding down the outside of the hill, the rest falling into the crater. We descend into the pit from which Surtsey arose, a torn and blackened wilderness touched with the gray moss *Rhacomitrium canescens*, rough and arid as the rock itself. It hardly looks alive. But in this place, desolate as the outer circle of Hell, the quarter-inch-high tufts, with their pointed leaves like hard little feathers, are a triumph of life.

Surtsey's mountain has a second crater, scene of a later eruption, attached to the first. The slope up to its rim is of fine ash, into which our feet sink. One of my feet sinks more than usual, above the knee in fact. When I pull it out a rush of steam comes from the dark cavity. I call to Jon that the mountain appears to be hollow, and that I've made a hole in it.

He was casual. "Sorry, I forgot to tell you about those," he said. "I'm always stepping in them."

Further evidence that Surtsey is still simmering at the roots is a convoluted cave at the edge of the crater from which issues a fog of sulphurous steam. Over the rim run smooth coils of lava quite different from the porous rock and pumice of the first crater, which are products of sudden explosive cooling. This lava, cooling more slowly, had a chance to harden as it flowed, giving it a look of sinuous aliveness. It might have stopped flowing just before we came. Within the crater is a lava lake of waves and billows still red and yellow, though the colors, intensely bright when the rock was molten, have faded with age and weathering. It is no longer soft, says Jon, but it is still hot. Nothing grows here, not even moss, not because the rock is warm but because its ropy surface, unlike the block lava of the first crater, offers no crevices for the root hairs to cling to, no tattered edges from which the plants can extract the chemicals they need for life.

The descent from the mountain is short: a stretch of fine sand down which we slide to the cliffs which surround all of Surtsey but the north end where the house and the beach are. A rock chimney leads down the west cliffs to a narrow beach of boulders rounded by the ocean and slippery with algae. It seems hardly possible that these smoothed cobbles have fallen from the ragged bluff we have just descended, and that only a few years ago they were part of a burning stream.

The only birds now nesting on Surtsey are fulmars. The black guillemots have not bred again, though a single one explores the cliffs regularly, flying close in, evidently to examine the ledges for nesting sites. Six fulmar nests are on the west side, where we walk, high in the accommodating wrinkles of the cliff. Each of these has a single egg except the one that was robbed by the black-back a few days ago. Jon wanted to kill the gull but he is not even allowed to drive it away. Climbing to each of the nests in succession, he finds that the remaining five eggs are still there. Six more pairs of fulmars have taken possession of the cliffs on the east side; he will check their nests later in the afternoon.

As we come around the corner of the west cliffs back to the level beach where we started, the north wind hits us. It is blowing harder. Our plane is waiting, a neat red and white anachronism on the primitive ash, and we take off at once. The pilot banks steeply and climbs close along the volcano's slope. Its texture is clear as an etching. He circles its craters and straightens for home.

24

From this height Surtsey appears young and fragile. The wild white waves creep up her sides, dragging at her unstable rock, while the wind whirls her new sand into clouds over the ocean. Surely the green plants cannot withstand much longer the pull of their blown sand, nor the birds the corrosion of their brittle rocks, nor Surtsey herself the surge of the North Atlantic and the intemperance of its winds. The beginning of the world seems no more than an experiment.

The other islands of the Westmann group, except for Heimaey, rise so sheer from the ocean that they have neither beaches nor harbors. They are all, like Surtsey, clearly daughters of the Fire Giant, each a smaller or larger replica of the others. They all blew out of the ocean roughly in the same shape, slab-sided and flat-topped, with minor variations due to weathering. While time has not much softened their outlines it has overlaid them with moss, grass and flowers and generously endowed them with animal life. Their angularities prohibit human habitation, and they have remained through the millennia the exclusive domain of several million cliff-dwelling seabirds. We spent a day on the ocean cruising among them in a small boat with a retired fisherman named Agust.

Agust's forty-foot lobster boat was named *Ran*. That is the name of the giant goddess, queen of the sea, a sister of Odin and Thor. Everyone who died in the ocean went to live with her in *Ran-bedr*, Ran's Bed, the bottom of the sea. There were times, this day, when it seemed that we also would end in Ran's Bed. The ocean had been alluringly calm from the heights of Heimaey the day before. Down in it waves towered over our little red boat. We lost sight of the islands in the troughs and saw them leaning outward from a vertical horizon as we slid down the pitches.

Leaving Heimaey we sailed around Heimaklettur, Home Rock, the bulky volcanic crag that guards the entrance to the harbor. Its dark red lava rose abruptly from the sea straight up to its grassy top. The rock was in some places pitted and wrinkled like rhinoceros skin, in others smoothly grooved, as if large fingers had raked down it while it was soft. On its upper reaches kittiwakes occupied the merest indentations and fulmars had taken over slightly wider crevices. Below them were the auks: murres, guillemots and razorbills on slanting ledges; and at the bottom, where the rock sloped into the sea, stood eiders. Halfway up, a pied wagtail was trying to land, fluttering against the smooth face of the cliff. It must have blown out there; it is a terrestrial bird, slim, long-tailed, unfitted for the ocean wind, a runner rather than a flier. It had a terrible time and finally it blew away, tossing helplessly. Around it the seabirds played with the wind. The air was full of spray and flying birds, and through the pounding of the surf came the voices: guttural cries of the auks, shrill mewing of the kittiwakes, homely chuckling of the fulmars.

The kittiwakes perched in pairs, breast to breast, one slightly above the other. Sometimes the lower one, the female, crouched and raised her head, beak open, in a suppliant gesture to her mate, a courting formality. A few nests had been started, untidy collections of grass and seaweed whitened by droppings, where soon the three or four greenish lavender-spotted eggs would precariously rest. Kittiwakes are gentle birds. Unlike their larger predatory cousins, the black-backed and herring gulls, they eat only small fish and plankton, which they gather near the surface of the sea. They do not even fight much with one another, probably because their nests, on nearly inaccessible smooth-sided cliffs, are isolated one from the next, and there are no rock bridges for trespassers. The eggs and chicks, however, are subject to massive depredations by their savage relatives, to such an extent that a few black-backs foraging in the neighborhood of a kittiwake colony will take as many as ten out of fifteen young or eggs from the nests. The kittiwakes overcome this hazard by nesting in places where, so far, the larger gulls have not established themselves. They are far more oceanic than most gulls, and have colonized islands in the North Atlantic out of the present range of most of the mainland-hugging herring and black-backed gulls. They rove as far north as there is land, and their colonies circle the top of the globe. But patterns change. The bigger, fiercer black-backed gull is driving the herring gull from many of its northern strongholds, and the displaced multitudes are invading islands hitherto safe for kittiwakes and terns, the far-flung colonizers.

Razorbilled auks perch on a rock near Heimaey, still and unafraid as their extinct relatives, the great auks.

27

In the Westmann Islands the big gulls have not yet taken possession and the kittiwakes, while not exactly safe, have few enemies. An occasional black-back hunts along the cliffs, but it has a wide choice, and may as easily take a young puffin exercising its wings at the entrance to its burrow, or a murre chick fallen from the overcrowded nest ledges to die on the rocks below. As we rounded Heimaklettur into open ocean a deadly predator, a flock of young parasitic jaegers, swept across the sea like sharks of the air, and where they had been the ocean was empty. These piratical birds are the terror of the cliffs. They seize their prey on the wing, swooping and grabbing, and are gone in an instant. But their population is minuscule compared to that of the nonpredatory seabirds whose numbers around the Westmanns are in the millions, and their depredations are relatively small.

Fulmars, birds of the cold seas of the far south, are relative newcomers to northern Europe and the Arctic. They were earliest known in Iceland. In 1640 the first written mention of a fulmar breeding colony made note of that in Grimsey, Hooded Island, off the north coast of Iceland, the only part of the country within the Arctic Circle. The immense fulmar colony on Heimaklettur is even newer. Before the eighteenth century there were none; in 1753 a few nests were noted; by the middle of the nineteenth century it was the commonest bird of the Westmann Islands, and for Heimaey's population it was a mainstay of life. In 1852 30,000 fledglings were taken from the nests. By 1900 the figure had risen to 56,000. No part of the bird was wasted. The meat was salted or, as a special luxury, smoked; the head, wings and guts were dried and used for fuel; the fat became both lamp oil and butter substitute; the feathers were used for clothing and bedding. By 1930 there were almost no fulmars left in the Westmann Islands. Chance saved them. In 1939 psittacosis was discovered in the colonies and the government put a total clamp on the taking of fulmars anywhere in Iceland. The birds not only survived the depredations but quickly increased, and today the population, overflowing its cliffs, is crowding out the other birds.

The increase of fulmars all over the globe, to the extent that they are probably now the most numerous birds, follows in an exact line the rise of the whaling industry. The chief fulmar food before the dominance of the seas by man was the free-floating animal life of the plankton, plus jellyfish and small shrimp which they took from the surface of the sea. They caught fish only when schools were driven up within their reach by underwater predators. Dead whales offered an easy bonanza of strong oily food, which the birds loved above all else, and the well-fed fulmars began to multiply exceedingly. When the whaling industry languished due to the inordinate greed of the whalers, trawler-fishing took its place for the fulmars, offal from the fishing boats being almost as greasily delicious to them as the insides of whales. Their eating proclivities made their flesh oily and gave rise to the name given them by the Icelanders, their first discoverers. Fulmar means foul mew (a mew is a gull), and refers partly to the disagreeable odor given off by the bodies of the birds in their crowded nesting areas, and partly to the vile-smelling fish oil they disgorge in self-defense.

Fulmars, despite their name, are not gulls. They belong in the far more primitive order of Tube-noses, birds of the open ocean made for flying and little else. Their adaptive intelligence is of the most rudimentary, their legs are set so far back that they are almost unable to walk, they are too buoyant to dive easily, nor can they swim underwater. They do not care much for hunting and catching live food, and when disturbed, rather than counterattack they simply vomit. The nostrils, enclosed in horny tubes on either side of the upper beak, are not for breathing or for smelling nor even for ejecting fish oil at an aggressor, but only for preening the feathers with oil from the stomach.

They are born to fly. Their bodies are intensively specialized. A broad short tail and a big head with no neck make a continuous cylindrical shape offering no angles to break the wind. The wings are straight and narrow, exclusively designed for fast, delicate maneuvers over rough water. Gray and white like the oceans they inhabit, fulmars were believed by sailors to be spirits of the sea. Fishermen never caught them, regarding them as reincarnations of dead seamen (the superstition did not extend to the fledglings, taken not from the sea but from the nests). Around the ledges of Heimaklettur they wheeled and soared. Starting high, one would ride the air currents, circling on still wings swiftly downward until it nearly brushed the sea. Banking its wings it turned in the trough of the wave and began to rise more slowly, using the surface wind slowed by friction with the waves. A few wingbeats and it reached a height from which it could start the downward circle again. It never touched the water, though the dark wings seemed part of the reaching waves. On the upward flights it soared close to the cliff, circling so near that it seemed the wings must graze the rock. What was it doing? Looking for a place to land, searching for food on the water? It did not seem to be on any sort of quest. Besides, trained observers say that they have rarely seen fulmars pick up food on the wing, that they nearly always alight on the water near the floating offal or surface-swimming animals that are their food. It was hard to escape the feeling that this fulmar was simply enjoying itself. Birds, like all sentient creatures, have a perception of pleasure, and what could have been more pleasurable than this glorious flight?

Man is almost the fulmar's only enemy. Even that peerless marauder, the skua, cannot drive it from its nest. Fearlessly it sits on its ledge, plumped over its one egg, and spits oil three feet out toward the approaching invader. This is an instinctive reaction. The chick will begin spitting through the pipped shell and go on spitting at its parents for a few days after hatching (greatly inhibiting its feeding). Predatory birds are smart and cautious; they know the fulmar, and its nest is safe from them unless left unguarded. Since fulmar parents take turns at the nest, an uncovered egg or a deserted chick are rare. But the instinctive brain of the fulmar is unable to cope with the subtlety of a piece of fish offal with a hand-net hovering above it. This is not stupidity but inexperience. The fulmar is without fear of man because in all the ages when it roamed the southern seas it had nothing to fear. Only when it came north and invaded human precincts did the unguessed enemy attack it, and it has not been able to adjust its primitive reasoning powers to the new complex threat.

Another persecuted family of birds is the *Alcidae*, auks. Below the fulmars and kittiwakes on Heimaklettur they perched upright, fronts shining white, heads and backs velvet black: murres, guillemots and razorbills. Where the fulmars flew in endless circles the auks beat determinedly in straight lines. Some were streaming away from the rock with rapid, exact wing strokes as if they were under marching orders. Others were returning with the same air of purpose, many carrying small fish sideways in their beaks, seven or eight at a time. Though the wingbeats were fast they were not especially strong. Auks' wings, adapted to underwater swimming, are blunt and short-feathered and not much good in the air. The birds compensate with good eyesight and an unerring sense of direction. Their feeble flying ability has kept most of them small and light of body.

Razorbills and guillemots occupied the lower parts of the cliff, below the murres, almost at water level. Here Heimaklettur was deeply pitted by wave action, and these auks occupied eroded holes and crevices where their eggs and chicks would be safe from falling into the sea or being plucked off by predators. The murres nested higher, on such narrow ledges that it was a wonder they could stand, let alone brood eggs. Yet they not only perched at these exposed levels but shuffled around on large flattened feet, stout bodies upright. Their legs were so short, and set so far back, for facility in diving and in steering underwater, that they looked as if they were traveling on their seats. The gait was supremely awkward. But they never fell off. The eggs also are designed for their precarious habitat, pointed at one end, wide and blunt at the other, and blue-green scrawled with chocolate markings. If accidentally moved (which is often, because murres nest in such dense colonies that they are always overstepping one another's territories) they roll in a circle. The shape has the further advantage of presenting a larger surface to the bare warm brood spot on the parent's breast.

About twenty-five razorbills occupied a smooth-sculpted triangular rock, a piece of Heimaklettur separated from its parent cliff by water erosion. Agust cut the motor as we approached so we could photograph them, and in the absence of sound the birds were trustingly immobile. Every detail was visible: from wide black webbed feet up the large protruding front of pure white to the black head marked with a fine line of white over the eye.

The beak, also black, had a thin vertical white stripe. It was parrot-shaped for holding large mouthfuls of fish (though its capacity is below that of the outsized beak of the puffin, which can hold thirty).

Just so, still and unafraid, sat the great auks when sailors set on them with clubs. The razorbill is a near-exact miniature replica of the great auk, the only one of the family that grew large and heavy and lost its ability to fly. It was not doomed to a natural extinction because of this abnormality, as it was surpassingly efficient in the ocean, making regular migrations of several thousand miles from South America to its breeding grounds in the North Atlantic. Its only flaw was that it represented a helpless supply of fresh meat, and even that need not have sealed its fate. It had been eaten through history and before man was even modern man. Twenty thousand years ago Neanderthal Man ate great auks, probably taking them while they were on migration and making no serious dent in the population. It remained for us in our modern ships to search out and destroy the birds systematically on the lonely, near-inaccessible rocks which were their breeding haunts.

Icelanders were not the first to depredate the great auk population, nor the worst, but they were the last. That final boatload of seamen did not consider they were doing anything out of the ordinary; they acted in the hallowed tradition of men catching themselves an easy meal from flocks whose numbers seemed never to diminish, who, no matter how many nesting places were destroyed, always turned up somewhere else. The last known flock nested on Geirfuglasker, Gare-Fowl's Rock (gare-fowl is the old name for the great auk), a reef about twenty miles southwest of the mainland. There they were raided until the colony was down to about three dozen. In 1830 earthquakes shook the area and Geirfuglasker sank beneath the sea. The great auks, who were bothered less by cataclysms of the earth than by sailors, swam to Eldey, Fire Island, a high square volcanic rock ten miles nearer the coast. They clung there for fifteen years, a few less each year. On June 4, 1844, a boatload of fourteen men approached Eldey. The waves were high and only three could land. They found two birds and an egg. One sailor smashed the egg, which he said was cracked anyway, and the other two each killed and skinned one auk. They sold the skins to a taxidermist in Reykjavik, and that was the end of the great auk.

It didn't take long. The bird had been officially classified and named in 1758. Eighty-six years later there were no more.

In a corner of Heimaklettur yawned an enormous hole at least 150 by 150 feet, entrance to Klettshellir, Cave in the Cliff. Inside, its lower walls were eroded with algae-glossed holes in which murres roosted. The ceiling lowered as we drifted toward the back, and around a curve we lost sight of the opening. In the half darkness kittiwakes fluttered around us like large moths. They were nesting back to the very end of the cave, where the sea-polished vault descended to the water; the grass of the nests hung over the edges in white fringes. No jaeger would enter here. The big birds, dextrous fliers over the empty sands and seas of their preferred territories, cannot maneuver in small spaces.

On its north side Heimaklettur had been literally torn apart by the sea. Around its base lay disordered turrets and fingers and a grotesque perching bird and the head of a giant with long hair, all streaked with the dull green of moss that only stained, did not soften the contours. The ocean, worrying away at the cliff base, had succeeded in detaching some; others were still part of the cliff. We could only tell which were separated by the plumes of spray that flew up between the dark pinnacles and the darker bulk of the main crag. Agust aimed the boat directly at a tower which appeared still to be attached. It resolved into two towers with a narrow channel between them. They leaned inward toward us and we could not see their tops. The sky was gone and so was the sun. The water in the lightless passage swung wildly, throwing spray far over our heads. Agust raced the motor as the boat was flung into the eddies, and we lurched out the other side and away from Heimaklettur.

Out of the surge and swirl of the offshore currents the water was still rough but it was predictable. The Westmann Islands were scattered around us, their furrowed cliffs and flower-strewn roofs standing high against the attacking sea like fortified gardens. Surtsey, farthest south, was swathed in its brown sand cloud. Nearest us was an islet, Smaeyar, Little Island, whose sides were all cliff. Spires of dark red rock enclosed a green meadow touched with the yellow and purple of buttercups and sea vetch. In the middle of the meadow was a small wooden house, four walls enclosing a single room. Here lived a man for about a month in the summer, Agust told us, who collected the eggs of the sea birds that nested all over the cliffs. He also took a number of young birds, mostly puffins, which were the choice of the market. There were similar houses on other islands. A rope hung from the top of the cliff, swinging in the wind. Below were sharp rocks. Only in the calmest weather could supplies be landed for him to haul up. How he himself got up there to attach the rope in the first place was not explained. It was a place for a hermit with sensibilities: the prospect of the timeless ocean, the dark and green islands, the clouds of summer, flat-bottomed cumulus and high cirrus feathers made of ice, and birds and dolphins and seals for company.

A flock of eight gleaming white gannets flew with magnificent slowness close overhead in V formation, their six-foot, black-tipped wings beating in deliberate rhythm. They were making for the next island, Hellisey, Cave Island, which is known to have belonged to gannets for three centuries. The old pairs, mated for life, always return to the same spot on the grassy roof of the steep-sided island, where they raise their one chick per pair within touching distance of their neighbors. The younger pairs, coming back from their winter far out at sea in the middle and equatorial Atlantic, get the less desirable cliff sites where they are exposed to weather and jaegers. The island was enveloped in a cloud of flying gannets, and one could just see the crowded straw-yellow heads of the brooding birds above their seaweed nests. Sometimes a bird detached itself from the throng to ascend, then to plummet straight into the sea, wings stretched back behind the body. With the impetus of its high dive the gannet can go as much as fifty feet underwater. Coming up under the school of surface-feeding fish it had sighted from above, it seized a fish and swallowed it before surfacing, thus foiling any waiting scavengers.

Agust brought the boat into a narrow rock-bound cove of Hellisey, hoping to land so that we could climb to the gannetry.

Eddies whirled around the cove and ten-foot waves swept up its vertical sides. The place we were to climb was smooth and slippery and only slightly less vertical. We were not put to this test, because landing would have splintered *Ran* within minutes. Getting out was more difficult than getting in. The boat pitched so that the screw was out of water, and we slewed around helplessly, inches from the rock. Even Agust was disturbed. One great wave tossed us outside and we said goodbye to the gannets with no regret. Their three-century tenure of Hellisey is happily almost unchallengeable.

The wild ocean forever attacking the islands has gouged out caves, and at the island of Haena, Hen (named for its shape), we sailed into one of these, named Kafhellir, Cave of Deep Water. The ocean was suddenly calm and the sound of wind-slapped waves died behind us. The hollow was dim under a low ceiling but the water was bright blue-green as if it were lit from underneath — the effect of light waves traveling underwater. Down through the sixty feet of water we could see by this light belts of algae on the rock sides, green, yellow and orange. At the far end of the cave was another source of light, a small keyhole opening at surface level, where white water bubbled in from outside. No birds nested within this cave because at high tide its entrance was a slit too low for flight.

Going back we sailed along Heimaey's east side. The rock on this coast was rawly new, looking much younger than the age-rounded hill, the little volcano Helgafell, that had spawned it. Layers of dark gray basalt alternated with bands of cindery black lava. There were red columns with black stone warts on them, and purple-brown terraces of rough square blocks. Here was the prow of a boat headed downhill into water, there the head of an elephant with extended ears and even a white eye. Offshore currents evidently coursed away from this coast, as there was little erosion, and the rocks fell seaward as sharply as they must have done when they first left the volcano. There was no black lava sand at their bases, and the merest scattering of small green plants had managed to put out roots in crevices fertilized by bird droppings.

The cliffs exploded with puffins as we came close, and the stout

36

little birds flooded out over the ocean by the thousand, the rapid whirring of their wingbeats audible. Some took off underwater, red legs dragging behind them. Most flew, barely clearing the waves. One careened off its rock perch right in *Ran*'s path, and in panic it could neither dive nor become airborne. It beat at the water with feet and wings, keeping desperately just ahead of the boat. We overtook and passed it, but as long as we could see it, it continued to flap along the surface, still too demoralized to fly or swim. It was not a young one, to be so undone by fear, but a competent adult in full breeding plumage.

Puffins are intensely sociable. They breed in large colonies, honeycombing steep grass-covered slopes with long burrows so close together that sometimes a whole hillside is undermined and at a careless step will start slipping toward the sea. Not only do they prefer to live like human apartment-house dwellers but on summer evenings both male and female will abandon their egg or young for a while to sit or waddle about on the cliffside visiting with their fellows in a clubby human fashion. They have made Heimaey their own, and are by far the most numerous birds on the island. Their burrows are not only on the tops of the oceanside cliffs but on inland slopes facing away from the sea.

Their true home, however, is not island cliffs but open ocean. Coming to shore in April, they raise each pair its one chick and desert it before it is fledged, to disappear again into the watery wilderness. The youngster stays in its hole, living on its fat, occasionally coming out at night to have a brief look at the world. Finally, hungry and thirsty, it leaves its burrow and plunges down the hill to the cliffs or the sea, helping itself with its stubs of wings. Now, in June, the adults were still incubating their eggs or feeding their young, and they could not stay long away from the burrows. As we circled offshore they began to come back, many carrying a slew of squirming fish in their beaks. Some flew up over the cliff to disappear into the burrows on its grassy top. Others landed on rock ledges. Perched upright, they were plump and perfect, like stuffed toys, white breasts gleaming, black backs glossy as velours, triangular red, yellow and blue beaks, big as their heads, seemingly glued on for comic effect.

We sailed around the puffin cliff back through the narrow harbor gate of this largest of Surtur's children. Gentled by time as she is, further softened and civilized by man, Heimaey's stark lineaments are those of her sister islands. Like them she is ever subject to the potence from under the ocean floor.

THREE

Island of the West Men

WITHIN ITS HARSH precipices, the island of Heimaey, the only one of the Westmanns that is inhabited, is a tranquil garden, often green all year round. Protected by its cliffs, warmed by the branch of the Gulf Stream that encircles it, possessing a superb harbor, the ten-square-mile island is eminently habitable. Its rolling flowered fields rise to the bare hill of Helgafell, Holy Mountain, the volcano that gave it birth 7,000 years ago. Because of the appalling renascence of this gentle hill in 1973 we must now transfer the tenses of this account to the past.

Fifty-two hundred people, most of them directly concerned with fishing, lived in and around Heimaey township, which surrounded the harbor and climbed back toward Helgafell. Fish were Heimaey's entire reason for being. The waters off the south coast of Iceland are among the richest spawning grounds in the world for Atlantic cod. But Iceland's shallow, sand-filled southern shore has no adequate harbors, and Heimaey furnished convenient access to the teeming fishery. Its rocky profile provided a deep, protected roadstead, the only sizable harbor between Reykjavik on the west coast and the fjord country of the east. From here went, and to here returned, the several hundred fishing boats, large and small, that provided Iceland with 20 percent of her fish products. Heimaey was Iceland's wealthiest port.

It took Heimaey ten centuries to reach this eminence. High, rugged, isolated in a rough ocean, the island group appeared no paradise to early settlers. According to *Landnamabok*, the historic *Book of Settlements*, compiled in the thirteenth century, the Westmanns entered Iceland's human history by accident at its very beginning. One of the two first settlers from Norway brought Irish slaves, of whom the names of five are known: Dufthak, Geirraud, Skjaldbjorn, Halldor and Drafdrit. Objecting to what they considered unreasonable demands by their owner, the slaves murdered him. They took his boat and fled the mainland, heading for the tall islands offshore, which appeared proof against immediate pursual. There, some weeks later, the second settler found them on Heimaey, eating a meal of roasted puffins. The slaves scattered but none escaped. Some were killed by the sword, others jumped from the cliffs that guard the harbor, and died on the rocks below. Dufthak, Geirraud, Skjaldbjorn, Halldor and Drafdrit have given their names to some of Heimaey's most fearsome seaside crags. The island group itself was named Vestmannaeyar, Islands of the West Men, in honor of its unwilling discoverers.

During the next sixty years some 20,000 settlers came to Iceland from Norway, and Heimaey received a few of them. "Herjolf, son of Bard Bareksson, brother of Hallgrimur, was the first to live in the Westmann Islands and dwelt in Herjolf's Valley near Ægisdyr, where now lava is burned. His son was Orm the Rich, who lived at Ormsstadir down near the Namar, where everything is now bare, and he owned all the islands."[1]

Another version records that "Orm the Unfree, son of Bard Bareksson and brother of Hallgrim Singe-Beam, was the first settler of the Westmann Islands. Before that there used to be a fishing station, with hardly anyone living there permanently."[2]

Heimaey is a natural landfall for anyone sailing from Northern Europe around the southern coast of Iceland, and *Landnamabok*'s second version of its settlement, though not the one accepted by the Westmann Islanders themselves, has a ring of truth. Attrac-

[1] *Landnamabok, Hauksbok* version
[2] *Landnamabok, Sturlubok* version

tive as it must have been to the ocean-weary, the island had little in those days to attract permanent settlers. The Norsemen needed more territory for their sheep, cattle and barley. Wherever in Iceland they made landfall it was their custom to lay claim at once to as much land as one slave could run around in one day. Even a slow slave could not have stretched the circling of little Heimaey to that many hours. Further, there were no springs, streams or lakes. The only potable water was rainfall. No doubt voyagers stopped, attracted then, as now, by the greenness of the meadows, the softness of the air and the amplitude of the food supply. Birds and eggs would have been a welcome change after weeks of dried fish and sour milk. Many would have landed there, few would have stayed.[3]

After the first sixty years of the Settlement all Iceland's choice arable land had been claimed. Rocky Heimaey, only second best, attracted some of the overflow; and by the year 1000, when Iceland accepted Christianity, the island had enough inhabitants to rate a wooden church, a luxury in a land that had no building timber. Though the land was owned by small farmers, the living was difficult, and in the twelfth century they were easily persuaded to sell it to a bishop who intended to build a monastery there. The project was never realized, for monks had the same problem as farmers with a land so small, stony and difficult of access. The islands stayed under the jurisdiction of the church, presumably because no one else would take them, until an indigent

---

[3] The importance of the Westmanns as a travelers' way station was revived in the 1940s when transatlantic planes found it necessary to make a fueling stop there between Europe and North America. Heimaey's airstrip, on the island's only flat surface, a field of crushed red lava just below Helgafell, is in the form of a cross. The twin-engined Fokker Friendships that take the place of trains for trippers in Iceland can land there any day the wind comes from the northeast and is not too strong. It is preferable to do so on a sunny day. Clouds over the ocean may presage a sudden storm. The early transatlantic planes, however, had to find the small island through clouds, had to land in wind, had to take off in mist. A crosswind or a surface fog could not be allowed to deter pilots whose planes were simply unable to make the coast of Ireland from Canada in one hop. Passengers must have found those trips exciting.

bishop named Arni the Mild paid them in 1413 to the King of Norway, who then owned Iceland, in settlement of heavy debts.

Still no one could be found who had an interest in Heimaey. Its few inhabitants went their small peaceable ways, farming, raising sheep and fishing, probably happy not to be bothered by the ever-feuding cheiftains on the mainland, and totally unprotected. As Iceland was founded by a nation of fighters of whom all Europe went in fear, it never occurred to the settlers that now they were homesteaders instead of Vikings they themselves might become the target of other freebooters. If the farmers thought at all about invaders they must have felt secure on their northern island in the middle of a stormy, windy ocean far from commercial sea lanes. Besides, their people had always ruled the oceans. But by the fifteenth century a new power had arisen on the sea — England, as efficient and almost as rapacious as the progenitors of Iceland's founders. Unfortified and forgotten, Heimaey was among the first hit by the new marauding sea power. The British found the island's protected harbor a convenient roadstead, and their merchant and fishing fleets as well as their privateers used it as a northern headquarters. Their personnel were no more respectful of private property than had been the Norse raiders before them. Plunder and killing came easy. After some years the English found it more profitable actually to take over the islands. From them the buccaneers fished, traded and captured all merchant ships of other countries that were imprudent enough to venture into their northern preserve. Their presence on Heimaey was unsanctioned by any sort of legality, but had the tacit approval of the Tudor monarchs at home, accustomed to turning a blind eye on any seagoing activities, however shady, that might enrich the royal treasury. They fortified Heimaey and ruled there unpleasantly until the middle of the sixteenth century, when the Danes, who by this time governed all Scandinavia including Iceland, succeeded in ousting them.

Heimaey's troubles were not over. In July of 1627 Moroccan pirates from Rabat, called "Turks" by the Icelanders, landed some 200 strong, led by a ferocious Dutch religious fanatic named Jan Janezen, whose pirate name was Rais Murad. The defender of

Heimaey, a Danish merchant, fled with his family, and the pirates raged unhindered over the island. They cut people in half, snapped the necks of infants, raped girls, murdered one of the two priests, burned farms and the church. Heimaey had not much worth the pillaging, so in lieu of treasure they carried off 242 men, women and children. The idea was to hold these for ransom, but once they got back to Africa their prizes somehow evaporated. The remaining priest, who was released the following spring in order to arrange with the Danish king for ransom, reported that many had died, young men and women had been sold, the girls to be concubines, the men servants and galley slaves, a few had changed their beliefs to save their lives, and these had become pirates themselves. Five years later some ransom was paid, but only thirteen broken souls eventually got back.

The lot of Heimaey improved only slightly as time passed. In the days before steamboats the islanders were not able with their open rowboats to tap efficiently the rich resource of the fishery. The hilly, lava-strewn island was unkind to cultivation and too small to support enough sheep and cattle for food. No one starved: fish and birds were endlessly plentiful. But disease was rife, particularly a virulent form of scurvy that acted like leprosy and was almost always fatal. The skin turned blue and scaly, the hair fell out, boils came on the face and limbs, the breath was fetid, smell, sight, taste and feeling were destroyed, the whole body broke out in open wounds and an extremely painful death followed. This disagreeable disease, though it occurred also on the mainland, was a scourge only in places where the diet was restricted to fish and fowl. On Heimaey there was nothing else to eat.

In 1783 even the fish failed Heimaey. A tremendous volcanic eruption, the largest in Iceland's recorded history, covered the southwestern part of the coast with sheets of lava and poisoned the ocean, making it uninhabitable for miles around. It was many years before Heimaey's only industry recovered.

A British traveler in the early nineteenth century found the island a sad place: "The population of Heimaey . . . does not amount at present to 200 souls, and is almost entirely supported by migration from the mainland; scarcely a single instance having been known, during the last twenty years, of a child surviving the period of infancy. [The children were dying of a dysentery-like disease apparently caused by a diet consisting solely of the oily flesh of seabirds.] . . . Their chief article of food is the sea-fowl, called the Fulmar, which they procure in vast abundance, using the eggs and flesh of the bird, and salting the latter for their winter food . . . Of vegetable food the inhabitants have none . . . The people are by no means respected by their neighbors on the mainland, who represent them as being remarkably indolent, and depraved in their habits . . . There is a church . . . but it does not appear to be of much use in improving the characters of those for whose benefit it was intended."[4]

A further privation was the lack of fresh water. Heimaey has no surface water, and the deepest of bore-holes discovered none underground. Provision ships transported it sometimes, but stormy seas often prevented any boats at all from braving Heimaey's cliffs and negotiating the narrow harbor entrance. The islanders collected rainwater in roof barrels, but in times of drought there was none. Lack of cleanliness made even more miserable the lot of the unfortunate victims of disease and malnutrition.

With the invention of the internal combustion engine things started looking up. In 1902 the first motors were fitted in Icelandic fishing boats, and fishing conditions in Heimaey's rough waters improved immediately. The harbor was dredged, wharves and lighthouses were built and the home fleet grew to eighty boats with room for a hundred more from other parts of Iceland and from Europe. Right after World War II quick-freezing was introduced. Four plants were built at the edge of the harbor and the product rose to $14 million. At the same time water pipes were laid 13½ miles over land from Merkurland, on the mainland, where water comes from the glaciers of the interior, then under the ocean for eight miles, and it seemed that Heimaey's last problem was solved.

By 1973 Heimaey's troubled history was a distant memory. Its inhabitants lived comfortably from the produce of the fisheries,

[4] *Travels in the Island of Iceland.* George Steuart Mackenzie, 1812

and their newly rich town stretched over the fields to the flanks of Helgafell, the 678-foot volcano that scarcely dominated the island.

Helgafell had been extinct since the Settlement. While every Icelander lives with the possibility that he may wake in the night to find a stream of lava entering his front door, the people of Heimaey felt reasonably secure with their old gray hill. They had seen Surtsey rise from the ocean on their near horizon. That had been a matter more for pride than fear, even though they knew that the whole island chain was uneasily rooted in the same earth fault that had produced her. Surtsey was another Westmann Island. In fact the people of Heimaey claimed her as their own. They refused to accept the name given her, and shortly after her birth sent a couple of fishermen to plant a sign, Vesturey, West Island, on the new black shore. But Surtsey had not finished erupting and showered pumice and mud on the visitors, who retreated hurriedly, taking their sign with them.

Surtsey meant the beginning of new life on the earth. Seven thousand years before, Helgafell had also meant new life as it brought their own Heimaey into being. Now it was just a pretty little round hill made of loose stone. Snow buntings nested among its rim rocks and moss campion bloomed inside its sunny crater.

On January 23, 1973, the meaning of Helgafell changed. At two o'clock in the morning, after several small earthquakes, casually noted (earthquakes are unremarkable in Iceland), people were awakened by a vast rumbling. They went outdoors to see a red glow through smoke over the mountain. As they watched, Helgafell appeared to explode. A fiery column burst out of its side and was thrown some 1,500 feet into the air. Burning ash rained down and the watchers ran for shelter. But their houses were no shelter. Mingled in the ash were red-hot stones, and from the east side of Helgafell a stream of lava crept toward the sea. One house was in its path. The occupants saw the grass on fire outside their window and escaped in their nightclothes just before the slow flood covered their house.

All over the town people were running out of their houses now, carrying an armful of clothing, a small suitcase, some household ornaments, whatever seemed to them at that ultimate moment precious or necessary. One woman held a bottle of milk, her husband a half-eaten leg of lamb.

Everyone headed for the harbor except those who were too old or ill to walk. These were taken from their houses by firemen and driven around to the airfield behind the smoking mountain, where helicopters from the American air base on the mainland were landing precariously through clouds of smoke and ash. About three hundred people chose to stay behind: a few shopkeepers who tried to get their stock out, some police and town officials to guard the abandoned town, and firemen. Most of the cattle and sheep were slaughtered before they should starve, burn or be buried. The keeper of the aquarium, as showers of pumice rained on his roof and the stream of lava came close, took his seals and his tanks of fish down to the ocean and let them go home.

Fortunately the fishing fleet was in the harbor waiting for dawn. If the eruption had started in the daylight hours rescue would have been far more difficult. All the boats got away, even the smallest laden with refugees. There were no casualties and no panic, either among those who left or those who stayed behind. Icelanders have lost their entire life's treasure before this. Their country's history of volcanic holocausts is as fresh to them as if each disaster in the ten centuries past had happened to their own friends and neighbors.

Up on the meadow that slopes to Helgafell a horse stepped across a small fissure, the earth yawned and he disappeared, screaming. He was Heimaey's only casualty.

The eruption on January 23 opened a fissure two miles long in Helgafell's eastern flank, the side away from the town. From this rift eventually arose a new mountain 225 feet higher than its parent, and bigger in circumference. It was named Kirkjufell, Church Mountain, because here had stood Heimaey's first church. The initial eruption had sent fountains of molten lava soaring high in the air, but the west wind had carried the fiery debris out to sea. The next day a new eruption sent lava flowing westward toward the town, threatening to inundate it and seal off the harbor that was the fishing port's whole reason for being. Though the boats had left, there was $14 million worth of frozen fish in the dockside

46

warehouses. Many of the boats went back, braving the new danger, and they succeeded in bringing all of it out, as well as furniture, books, paintings and other belongings that could still be salvaged. The larger boats carried off the remaining sheep and cattle.

Still the lava streamed over the northeastern part of the town, engulfing streets and houses and spilling into the harbor in a flood nearly a quarter of a mile wide. For the first time in history an attempt was made to stem the molten river. Pumps and hose were flown from the mainland. The pumps were set up in an empty factory building at the edge of the sea and the hose laid from the harbor up the main street to the path of the lava. As it flowed seaward, water was pumped on it, 29,000 tons an hour, amounting in all to 5,500,000 tons. The liquid rock cooled and hardened into a wall ninety feet high that ran out into the middle of the harbor. When new lava flowed down it piled up behind the wall. Most of the eastern part of the town was buried under a sheet of lava 120 feet thick. But the harbor was saved.

For the five months of Kirkjufell's activity the fate of Heimaey was unpredictable. The disturbed earth might yawn wider and the whole island disappear under the ocean. New tremors might cause Kirkjufell to blow up, scattering the island in pieces all over the sea. Even if Heimaey did not disappear it could be years before it was habitable again. The grass was burned off, the soil destroyed by heat and cinders. About two million tons of pumice and ash covered the eastern area where the main fissure opened, and in some places this was fifteen to twenty feet thick.[5] One hundred and twelve houses were either burned out or buried. Other houses turned into giant flues as the vapors from the cooling lava penetrated their sewerage and ventilation systems and were drawn out through windows and chimneys. The heat inside these houses rose to 110° F. while the foundations, much hotter, began to crack and melt into the surrounding earth. Every east wind brought a storm of flaming dust to set new fires.

[5] Pumice is lava so full of gas that it is frothy. As it congeals, the gas is trapped and the resultant rock is porous and lighter than water. Ash and cinders are pumice that has exploded, the rock froth shattered into fine glasslike shards.

This time the fire giant brought not life but destruction, as foretold in the Edda: "Surtur from the south comes with flickering flame. . . . The stony hills are dashed together, the sun darkens. . . . Men tread the path of Hell, and heaven is cloven."[6]

[6] *The Vala's Prophecy: The Poetic Edda* of Sæmund Sigfusson

FOUR

Heimaey: A Memory

WE KNEW HEIMAEY before the eruption and afterwards, for a time, it seemed to us to have lost existence except in the past. In memory the island had a special beauty. Its grass was greener, its flowers larger and brighter than those of the known world. The blue sky had incomparable clouds, like silver feathers. The sunset near midnight was clear gold and Heimaey's red cliffs shone as if with their own light. Was there really such an island? It came to seem a place heard of in a traveler's story, once seen and never found again.

Deceptive memory can surround a scene with an aura of legend. But Heimaey is still alive in the pages of a notebook. As I turn them I see the island again, and indeed it had a special beauty.

We flew from Reykjavik in the morning, east and south into the sun. On the left were snow-covered table mountains, on the right the ocean, shallow here off the south coast where subglacial volcanic eruptions had spread lava and sand. The shadows of clouds lay on the sea, dark gray-green on the pale green water. Beyond the coast the ocean was deep flat blue with white flecks. The Westmann Islands were a scattering of rocks in the blueness, dark and jagged, rimmed with white lines of surf.

Close to, Heimaey's slopes were very green, misted with yellow clouds of flowers. Darker green squares patched the fields, sharply furrowed. The plane flew over the many-colored town, circled Helgafell's low cone and came to earth on the crushed-lava runway.

Outside the plane the sun shone hot on the red dust and a golden plover called through the quietness. Around the airstrip were grassy fields touched with color: beach pea purple and mauve, mountain avens white and yellow, daisies, dandelions, buttercups, all tall and large-blossomed in the soft moist air. Below the airfield the island's one main road, circling Helgafell, had a lot of traffic. Fourteen hundred cars were owned by 5,200 people — and they could not go anywhere off the island. But cars are so new to Iceland, most of whose roads are less than fifty years old, that they are still exciting toys and everybody wants one. The road wound south around the gentle curves of the meadows, whose green was interrupted by outcroppings of porous lava, to remind one that long ago Heimaey was another Surtsey. Walls of the same burnt rock, painfully dislodged by farmers of old times to clear their land, delineated the tilled fields. Here and there a low building of lava roofed with sod, to keep the hay dry in winter, looked like yet another bit of volcanic debris. Potato patches, their dense-leaved plants in flower, were strewn over the hilly pastures, elongated mounds with ditches between them so the frequent rain could run off. The potato plots alternated with acres of tall wooden fish-drying racks.

The tilled fields gave way to a green bowl, Herjolfsdalur, Valley of Herjolf, a lake of grass under an encircling precipice called Ægisdyr, Sea Gate. Between the cliff and the hills to the south the sea was just visible, its spray misting the clear air. There was a strong wind out there but in the valley the air was still and hot. Puffins crossed and recrossed from the ocean to their burrows on Ægisdyr's turf roof, many with five or six small silver fish drooping on either side of the triangular beaks. Fulmars had nests there too, and these ever-flying seabirds, voiceless shadows over the water, talked in continuous husky chuckles as they met their mates and the fat chicks spread comfortably far back in the ledges.

The green bowl was Heimaey's meeting place for the three-day festival of Thjodhatid, People's Feast, Heimaey's special celebration of Independence Day a month later than that kept by the rest of Iceland (because bad weather had prevented the islanders from attending the original jubilee on July 1, 1874, the day the Danish king granted Iceland a new constitution with home rule).

People came to Heimaey's festival from all over Iceland, to set up tents and eat, drink and dance. The rest of the year Herjolfsdalur was the golf course, a strenuous one full of sharp hills and sudden valleys, and interrupted with terrible little volcanic rocks and sand traps of lava cinders. At one side of it was the soccer field, a necessary adjunct of every town in Iceland, its grass smooth as a bowling green.

At the edge of the golf course, on the slope of a hill with a clear view of the sea, was the red gash of a fresh excavation, a rectangular hole in the ground lined with large stones. This was the foundation of a tenth-century dwelling. Here lived Herjolf, whose valley this was. The main hall was about thirty feet long and fifteen wide. A room about half that size opened off one side and a third room, even smaller, now marked by stakes in the grass, was going to appear on the other side. This was small by some Norse standards; there were halls in which fifty people could be entertained at dinner and later sleep, the raised shelves along each wall doubling as bench and bed. But if Herjolf's house was modest its location was breathtaking. Behind him was the cone of Helga-fell, before him his meadows, protected by the towering wall of Ægisdyr, swept down to the shining sea. He had built facing south, the direction of good omen for the Norsemen, his door open to the sun. To the north, not far away, was the sheltered harbor where his boats lay at safe anchor. Heimaey may have been second-best for the land-hungry Norwegian emigrants, but there must have been some compensation in the heart-stopping beauty of this small island.

The meadows flowed around the flanks of Helgafell and continued to within a mile of the southern headland, where the island contracted to a narrow neck covered with sand. Under this defile passed the transatlantic cable, laid in 1906, that connected the United Kingdom with Iceland and went on to North America through Greenland. There was a small shack here by the sea that housed the equipment to service the cable. (Though the main force of the 1973 eruption was to strike well to the north, the shack would be buried in pumice and the transatlantic cable would have temporarily to fend for itself. It continued to function but an alternate site, less vulnerable, would be sought on the mainland.)

Within the neck was a protected bend of the coast where the ocean lapped gently on a curve of fine black sand. The warm Irminger Current that keeps the Westmann Islands green all year round and brings their prodigious rainfall (49.4 inches a year) gives the ocean a summer temperature of around 57° F. On a fair summer day when the wind was a clearing breeze from the north the islanders used to sun on this pleasant arc of beach and swim in the moderate ocean.

The island widened again at its southern end to Storhöfdi, Big Headland, a round bulb of deeply eroded weather-marked volcanic rock about 300 feet high and descending precipitately to the sea. A hard south wind usually blew here straight out of the open Atlantic. Nothing lies between the Westmanns and Antarctica but the continental shelf of the Spanish Sahara on the bulge of Africa, and untrammeled waves fifty or sixty feet high pounded on the old lava, carving it into fierce shapes and sending clouds of spray even over the top of the cliff. A man could not stand up straight here, let alone build a house. This was puffin country. Hundreds of thousands had their burrows here, and the puffin catchers used to come down in July and August when the young were out of the nests. Holding a pole eighteen feet long ending in a net, the catcher lay in the grass at the top of the cliff. As a puffin came beating over the edge from the sea it found a startling journey's end. In silence it fluttered and kicked against the net until the catcher disentangled it and broke its neck with a quick twist. On a good day a clever catcher netted a thousand puffins. They claimed they never took breeding birds, which they knew by the beaks full of fish. Those caught were mostly two-year-olds, full-grown and fat, which have the habit of visiting the nest colonies after their first year of adulthood, spent on open ocean far from land. The young puffins were cured, either by salting or smoking, and sold as a special delicacy on the mainland. They were not exported.

At the northern end of Heimaey, six miles from the puffin cliffs, was the pretty town. Perched on the terraced hillside over the harbor, it looked Mediterranean. The spacious older houses along the main streets were of whitewashed concrete with red and green roofs. Fanning out toward the cliffs and back into the rising

Before eruption: Heimaey's town rose clean and bright to the flanks of the ancient volcano Helgafell, quiescent for 7,000 years.

land of the interior, even on the lower slope of Helgafell, were new houses of painted concrete, clean and bright as field flowers: coral and gray, blue and burnt orange, chocolate and pale green, with split levels, studio-height picture windows and flat roofs. (Pitched roofs were unnecessary, as ocean-bound Heimaey got little snow.) Most of the houses had gardens of tulips, daffodils and early roses. Streets of red lava gravel ran between the houses, up through the fields and down to the water. The focus of the town was the harbor, protected by its guardian cliffs, Heimaklettur, Dalfjall, Dale Hill, Storaklif and Litlaklif, Big Cliff and Little Cliff. Heimaklettur was 925 feet high, taller than the volcano that gave it birth and far more imposing. Sheep grazed on top of it, on the grass slope of Dufthaksskor, Dufthak's Rift, from which the Irish thrall leaped to escape the avengers. It was hard to see how the sheep got up there, let alone a fleeing murderer. Dufthak was aided only by desperation. Later a rope was put up one side where the steepness was broken by diagonal ledges. Iron ladders spanned the perpendicular spaces. Men had to scale Heimaklettur to place and keep in repair the cable that brought electricity from the mainland. The sheep were hauled up in slings at the beginning of summer and slung back down when the weather got cold.

On the land side of the harbor was another, milder eminence, the Skanzin Fortification overlooking the harbor's narrow entrance. It was built in 1630, three years too late, to protect the islanders from pirate attacks. It used to be of stone, its walls lined with cannon. That summer it was a rectangular depression with wild flowers growing in it. Its walls were soft mounds of grass where one could sit and watch the boats go in and out of the harbor. Beyond the seawall, a natural bridge of rock connecting Heimaklettur and Storaklif, the ocean was usually dark and rough. Waves broke ten to twenty feet up on the cliffs, geysers of spray flew into the air and water streamed over the rock wall. Within the protection of the crags the water of the harbor was quiet and the boats barely moved at their moorings.

This was Heimaey as we remember it. The day before we left we climbed the little volcano to view the island a last time. Helgafell was a round pointed mountain ascending slowly to an upper pitch of about forty degrees. Sheep, cattle and potato plots inhabited its lower fields, where the slope was so gradual that soil had been able to accumulate and the roots of grass and flowers kept the earth from slipping downward. Green streaks continued into the steepening flanks, but few plants could keep a foothold on the shifting gravel of the mountain's upper half. A golden plover ran ahead of us up through the green streaks, flying when we came close, alighting to run again, uttering short mournful cries. It left us at the steep incline. These handsome Arctic-breeding birds are used to upland and tundra, and do not need much for their ground nests. A little dry grass and leaves to line a shallow depression, and they can breed on the coldest, unfriendliest ground. But Helgafell's upper reaches were unsafe even for plovers. Everything slipped downward at the merest touch. You set a foot into lava cinders and it slid two steps back. You tried to make headway by seeking out larger stones, and they turned over and started to roll. In the 7,000 years of its existence it was a wonder that any of the mountain still remained at the top. The only plant that inhabited the slithering pebbles of the sharpest pitch was Surtsey's colonizer, seaside sandwort.

Above us a snow bunting sang from a rock at the crater's rim. As we crawled over the edge he flew, to alight a few yards away and sing again. Vividly black and white, he perched on his stone and watched us, warning us away with the only vocal anger a snow bunting can show, a long ripple of heartbreaking sweetness. Somewhere deep in the rimrocks was the nest, lined with moss and feathers, where his brown and white mate sat silently, her breast bare of feathers so she could keep warm her six or seven small eggs on the windy mountaintop.

In the shallow crater grew grass and a few bright pink clumps of moss campion. From the burnt, eroded boulders of the rim all the Westmann Islands were visible, some tall and green-thatched, others stark rocks breaking through the spume of surf. Beyond them in every direction but north stretched the ocean, gray and misty. To the north, nine miles away, was the mainland of Iceland, a long brown and green coastline with mountains of ice rising behind it.

It was hard to conceive that out of this small grass-filled

58

crater could have flowed this solid island. Heimaey seemed part of earth's creation, unimaginably long ago. Equally impossible was the thought, which did not even occur, that destruction, corollary of creation, was very close to us as we stood on Helgafell.

We returned to Heimaey in the summer of 1973, flying in a one-engined plane from Reykjavik. The ocean was dotted with fishing vessels, Heimaey boats come back to fish in their home waters. The Westmann Islands were high blue shadows on the horizon back of the gleaming sea. Smoke puffed upward suddenly from them and in a few seconds a brown mushroom-shaped cloud hung in the still sky.

We flew around the cloud, and there was Heimaey below us, all black. From the flanks of the new mountain, Kirkjufell, oozed continuous streams of smoke, flattening over the land. The whole northern end of the island was larger (by nine-tenths of a square mile). The puffins' cliff on the east was gone; the new mountain had swelled out over it into the ocean. The northeastern part of the town had disappeared under a flood of lava, which had spilled a rough cover over half the harbor entrance. Blackness had spewed over the rest of the town, obscuring some of it, leaving the rest a soiled patchwork. All the fresh fields were darkened. The only green left was on the rocky southern elevation, beyond the neck of land where lay the transatlantic cable.

The runway was ankle deep in black ash. The ash was deeper as we walked down toward the town, a fine dust that rose in clouds as we waded through it, seeping through clothing and getting into eyes, mouths and noses. It was very quiet. There were no birds. Even the gulls had abandoned the wasted fields. All of little Helgafell was covered with ash. The great new mountain that had risen from her side still had gaping yellow craters in its sides from which came smoke with a strong smell of sulphur accompanied by a sharper odor which we could not identify but which was probably the poisonous gas fluorine. There was still danger on the island. We carried with us official identifications and instructions as to what to do in an emergency, including the warning that we must be prepared for a possible stay of twenty-four hours in the open air.

Before us a three-foot post stuck out of the black sand. Near it a square of cement rested on a bulge. We were looking at the top of a telephone post and the chimney of a house. It was the edge of the town. Parts of more houses became visible, crushed eaves, caved-in roofs, an occasional shattered window frame. Farther into the town the streets defined themselves, their concrete pitted and buckled. Everywhere was the smell of burning, and from nearly every house smoke came gently, lazing into the air.

There was no sign of a human being in this devastated part of the town, but a steady pulsing sound filled the deserted streets. As we neared the harbor it grew stronger. It came from the pumps still running in a dockside factory. The heavy rubber hose, a foot in diameter, still ran up the street. The pumps were kept going all the time to keep the water pressure up in case of another eruption. The entrance to the harbor from the ocean was much narrower than before, but the new seawall afforded better protection than the old low one. For some years to come, however, the islanders would have a hard time growing anything in their gardens. The spraying of the lava left behind 180,000 tons of salt.

The western part of the town was all there, though no house had escaped the rain of black ash and many breathed smoke from their overheated pipes and vents. There was human activity around the secondary school where offices had been set up. The three hundred remaining inhabitants had here their town council, police, civil defense, telephone and telegraph company and geological survey. Trucks and earth-moving machines crept up and down the potholed streets. It was planned not only to remove some of the millions of cubic feet of tephra that covered the inhabited regions but to level an ancient lava bed to the west, out of Kirkjufell's path, and dump the debris there for foundations for new houses. The tephra would be valuable foundation material for new roads also.

We went back to the harbor to find the little street down which we had walked every evening to watch the life of the docks. Its beginning was there. But right beyond the fish factory we were stopped by an unkempt fifty-foot wall of red and yellow lava unbelievably ragged and burnt. On top of it were the sole human signs: a chair with only two legs and a broken baby carriage. Some-

After the eruption: much of the town was buried under lava, pumice and ash. By the following year 900,000 tons of debris had been removed and most of the inhabitants had returned.

where under that bristling rampart was our small congenial hotel. Over to one side had been the town swimming pool, the grass-grown seventeenth-century fort and the oceanside path where we had walked, picking wild flowers, studying the tidal pools and watching the fulmars of Heimaklettur hunting. Heimaklettur was stained black and the fulmars had gone.

For the first time the loss came home to us. None of our friendly corner of Heimaey was there anymore. It was lost forever. Forever. The word had unqualified finality.

But most of Heimaey rose again. Five months and five days after it had started the eruption was officially declared over. A group of scientists descended into the crater and had their pictures taken there to show that the earth beneath the mountains was quiet at last. It had been an "average" eruption, twice as large as Hekla's in 1970 but only a quarter the size of the emergence of Surtsey. However, it had had a human effect far out of proportion to its size. All Heimaey's population had had to be temporarily resettled; Iceland's largest fishing fleet had been scattered to inadequate ports on the mainland far from their home waters; 20 percent of her fish production had been halted. New tax measures costing the average Icelandic family 10 percent of its income had had to be levied to meet the cost of Heimaey's losses, of $20 million, or 2 percent of the gross national product. A relief fund totaling $50 million was raised nationally and internationally. This money was used first to take care of the refugees, later to help in the rebuilding.

In July, 1973, people began trickling back. They found an eerie, sullied island almost unrecognizable under its cloak of ash. With the spirit of pioneers — almost happily, so glad were they to be home again — they began to dig out. A year after the eruption all the fish processing and fish meal plants were operating again except for one which had been buried under the lava wall. Most of the boats returned and Heimaey was on its way back to its position as Iceland's biggest fishing port. Schools were reopened and a new hospital was built, the most complete in the country outside Reykjavik, to replace the old one lost under the lava. The new housing quarter on Helgalfell's old lava bed was fairly begun, with 450 row houses and single-family dwellings planned to succeed the 400 burned or buried. Nearly 900,000 tons of ash, pumice and lava bombs were removed from the town, much of it being used for foundations, road repair and an extension to the airport runway. Another useful by-product of the eruption was underground heat, which would last for a long time. Lava, protected by its own crust, stays molten inside for many years. Pipes were laid through the lava's sheath and water sent through them was converted to steam to heat the new houses. Plans were made to build greenhouses using this free source of energy. The main electricity cable, severed by submarine volcanic activity, was repaired and two new 650-kilowatt diesel generators were added to the two emergency ones that had been set up during the eruption.

Most of the island's arable land was covered with tephra, soured by poisonous smoke, or scorched by fire. It would be a long time before the soil would regain its fertility. But a start was made. Fertilizer and grass seed were first dropped unsuccessfully by plane, most of it being blown into the ocean by the sea winds that almost always blow over Heimaey; and later was spread with a seeding and fixing machine used on the mainland to establish grass verges along highways. There was no land yet fit for the grazing of cattle and sheep. But one chicken farmer came back. All his stock had died while being moved to the mainland. He had left behind, however, knowing he would return, a rooster and two hens. Now he had several hundred chickens, some imported, most bred from his three survivors. Turf was brought in to cover the ashy, salty soil around the houses, so backyard gardens would bloom once more.

Two thousand, six hundred people went back. They worked twelve hours a day seven days a week to make their island livable again. It will be. It would have been even if none of them had gone back. Earth destroys itself and regenerates itself over and over. Heimaey and Surtsey are beginnings and ends at the same time; Iceland is still creating herself out of the sea, and still annihilating her flowering old volcanic earth with new floods of liquid rock from her shifting foundations.

In these two volcanic islands we can see, as if we were standing on an ocean rock back there in the darkness of the Eocene dawn fifty million years ago, the Thulean subcontinent break the surface all over the northern seas like a school of unimaginable leviathans rising from depths altogether alien.

FIVE

A Desert in the Ocean

WHILE SURTSEY AND Heimaey struggle for survival above a widening crack in the ocean floor, Iceland's southern mainland, opposite them, is subservient to another of earth's primal forces, ice. When the ice sheets covering most of northern Europe retreated during the period from twelve to eight thousand years ago, the Iceland that emerged was a totally different land from that which had been buried some three million years earlier. The volcanoes that had been erupting throughout the glacial age gave the interior a landscape of sharply irregular peaks made of the glassy rock, palagonite, that forms when lava erupts under the pressure of ice. The retreating ice, gouging out innumerable fjords, bays and inlets, left an extravagantly wrinkled coastline 3,700 miles long. Water was abundant, tumbling from the heights in prodigious waterfalls, sluicing through deserts of volcanic ash in rapids milky with glacial silt, hollowing deep channels and caves and potholes in the fragile rock. Water below the still-hot earth erupted in hot springs and geysers, creating swamps and staining them pink and yellow and blue. The new Iceland was, in short, today's Iceland, violent and vivid and youthfully unfinished.

Eleven and a half percent of Iceland is still covered with ice left over from the Pleistocene epoch. The largest remnant is Vatnajökull, Water Glacier, in the southeast, covering 3,240 square miles, more than all the glaciers of the Alps and Scandinavia together. From Vatnajökull flow most of Iceland's rivers, and its southern outlet glaciers nearly touch the ocean. Glaciers generally have chilly associations with mountaintops or tundra, but Vatnajökull has its being on top of volcanic fire. At its core are lakes of hot water, from which its name is derived. The biggest and most dangerous of these is Grimsvötn, Water of Odin (Grim was a name for Odin when he visited earth in masked disguise, a reference to the lake's mask of ice). The hidden lake is thirteen miles square and 1,600 feet deep. Its warmth melts the ice above it, enlarging the lake's volume, until the warm water rises so high that it breaks the ice dam at the mouth of its hanging valley. The overflow forces its way under the glacier down toward the sea, to burst into the open forty miles south in a rampageous torrent of water, mud and stones that destroys everything in its path. This used to happen about every ten years. But the earth's climate has been warming since the late nineteenth century and glaciers are shrinking. Vatnajökull has become thinner, though it is still more than half a mile thick at its bulkiest, and nowadays it only takes the hot water five years to rise and break its barrier.

Vatnajökull also contains active volcanoes. Since they are all or partly under ice their eruptions hold a peculiar terror, bringing not only lava and tephra but killing floods of ice, water, earth and rocks discharged by the explosions under millions of tons of glacier.

The biggest of these volcanoes is mostly under Öraefajökull, Glacier of the Unsheltered Coast, an outlet of Vatnajökull. Only one part of it reaches the air, a nunatak (mountain summit protruding from ice) called Hvannadalshnukur, Peak of the Valley of Angelica, named for a valley below it where angelica grows tall in earth perpetually moist from glacial runoff. Hvannadalshnukur, 6,954 feet, is Iceland's highest peak. Öraefajökull has erupted twice since the Settlement. The first eruption, in 1362, was one of the biggest in recorded history. It is said that a shepherd named Hallur in the valley below heard a powerful crash one morning at milking time. There came a second, stronger crash and the shepherd, saying to the milkmaids that it would not be wise to wait for a third one, ran away and hid in a cave. He was the only one in the area to survive. At the third crash the glacier exploded, sending over the countryside millions of tons of water and ice that washed away all the people and the livestock. Forty farms were buried in mud and glacial debris. There was enough tephra from the eruption to have covered all of Iceland with a layer four inches thick, but most of it fell in the sea. The detritus that was spewed forth from under the glacier, however, created the vast waste of the Skeidararsandur, Sands of the Open Spaces, and the Breidermerkursandur, Sands of the Broad Boundaries, covering much of the arable land that the early settlers had found so attractive.

The second eruption, in 1727, started with two earthquakes. They loosened two small outlet glaciers, which suddenly slid down toward the sea, while ash from the ensuing eruption darkened the sky for three days. The eruption continued for ten months, laying waste the land all over again.

Under Myrdalsjökull, Glacier of the Moor, is another potent volcano. This glacier, once a western outlet of Vatnajökull, has retreated so that now it is surrounded by dry land. Its volcano, Katla, a name derived from the word for kettle, is entirely hidden by ice. The Kettle has boiled over thirteen times since the Settlement, causing discharges of water five times that at the mouth of the Amazon, or 65,000 cubic yards per second, and wiping out all traces of life on the plains at the edge of the sea below it. The volcano has been roughly predictable in the timing of its eruptions. The last one was in 1918, and 1973 was to have been its year. But the scheduled explosion hit Heimaey instead. The pressure under the earth's crust was relieved and the south coast farmers are safe for a few more decades.

The *jökulhraups*, glacial bursts, occasioned by the mighty clash of fire and ice, have altered, and continue to alter, the shape of Iceland's southern coast, filling in harbors, flattening hills, submerging headlands. All along that shore the ocean is shallow, and ships have been coming to grief on its shoals and reefs for 1,500 years. Between the heights of the ice-hidden mountains and the unimpeded surf of the open ocean is a constantly changing strip of flat land. Much of it consists of wide plains of muddy sand with multitudes of braided streams creeping over the dark expanse. Some of it is thickly green, its healthy grass nourished by the eternal dampness of the glacial air and the closeness of the warm-

67

ing ocean. Farms are scattered through these fertile reaches. Gnarled fingers of outlet glaciers touch the upper pastures, and ocean waves sometimes pound up to the front yards, and tomorrow or next year the houses may be swept away and the fields buried under mud and rocks in a new glacial burst. But the farmers of the south coast have a deep attachment to their wet green land. No other part of Iceland pleases them as does this verdant strip squeezed between ice and ocean.

The south coast was the first natural landfall for boats from Europe. Those who saw it, whether blown there by mistake in a storm or sailing on purpose to escape from the turmoil and misery of Europe in the Dark Ages, were attracted at once to the gentle green shore under the shadow of the mountainous ice. Those seeking sanctuary were comforted to find a land entirely free from the taint of human occupation. Since the advent of man on earth Iceland has not been connected with any land, nor had it an indigenous population. Four hundred and ninety-five miles from the nearest point in Europe, beyond reach of primitive oars, sails or rafts, it was not on the path of any prehistoric migrations, and it remained empty while over the rest of Europe civilizations grew and died.

The first to find it were Irish monks. After the fall of the Roman Empire and the occupation of most of Europe by barbarians, Latin culture was dissipated, to be kept alive only in isolated, often beleaguered monasteries. Christian scholars found no place left in Europe to spread their knowledge, hardly even to hide. Some of them, fleeing the rule of the heathen, found their way to Ireland. Saint Patrick had returned there in 432 from studies in Auxerre to organize the scattered minority of Christians, convert most of pagan Ireland and bring the country into touch with the rest of Europe, introducing Roman culture and the Latin language. Insulated by sea, Ireland escaped most of the holocaust that accompanied the fall of Rome, and she became a haven for the hard-pressed scholars. The refugees founded monasteries, educated the people and maintained constant touch with Christian headquarters in Byzantium. From 500 to 800 Ireland was the only truly civilized country west of the pope's enclave. The Dark Ages never touched her. The chieftains of her seven kingdoms ruled by common consent, and education was more important than wealth. Though her people were mainly poor farmers they were endowed with poetry and a love of beauty. There was no religious strife as the new Christians, easy-going and tolerant, never minded a touch of Druidism in the background (it lingers today in the form of elves). Schools were important and scholarship was honored. All monks spoke Latin, many Greek; they read Homer, Aristotle, Plato and the Greek Fathers of the Church; and they made remarkably beautiful illustrated manuscripts on the finest vellum. For three hundred years, while the rest of Europe lay under the pall of despotism, paralyzed in ignorance, Ireland was a place of light in the surrounding darkness.

But even in this paradise there was discord. Today's bitter struggle between north and south is not a new phenomenon. It had its counterpart in the jealous bickering of a thousand years past and more. Ireland's seven kingdoms were joined loosely in two confederacies, Tara and Cashel, dividing the country into realms of north and south. The king of Tara was the titular head, the high-king of all Ireland, but he had no power, and fighting between the two sections became increasingly vicious. By the ninth century Ireland, hopelessly divided, was an easy prey to Norse invaders. The priests and monks, now wealthy landlords, whose precursors had fled the ferocious barbarism of post-imperial Europe, found themselves beset in their blessed isle by a new kind of barbarian. The Vikings were tough, skilled pagans with a set of warlike gods, an overweening belief in physical strength and personal heroism, and an inexorable devotion to family solidarity. This combination made them practically invincible wherever they went, and they went everywhere. The monasteries of weakened Ireland were fat prizes, and the terrorized monks, faced with the prospects of slavery or death, began to leave the country.

Irish monks had a tendency to roam. They were always wandering off looking for havens. They did not travel as missionaries; with a notion of penance they "sought with great labor . . . a desert in the ocean"[1] where they could lead hard and holy lives away

[1] *De Vita S. Columbae*, Adamnan, *circa* 700

69

from the worldliness that beset even their quiet sanctuaries. The sea held no terrors for them, and in an age of almost total geographical ignorance they knew the earth was round. This knowledge had come to them from the writings of the Greeks by way of two fifth-century Latin scholars, Macrobius and Marianus Capella, and they had kept it alive through the benighted centuries. Long before the coming of the Vikings the frail curraghs of Irish monks had touched on islands in the North Atlantic from the Shetlands to the Faeroes and beyond. They knew of Iceland as "Tila," a corrupted spelling of Thyle, or Thule, from their classical reading, wherein they had found accounts of the journeys of the Greek explorer Pytheas of Marseilles. In about 300 B.C. he discovered "the farthest island of the ocean, lying between north and west six days voyage beyond Britain, getting its name [Thule] from the sun, because at the summer solstice there is no night, when the sun passes out of the Crab."[2]

Though it is not now believed that Pytheas's Thule was Iceland, the Irish monks so believed it, and by the time of the voyage of Saint Brendan in the early sixth century Tila was already known, though not settled, by would-be hermits. Brendan, in his curragh, a "very light little vessel, ribbed and sided with oak-tanned ox-hide strips and caulked with ox-tallow"[3] set sail with seventeen monks on a voyage of forty days (the standard time generally allotted by the scribes to holy voyages) with water, wine for mass in goatskins, cured meat and fish, and dried heather to sleep on. He was not looking for Tila but for a land across the sea promised him one night in a visit from an angel, which knew neither death nor decay, where saints could live in perpetual joy.

Brendan's vessel, his supplies and his comrades seemed more suited to a trip across a lake than a journey of some 750 miles over the unfriendly North Atlantic. The voyagers were not seamen nor warriors; they came out of cloistered monasteries to plunge directly into the most elemental dangers. Their courage was incredible, the more so since they took no note of it. Doubtless these unworldly monks held that faith alone sustained them,

[2] *Liber de Mensura Orbis*, Dicuil, 825
[3] *Navigatio Sancti Brendani, circa* 575

but their physical stamina must have been equal to their spiritual fortitude. Cold and hungry and battered and exhausted they surely were, but asceticism pleased them. Their little basket-weave boat bobbed in the waves like a cork; where a heavy wooden vessel might have been swamped in a storm theirs was always dry. Unbelievably, they journeyed, they arrived at various destinations, and they lived to return and to record their adventures.

Tila, when Saint Brendan's boat was blown onto its shores by mistake, smacked more of hell than of the heaven he was seeking. "There came into view a large and high mountain in the ocean . . . toward the north, with misty clouds above it, and a great smoke issuing from its summit . . . Then they saw the peak of the mountain unclouded and shooting up flames into the sky which it drew back again to itself so that the mountain was a burning pyre."[4] The wind drove them toward the shore and with great difficulty they got away from the dangerous island, only to come on another part of it "which was very rugged and rocky, covered over with slag, without trees or herbiage, but full of smiths' forges . . . They heard the noise of bellows blowing like thunder . . . Soon after one of the inhabitants came forth . . . he was all hairy and hideous, begrimed with fire and smoke."[5] Saint Brendan made the sign of the Cross and urged his brethren to ply their oars briskly. Seeing this "the savage man . . . rushed down to the shore, bearing in his hand a pair of tongs with a burning mass of slag of great size and intense heat, which he flung at once after the servants of Christ . . . Where it fell into the sea it fumed up like a heap of burning coals and a great smoke arose as from a fiery furnace . . . 'Soldiers of Christ,' " said Saint Brendan, " 'be strong in faith unfeigned and in the armor of the Spirit, for we are now on the confines of Hell.' "[6]

It is conjectured that the monks had witnessed an eruption of Mount Hekla, which later was assumed even by the most respected explorers to be the gateway to hell. The fancy of the smiths' forges could have been the monks' observation of a predecessor of Surtsey, an island that came up out of the sea with a great smoking, only to sink back under the waves a few hours or a few days later.

[4] Ibid.
[5] Ibid.
[6] Ibid.

This has happened more than once in historic times off Iceland's southern and western coasts.

The voyages of Saint Brendan, fanciful as were his descriptions (and they became ever more fantastic the farther he got from home) gave heart to monks of the following centuries fleeing from this or that discomfort in Ireland. Presumably they ignored his warning about the confines of hell, and found in stormy Tila the "desert in the ocean" for which they had always longed. For by the year 793, when the explosive Norse migrations started that would take Vikings all over the known world, there was already an establishment of Irish monks on the southern coast of Iceland at Kirkjubær, Farm of the Church, today a green oasis between lava and glacier. New refugees joined them, forming monastic cells all along the south coast and its islands. The monks' sanctuary evidently pleased them, for they stayed. A contemporary account by an Irish monk states, of Tila, "It is now thirty years since clerics, who had lived on the island from the first of February to the first of August, told me that not only at the summer solstice, but in the days round about it, the sun setting in the evening hides itself as though behind a small hill in such a way that there was no darkness in that very small space of time, and a man could do whatever he wished, as though the sun were there, even remove lice from his shirt, and if they had been on a mountain-top perhaps the sun would never have been hidden from them."[7]

The lonely green land under the shield of ice mountains, headlands of dark lava guarding its shore, must have seemed to the harried monks a retreat forever safe. Its closest neighbor was Greenland 180 miles to the west (also discovered in their wanderings by Irish monks, who reported on "loathsome stinging creatures" found there, nearly as large as frogs, a somewhat baroque reference to mosquitoes), but its primitive inhabitants seemed unlikely to venture far from their own shores. Europe was almost beyond reach, far to the southeast.

But for a storm and a chance landing Iceland might be Irish today. For eighty years the monks were undisturbed, and by 874 there were probably more than a thousand scattered along the

[7] *Liber de Mensura Orbis*, Dicuil, 825

72

south shore. It is probable that the anchorites did not know of the coming of the first Viking. Naddodd, about whom little is known but that he was the first Scandinavian to set foot on Iceland, set sail from Norway around 860 with the intention of going to the Faeroes. His ship was caught in a storm and blown hopelessly off course to the west. His eventual landfall, some 1,000 miles from his point of departure, was Reydarfjord, Whale Fjord, on Iceland's east coast, a narrow arm of the ocean with steep rocky sides. He beached his boat at the head of the fjord and climbed a hill to reconnoiter the land for signs of habitation. Being far north of Irish territory he saw no smoke or any other evidence of people. Though it was summer, snow began to fall and the newcomers, as they sailed away, named the place Snowland.

In spite of the weather they brought home a good report of what they had seen, and a few years later a Swede named Gardar Svafarsson went to see what he could see — guided by his mother, reads the account, who had second sight. He made land in the southeast, and perhaps his boat was seen, for his landfall was at Hornafjord, Horn Fjord, named for its shape, one of the few harbors on the south shore, a calm anchorage and a flat shore where monks would likely have settled. He did not stay at Hornafjord but sailed right around the country, the first to discover that it was an island. He built a house at Husavik, House on the Bay, on Skjalfandi, Shivering Firth, a broad inlet in the north bordered by green hills and valleys and wooded (then but not now) from the mountains right down to the sea. There he stayed for one winter. When he sailed home he was full of praise for the new land, which was renamed Gardar's Isle.

A Viking named Floki Vilgerdarson was the next explorer. He and his comrades, intending to settle, took cattle with them, though knowing nothing about the nature of the land they brought no women. Three ravens sailed with them, for which their leader was later called Raven-Floki. A few days out of Norway they set free the first one, which flew directly home. The second raven, released in mid-ocean, flew up into the air and came back to the ship. With the last bird they were lucky. It flew straight ahead and they followed it to land, which was again Hornafjord. They sailed close along the coast, undoubtedly watched by fearful monks, rounded Reykjanes Peninsula and entered the wide deep bay where now Reykjavik stands. One of the warriors, Faxi, said, "It must be a big country we've found; the rivers are big enough,"[8] and Reykjavik's harbor still bears his name, Faxafloi, Faxi's Bay (originally Faxi's River).

They did not land there but kept sailing north and finally came to land in Vatnsfjord, Water Fjord at Bardaströnd, Shore's Edge, on the mountainous coast of the Northwest Peninsula. There were so many fish in Vatnsfjord that the men got caught up with fishing and forgot to cut hay, so all their cattle died in the winter. The party was further discouraged by an extremely cold spring. Floki climbed a mountain, and north across the range he saw Fossfjord, Cataract Fjord, southern arm of Arnarfjord, Eagle Fjord, packed with the floe ice that used to drift from Greenland every spring. When he came down he told his men that the whole country was nothing but ice, and they decided to go home. But it was winter again before they could make ready. Then they lost their towboat in a storm while tacking around Reykjanes. One of their companions was on it and they didn't find him until springtime, after wintering in Borgarfjord, Fjord of Hills, in sight of the beautiful but icy Snaefellssnes, Cape of the Snow Mountain, a peninsula with an extinct volcano buried under a glacier in the middle of it. Back in Norway at last, Floki had nothing good to say about the new country, which he called Iceland.

One of his men, Thorolf, had a different report. The land was so rich, he said, that butter dripped from every blade of grass. His name became Thorolf Smior, Thorolf Butter. He is not known for anything but this remark, but his words led to the founding of Scandinavian Iceland.

Two blood-brothers, Hjörleif and Ingolf, who had traveled and plundered and fought long enough, needed to settle. They could have chosen civilized Ireland, as had many of their friends, but the unknown attracted them. A lonely island far out in the ocean, whose very grass dripped butter, seemed an ideal final landfall for two war-weary Vikings. Only one of them, Ingolf, survived, to become Iceland's first permanent Norse settler. "The

[8] *Landnamabok*

summer Ingolf and Hjörleif went to settle in Iceland . . . was 6073 years from the Beginning of the World, and 874 years from the Incarnation of our Lord."[9]

Eighty-one years before this a band of Norse pirates had plundered the island monastery of Lindisfarne, off the Northumbrian coast of England. That was the first Viking raid, the beginning of nearly three hundred years of successful piracy. It was not all brigandage. A large majority of the Norsemen eventually went back to become responsible citizens of countries they had ruthlessly pillaged, and the Viking Age was the period of the blending of the Norse with the English, French, Russian and Irish peoples to produce the modern nationalities of those countries. Colonization, however, was secondary to the early Vikings, and secondary in the view of their victims. In their own day the Norsemen were known and feared primarily for their flamboyant success as seagoing bandits. The monks on Iceland's pristine shore, when the first long ship appeared, unmistakable with its red and blue checked woolen sail swelling in the wind, saw not possible friends or future settlers but those same infamous robbers from whose depredations they had but recently fled. Vikings, to the Irish as to the rest of Europe, were synonymous with bloodshed.

The people of Scandinavia were actually no more greedy or bloodthirsty than most Europeans of those centuries. Men were in the habit of fighting for kingdoms, for family honor, for plunder, for revenge, or just for the sake of fighting. The young Norwegian of distinguished family who went "on his viking," or freebooting by ship to foreign parts as a sort of *grand tour* to gain experience in warrior ways, was little different from the itinerant knight seeking out other knights to engage in armed combat on flimsy excuses. The word "Viking" points up the only real difference. It is derived from "*vik*," bay, and refers to the "men of the bay" because the raiders always came by water. In this lay much of their invincibility.

Those early Vikings who found the undefended monastery on the English coast uncovered for their friends and relations a source of continuous bonanza. It was not customary in ninth- and tenth-

[9] Ibid.

century Europe to people the churches and monasteries with armed defenders because hardly anyone would attack them. This was partly on account of the force of spiritual sanctions in the Christian world and partly because any unscrupulous ruler who wanted the wealth of a monastery had only to confiscate its land and privileges and take what he wished without bloodshed. The pagan Norsemen, immune to the strictures of an alien religion, found the defenseless monasteries absurdly easy game. With their highly maneuverable ships they got into the shallowest bays and narrowest estuaries, pounced swiftly and were gone before anyone could raise enough outcry to summon help.

The explosion of the Vikings over northern Europe was partly due to a dramatic increase in Norway's population and partly to increased technological skills. Around 350 A.D. the people of Norway, which had never been occupied by the Romans, came under Roman influence to the extent of learning the use of iron for tools and weapons. These northern Teutons, hardly beyond the Stone Age, inhabited only the coastal regions, and the new knowledge gave them access to their rich interior. Norway had immense natural resources of iron and wood, and her primitive population soon learned how to reduce the native ore. The resulting abundance of cheap tools made it easy to hack farms out of the virgin forests. The new lands were uncommonly fertile. Living was easy, families were large and healthy, and by the seventh century the third, fourth and fifth sons found there were not enough fields to go round. They turned to the sea. The same combination of iron and wood served them in their new pursuits of boat-building and the construction of fine weaponry. Norway's shoreline of deep, calm fjords seemed created especially for ships. Add to this an apparently endless supply of lumber and a floating population of younger sons with excellent tools and weapons, and Norway's destiny as a major sea power — and the resulting barbaric magnificence of the Viking Age — was inevitable.

At first the sailors were out only for what they could grab and return home with to decorate their fathers' halls and adorn their wives. As land became scarcer the voyagers found themselves coming home to a less certain welcome. There was jealousy over ownership and inheritance, anger between brother and brother, and feuds that split families down the middle. Excessive bloodshed led to lawsuits and exile. Some of the Vikings became permanent freebooters. Many others, forced to leave home, decided to settle somewhere else. Though landless, they were still basically farmers. Tilling the land was a more congenial tradition to them than indefinitely wandering the sea. By the beginning of the ninth century the helpless inhabitants of England, France and Ireland became unwilling hosts to a quantity of buccaneers turned homeowners.

Around this time a new element appeared in the Norwegian picture: government by king, better known to the ninth-century Norwegian landowner as centralized tyranny. The children and grandchildren of the simple farmers who had cleared and plowed were not themselves simple farmers. Families had joined properties through marriage, younger sons had brought home the wealth of European monasteries, and a hard-working peasantry had become an oligarchy of rich *jarls*, earls, with vast holdings, subservient *karls*, farmers, and trains of *thræls*, slaves, from the countries they had pillaged. Family was supreme, and the heads of families ran the country, kings in practice, while the elected king was a figurehead.

In Norway of the Middle Ages he could be nothing else but a figurehead. Among the early Teutonic peoples land was held in absolute ownership without acknowledgment to any superior. Title was transferred automatically from eldest son to eldest son in a hallowed tradition of *"odal* rights."[10] This unconditional hereditary ownership made it impossible for a king to rule. He could command nothing from his wealthy, powerful subjects, not money nor arms nor any sort of service whatever.

Harald Haarfager, Fairhair, who ruled Norway from 862 to 930, decided to become king in fact as well as in name. There was no legal way in which he could undermine the power of the family

---

[10] *"Odal"* is the parent word of *"edel,"* noble, for early nobility was based on the ownership of land. Norway still adheres to the ancient system of *odal* rights, and the old laws can be extremely confusing in modern real estate transactions.

chieftains, so he attacked the very base of the problem, the *odal* rights, disputing titles and abrogating inheritances. The enraged *jarls* responded by attacking the king's men whenever they appeared, and there was open warfare throughout Norway. Harald's mercenaries and berserkers[11] were better organized than the motley crowds of *karls* and *thræls* pressed into service by the noblemen, and wherever he chose to do battle he was victorious. But the oligarchy did not give up easily, and in 872 their finest warriors were summoned by the *jarls* Kjotvi the Wealthy, Thorir Long-Chin, Onund Treefoot, Geirmund Swarthyskin, Soti and King Sulki for a full-scale encounter in Hafrsfjord, Whale Fjord. Harald's forces won decisively, most of the leading opposition was killed or wounded, and the *jarls'* power was finally broken. Harald's next step was organized taxation. The defeated nobles' reaction to this latest insult was to emigrate. This was more than the king had envisioned in his bid for strength, and he tried unsuccessfully to stem the exodus by laying a visa tax of four ounces of silver on each emigrant. His enemies paid, and departed in crowds.

The proud men who left Norway to escape what they considered outrageous infringement of their rights were not interested in going to another country where they might encounter more of the same. The living was easy and the pickings were good in the countries of Europe where their friends and relatives had settled. But they had no wish to exchange one bossy government for another. They were not poor farmers who had to scramble anyhow for a living, but men of property who could choose their land and their style of life. They chose a new land which they could shape to their desires.

So it was that in 874, two years after the defeat at Hafrsfjord, Irish monks on the south coast of Iceland looked up from their

---

[11] Berserkers were warriors subject to fits of frenzy during which they howled like wild animals, foamed at the mouth and gnawed at the iron edges of their shields. At these times, suffering neither pain nor fear, they were invincible. The word *berserk* means bearskin. Instead of armor they usually wore the skin of a wolf or a bear, and it was thought that in the fever of their rages they were transformed into the animal whose skin covered them.

devotions and saw a fleet of businesslike wooden ships nosing around the headland, heard the lowing of cattle and the crying of children, and knew that their retreat was irrevocably invaded.

The ships, called *knarrs*, designed for ocean travel, were simple, broad-beamed and heavy. No carved dragons adorned the prows nor painted overlapping shields the sides as on the swift, showy warships. Each weighed about twenty tons, measured about fifteen feet in the beam and fifty-five feet from stem to stern. The prow curved upward to a high point, the better to breast the waves. A single square woolen sail was hoisted on a central mast by walrus-hide lines and rings of willow-wood, and fifteen pairs of sweeps with narrow blades protruded ten or twelve feet from holes below the gunwales. The ships were partly decked fore and aft. Each held about thirty people as well as cattle, sheep, horses, tents, cooking utensils and all the cargo needed to sustain life on the ocean and make a start in an empty land.

Comfort was no part of the Norsemen's new venture. Seaworthy as they were, the *knarrs* shipped water even in moderate seas, and the half decks were little protection. The men had *hudvats*, hide vats — hammocks in the shape of bags, made of cowhide — in which they carried tools and weapons and which, emptied, served as sleeping bags to keep two warm and dry at night. No fires could be lit at sea, and the adventurers subsisted for the journey of many weeks on dried and salted fish and meat, with sour milk and beer to drink. Water was carried in large skin bags, and fodder for the livestock was stored under the decks.

Any monk who had missed meeting a Viking before he left Ireland must have been terror-struck at the appearance of the men who stepped out of their beached boats. They were enormously tall. Scandinavians are now among the tallest people in the world and in the ninth century, before they mixed with smaller neighbors and captives, they were even larger. Blond or red curly hair fell to their shoulders and framed ruddy bearded faces with strong long noses and extraordinarily light eyes, blue or gray.

Even more frightening than the size of the intruders were their weapons. Some carried huge two-edged swords; most had slung over their shoulders long-handled broad-edged battleaxes, one of barbaric Europe's oldest weapons, specifically Nordic and a well-known symbol, even if the monks had never seen one before, of the bloodthirsty Viking.

It was entirely evident to Iceland's older inhabitants that the Norsemen were moving in. What did the newcomers think about the monks? History is silent. How a thousand or so holy men, established for eighty years or more, managed to disappear immediately after 874, leaving hardly a trace, is a deeply shrouded secret. The contemporary accounts are noncommittal. "The Christian men," states the most explicit of them, "whom the Norsemen call Papar were here; but afterwards they went away, because they did not wish to live here together with heathen men, and they left behind Irish books, bells and crooks. From this it could be seen that they were Irish."[12]

Had the monks built no churches out of the loose stone with which that coast is littered? None is recorded, nor was note made of any kind of shelter from the weather, any domestic animals, any agricultural activity, any sign at all of their having to wrest a living from a cold harsh land for the whole span of a man's lifetime. For all the historical record the Irish monks might have lived thriftily on manna from heaven for all those eighty years.

But the comely oasis of Kirkjubær, where the monks had had their earliest community, could not be settled by pagan Norsemen. It was a coveted acreage, lying protected at the foot of a wooded hillside, its green fields stretching south and east to meet the black sands. But a spell was on it, bringing ill luck and death to any non-Christian rash enough to settle there. "Ketil [a Christian] made his home at Kirkjubær, where the Papar had been living before and where no heathen was allowed to stay . . . Hildir wanted to move house to Kirkjubær after Ketil died, not seeing why a heathen should not farm there, but as he was coming up to the fence of the home meadow, he dropped down dead."[13]

Landnamabok never comes right out and says it, but the hint is there. The Norwegian immigrants brought from home a legion of superstitions regarding death, among them the vengeance of the

---

[12] *Islendingabok*, Ari Thorgilsson the Learned, *circa* 1130
[13] *Landnamabok*

slain. The spirits of the dead, if they had not liked the manner of their death, did not simply haunt the living, they afflicted them with sores and sickness, drove their livestock crazy, set their hay-ricks on fire, dropped rocks on their roofs and tore to pieces any-one foolhardy enough to challenge them. The sagas are full of accounts of malicious acts by the spirits of men whose corpses did not lie easy, and whole villages were known to have been deserted following the mayhem committed by belligerent ghosts. Kirkjubær may have been taboo to the heathens for a good reason. The curse did not extend to Christians. Later a convent was founded there, and the place became Kirkjubærklaustur, Church Farm Cloister.

Ingolf Arnarson and Leif Hrodmarsson, who came to Iceland in 874 with the intention of permanent settlement, had become blood brothers in youth. Together they had knelt in Thor's tem-ple. Each had drawn his sword and opened a vein in his arm. Their blood mingled and sank into the earth as if it were the blood of one. Asking all the gods to hear their oath, they swore to share the same dangers and to defend each other to the death. "May one and the same fate come over us," they said at the end. They engaged in Viking raids together, and after a particularly success-ful one they gave a feast for their companions. One of these, deep in mead, bragged that he would marry the girl who was Leif's intended. Leif flushed red and, when the feast was over, called on his blood brother to help him avenge the discourtesy. There was a battle and the boaster was killed. In Norway of the ninth century battles over trivial insults were frequent, but killing was not gen-erally condoned. The killer had to pay compensation to the vic-tim's family, and in this case the judgment was that Leif and Ingolf had to give the young man's father everything they possessed.

There was nothing left for the blood brothers in Norway and they decided to emigrate. Floki's land of ice appealed to them but they were destitute. In order to recoup some of their losses, Leif went west, to Ireland, and plundered for an entire summer, return-ing with enough wealth to outfit ships for the new life. During one of his raids he found a cave, entered it and saw in the darkness a streak of light which came from a sword. He took the sword, killing its owner, and after this he was called Hjörleif, Leif the Sword. Among the loot he brought back from Ireland were the ten slaves, the Westmen, who involuntarily gave their names to the Westmann Islands.

Ingolf and Hjörleif set sail for Iceland in the summer of 874. Before they left Norway, Ingolf held a sacrifice in the temple of Thor to propitiate the gods. Then he dug a shovelful of earth from beneath the temple to plant in the new ground. On his boat he carried the high-seat pillars of his old home. The high-seat pillars were dedicated to Thor, and they were the emblem of tribal chieftainship. In the ancestral hall benches were placed along the walls, with two large seats of honor in the middle, facing each other. The northern seat, facing the sun, was called the *ærdra*, the higher, and it was the master's. The southern seat was the *nædra*, the lower, and here was placed the most honored guest. The side supports of these thrones were pillars of wood carved with runes relating notable exploits in the family history. When a Norseman emigrated, the pillars were an indispensable part of his baggage, religious and authoritarian symbols to guide him to land and take their place in the new hall.

Hjörleif, who had come briefly and bloodily in contact with Christianity in Ireland, had learned just enough humanity to forswear heathen superstition. If he had learned more, or less, his life would have been longer.

The blood brothers sailed close together until they sighted land, then lost each other along the foggy southern coast. Ingolf threw his high-seat pillars overboard, vowing to settle wherever they washed ashore. He lost sight of them and steered for a promontory looming through the mist. On its landward side was a wide but shallow harbor, and there he made landfall, at the place now called Ingolfshöfdi, Ingolf's Headland, a long green-topped bluff 250 feet high forming a barrier island offshore. Beyond its protected harbor the shore was lined in both directions as far as the eye could see with rolling fields. A few miles north of the coastal plains rock ridges rose to the mountainous glacier of Öraefajökull.

Hjörleif sailed along the coast, and 72 miles west of Ingolf's anchorage he found a fjord cutting deep into the country. At the mouth of the fjord another green-thatched headland thrust into the sea, and there Hjörleif came to land. Hjörleifshöfdi, Hjörleif's Headland, as it was called later, was an unevenly flat-topped hill two miles long and 725 feet high. The fjord allowed him safe anchorage, and the country around his headland had pasture and woodland enough for all his large party with their cows, sheep and horses.

It was autumn, and Hjörleif immediately set his ten slaves to building two large houses in time to shelter the party in winter. One was eighteen fathoms across, the other nineteen. (One fathom is six feet.) When spring came he wanted to sow. He had only one ox, so he commanded his slaves to pull the plow. They were only poor Irish thralls, but they came of a race at least as proud and a civilization more sophisticated than that of Hjörlief. They had not done the work of animals at home, and they rebelled. When Hjörleif and his men were in one of the houses feasting, the slaves killed the ox. They went to their master to tell him that a brown bear had killed it. There were never any brown bears in Iceland, only an occasional polar bear that crossed the ice from Greenland in an exceptional winter. But neither the slaves, Hjörleif, nor the narrator of this tale, recorded in *Landnamabok*, knew that. Hjörleif and his men went to hunt for the bear. They spread out in the woods, and the slaves set on them and murdered them all, one after the other.

Ingolf was still looking for his high-seat pillars. He sent two of his slaves to search west along the coast and they came on the bodies scattered through the woods. More loyal or perhaps better cowed than Hjörleif's slaves, they went back to report to Ingolf, who hurried to the spot. When he saw his blood brother lying dead he exclaimed, "Little indeed went here to the undoing of a brave man and true, that slaves should have put him to death!"[14] The end of a life devoted to heroism should be, to a Norseman, a death at least equal to the most valorous of his life's deeds. A slave was hardly a soul, and a man killed by his thralls could not hope to enter Valhalla.

[14] Ibid.

Ingolf added a pious afterthought, decrying the taint of Christianity which had all too inadequately touched his friend: "But thus I see it goes with everyone who will do no sacrifice."[15]

For many years the fair hill of Hjörleif's landing was shunned. "No man dared to settle there on account of the guardian spirits of the land since Hjörleif was slain."[16]

The high-seat pillars had floated all the way around the southern tip of Iceland and come to rest at last on the shore of Faxafloi, the great bay discovered by Floki. Two of Ingolf's slaves, Vifil and Karli, found them at Arnarnes, Cape of Eagles, on the site of today's Kopavogur, a suburb of Reykjavik. In the third spring Ingolf moved all his families there, including the widows of Hjörleif's murdered companions, having spent the intervening year on the fertile plain of Hveragerdi, Garden of Hot Springs, where warm underground water irrigated the greenest fields in all of Iceland.

The thrall Karli said, "To an evil end did we pass through goodly countryside that we should take up abode on this outlying cape."[17] He ran away, taking a slave girl with him. But Ingolf looked beyond the desolate tumbled lava of Arnarnes and saw a deep, calm harbor, steam rising from gently rolling flower-strewn meadows that came right down to the water's edge; above this a rim of mountains widely enclosing the bay. Reykjavik, he called it, Bay of Smoke, and knew that this was the best place he had seen in Iceland.

Hjörleif's death and the departure of Ingolf left the south coast deserted. But news of Ingolf's successful settlement gave rise to a flood of wealthy and well-born emigrants anxious to escape what they regarded as an increasingly oppressive rule at home. First landfall, as with the earliest explorers, was usually the south coast.

Earl Rognvald had six sons, three of them illegitimate. His eldest legitimate son was killed in battle. The second, Hrolf (Rollo), later deprived of his inheritance by Harald Fairhair, went

[15] Ibid.
[16] Ibid.
[17] Ibid.

a-viking to the continent. He conquered Normandy in 911, turned Christian and was baptized Robert. He became the first Duke of Normandy and was a direct ancestor of William the Conqueror. From Hrolf are descended the kings of England.

Though the earl recognized his illegitimate sons, Hrolf's half-brothers, he did not think much of them. When one of them left on an expedition to the Orkneys his father said to him: "I am very glad you are going away, but I do not expect much of a man whose mother is descended from slaves on both sides."[18] Hrollaug, the eldest of the illegitimate sons, asked his father if he could accompany his brother to do battle in the Orkneys. Earl Rognvald answered: "You have a temper which is not suited to warfare . . . Your destiny does not lie here."[19] In effect driven from home, Hrollaug threw himself on the mercy of King Harald, who aided his emigration to Iceland. Harald, unable to stem the wholesale departure of his enemies, was already looking for allies who would advance the royal cause in the new country.

With his wife and sons Hrollaug made landfall at Hornafjord, after some months of the usual drifting around to hunt for his high-seat pillars. Southwest of Hornafjord were the fields and woods of Breidamerkur, Broad Boundaries, a lovely wide vale open to the sun and the sky and the unusual warmth that is caused by glacial reflection. There Hrollaug established his farm and became a great chieftain, the chief landowner of the south coast. To the end of his life he stayed friends with King Harald, who sent him a sword, a drinking horn and a gold ring weighing five ounces. South coast families descended from Hrollaug to the thirty-fourth generation (the 1970s) legitimately claim cousinship, although through the bar sinister, with English royalty.

Breidamerkur, generously fertile at the time of the Settlement, is today a long gray waste of watery sand. The tremendous eruption of Öraefajökull in 1362 flooded parts of the shore with mud and rocks and buried others under a thick layer of volcanic ash and pumice. In the increasingly deleterious climate of the eighteenth

[18] Ibid.
[19] Ibid.

and nineteenth centuries the glacier Breidamerkurjökull, another outlet of Vatnajökull, advanced, swallowing the remaining farms and reaching down to within 650 feet of the ocean. The glacier has receded in the warming trend of the past 75 years but the green vale of Breidamerkur has vanished. Now it is called Breidamerkursandur, the Sands of Breidamerkur, and aside from being home to thousands of pairs of nesting skuas it is an abandoned wasteland.

SIX

The Southern Sands

HORNAFJORD, WHERE THE Swede Gardar and the Viking Floki made their first landfalls, is a shallow fjord in southeastern Iceland about six miles wide at the ocean, bounded on its landward sides by low-lying green fields and a broad expanse of sandy gravel. At the threshold of the sea is a barrier island of sand nearly closing off the waters of the fjord. There is a narrow opening between the island and a ridge of rock to the east, through which ships can pass to enter the protected harbor of Höfn, Haven, one of the few fishing ports on the south coast.

The town of Höfn is on a thin spit of land pointing at the entry to the sea. It appears from the air to be more in the water than on land. On the black sand of the barrier beach just beyond it long layered breakers roll in over a barely sloping shore. On the inland side of the fjord more water, seeping slowly and endlessly from the ocean-reaching fingers of Vatnajökull, seams the gravel plain which itself was ice not long ago. The outwash plain merges imperceptibly with the fjord, and the green fields on both sides look from above like reclaimed ocean bottom. Höfn's mouse-colored houses, surrounded by water, could be low hillocks in a marsh.

Höfn bears a fleeting resemblance to a cowtown in the western United States. Wide unpaved streets are full of puddles on rainy days, dusty under the sun. The houses, mostly one story high, are of concrete unpainted or thinly whitewashed, and they look like wooden buildings, from the marks of the two-by-four frames into which the cement was poured. Each house is set back from the road in its plot of sparse grass with earth showing through. Toys and baby carriages, bicycles and pieces of old car motors litter the backyards as in countless backyards of rural U.S.A. There are a few chickens, and an occasional cow nibbles the gray grass at the roadside. Everything looks old and comfortable.

An oyster catcher flies screaming down the muddy street, and at once we know we are far from home. At the end of the town the masts of fishing boats swing as a sudden wind roughens the harbor. Scudding rain clouds part on the western horizon and the sun's rays, low at ten in the evening, shine through gusty rain. Two rainbows appear over the water, one above the other, the lower one brilliant, the upper broad and fuzzy. A skua chases a raven out of a field, stooping down out of the sky like a hunting falcon, and a snipe walks tamely through a patch of grass at our feet.

The countryside around Höfn is not flat, as it looked from above. The pastures flow steeply down to Hornafjord. Back of the fjord mountains rise, ridge on ridge, to the white peaks of Vatnajökull. Dark clouds roll across the tops of the hills and the reflection of cloud and sky flies over the water, gray and blue. The tall grass of the pastures, almost ready for haying, streams under the wind in long ripples. Everything moves in sweeping curves, from the dark of the sky to the lightness of the earth. A group of horses, chestnut, roan and dappled gray, blends into the wind-tossed scene, galloping across the side of a hill, heavy manes flying, long tails flowing behind them.

The sloping fields where the horses run give way, at the head of the fjord, to the outwash plain that once was glacier. Now it is water-washed gravel with areas of mossy bog and a scattering of low green mounds. Arctic terns hunt down the slow streams, diving after the small fish and crustaceans that started their lives in the comparative safety of the swamp. A pair of skuas, dark brown and heavy-bodied, appear in leisurely flight and the terns fly off at once. The clumsy-looking flight of the aerial pirates can change in an instant to a twisting, darting attack almost impossible even for the lithe terns to escape. With their sharp talons and hooked beaks the skuas will play havoc in the nesting area when the terns begin to lay their eggs. They will pluck the eggs from the open nests in sand or gravel; assail the parents bringing food to their young; chase them at sea to force them to drop their fish catch; will even seize a bird by the tail, drag it down to the water and hold it there until it gives up its food. Entire colonies of Arctic terns are sometimes harassed beyond endurance by the activities of one pair of skuas, and disperse without laying a single egg. At other times, of eggs successfully laid and chicks hatched, not one will reach maturity.

This pair of skuas, after quartering the ground, hawklike, comes to rest fearlessly near us. One settles into the earth as if on a nest while the other stands guard on a nearby hillock. We walk with caution. Nothing frightens a skua. It will not only dive at an intruder from the air but will make an alarming frontal charge low over the ground at anything, no matter how large, that approaches its nest. But this pair does not attack. The guardian bird flies as we come near, while the other waits until we are within a few yards before it too takes off. No space has been hollowed in the grass of the mound; the pair has not yet started to nest. They have probably only recently arrived from their wintering far out in the Atlantic. Soon the gravelly swamp will support a colony of skuas, as will the Breidamerkursandur to the west, the biggest skua nesting ground in the northern hemisphere.

There are no other birds on that great expanse. At the back of the empty plain is a farm, several buildings of corrugated iron painted white, with red roofs, set in the midst of a few acres of fields reclaimed from the swamp. It lies at the foot of Hoffellsjökull, Temple Hill Glacier, an outlet of Vatnajökull which until about a hundred years ago covered the plain down to the edge of Hornafjord seven miles distant. The farmer has chosen a place of, at first sight, appalling loneliness, a swamp at his front door, a glacier at his back, no companionship but that of skuas. There are many such farms in Iceland, in the midst of lava flows, on desert sands, tucked away between stony mountains. Wherever the grass touches, there are the farms, with their sheep and their few milk cows, eking a subsistence. The life is very hard. Even where the earth is good to begin with the farmer has to dig out the ubiquitous lumps, earth mounds thrown up by frost action, before his fields are level enough to till. In bogs and low-lying areas he has to dig miles of drainage ditches. To make the desert bloom he must transport sod and lay it in rows of squares over arid sand. In the lava fields he must gouge out acres of sharp-edged rocks. A stone wall of lacy burnt lava, red and black, lining a flowered field, is a lovely sight but it represents a painful labor.

The farm under Hoffellsjökull is marked by lines of grass-grown mounds along the drainage ditches. Marsh marigolds, heavy-flowered and bright gold, line the ditches, testimony to the fertility of the earth. Cows graze in fields of grass and buttercups. Dense-fleeced sheep, black, brown, white and piebald, wander over the boglands, finding sustenance enough there. Across the plain the farmer can see the rock ridge at the ocean's edge to the east of Höfn. Surf flares up in white flames beyond it. On either side of him are bare rounded mountains with snow on their tops and clouds flying through their valleys. Drifts of sunlight move over the mountains, reflected momentarily in ice and shining black rock. From his house only the tongue of the glacier is visible, dark brown and wrinkled. It does not look like ice, but from it flow eternally the fresh streams that give life to his land. All his prospects are unimpeded, and wherever he looks there is life and motion. It is possible to understand why the farmers of the south coast do not want to live anywhere else.

The early settlers had sailed or drifted west along the south coast, and we parallel their course on the single road that runs on the flats between ocean and glacier. The strip of verdure is varyingly wide, bordered on its inland side by long, curving palisades of columnar rock. Above them are stony ridges, and down the valleys between these run the tongues of Vatnajökull's outlet glaciers. To the north there is nothing but the Pleistocene ice, its monstrous gray-white heights usually lost in rain clouds. On the glacier it rains 150 to 200 inches a year.

The columned escarpments look like dikes to hold back the creeping glaciers and protect the farms beneath. On the ocean side the land is buffered by the barrier islands, some of rock, some of black sand dunes, that stretch almost without interruption from Höfn to Ingolfshöfdi sixty miles to the southwest. Between glacier and ocean the plains are dotted with the oases of the farms, their meadows rich with grass and flowers. The houses, surrounded by trees, lie in sheltered hollows. Of the forests that covered the country when the first settlers came, only a few patches remain. The trees that shade the farm buildings, mountain ash and larch and spruce, are lately planted. Outside these groves the countryside is open. The eye travels unendingly over the bare bones of the land. Lines of headlands and ridges are superimposed on one another, the nearest a sharp black outline, beyond it one sharp gray, then dimmer hazy gray shapes far into disappearing distance.

The sand and gravel plains are scored with water, wandering trickles and racing rivers. The lagoon between land and barrier beach is so shallow that the shapes of the rivulets continue right across it, like separate water within the water. Some of the streams on land have dried up and their courses are full of flowers. Others are new, cutting channels over the road. The bigger rivers change course continually. We keep passing remains of old bridges, crossing nothing, their erstwhile rivers half a mile away. The road, of dirt and gravel, needs constant repair; in fact almost the only signs of life on a rainy day are the villages of green prefabricated huts for the road workers being transported around the country by trailer truck.

One of the big rivers is the Jökulsa, Glacier River, a very short stream that carries more water than most of Iceland's rivers. It flows from a glacial lake directly into the ocean less than a mile distant. At the far side of its source lake is the tongue of the Breidamerkur Glacier, large pieces of which break off to float through the lake and down the river into the ocean.

About the year 900 Thord Illugi, shipwrecked on the Breidamerkur beach, was given land by the powerful chieftain Hrollaug. He built his farm at the foot of Breidamerkur Mountain which rises, stark and steep, beside the lake. Thord's land was fair and forested. His daughter married Hrollaug's son, and their descendants farmed there for nearly 800 years. During the seventeenth century the climate all over the world grew colder and, among others, Breidamerkur Glacier expanded. In 1695 its cold fingers touched Thord's farm, and fourteen years later houses, fields and woods were gone. The ice had reached the ocean.

The glacier started receding in the middle of the nineteenth century and its tongue, now a few miles above the site of Thord's farm, looks like a relief map of an unearthly mountain range, a million wrinkles, brown and white. The pleasant fields of his farm are a glacial moraine of mud and stones. Bare rock slopes down to the lake, once framed in trees. Now it looks Arctic. Hills of ice float in it, some mushroom-shaped, some tall and angular, all dark gray from the dusty tongue of the glacier. Near the lake's outlet the river current catches the little icebergs, turns them over and over and washes them to pale blue.

Even the beach across which the Jökulsa tumbles into the sea is empty of life. It is of black volcanic sand scattered with stones of gray basalt scoured and rounded by water. Mountainous waves pound in, twenty to thirty feet high as they break, their curling edges grayed by sand. There are no seashells or seaweed on the beach; no mollusk could live in that surf, no plant could cling to the rolling, water-polished rocks. The only jetsam is one of Breidamerkur's icebergs, brought down by the river, washed out to sea and tossed back on the beach by the breakers. The ancient ice was stone-hard from centuries of pressure. Even the ferocious waves could not break it, but they pared it down. Now it is futuristically concave, thin and transparent as glass.

A few black-backed gulls hunt low over the waves and one seal shows its head far out. But the water is not kind even to seals. On the beach lies a dead one with blood on the side of its head where it has been hit, probably by a heavy bit of flotsam in the surf. It has not been dead long, possibly only minutes, for the scavenging black-backs have not discovered it. It is a hair seal, silver-colored with darker silver blotches on its back. The hair seal is the common seal of Iceland, about five feet long, with no external ears on its smooth head, and large eyes that easily fill with tears. Like all the members of the *Phocidae*, so-called true seals, it cannot turn its hind flippers forward, so is unable to walk on land. In order to navigate out of water it has to wriggle clumsily on its stomach. It makes up for earthly awkwardness with extraordinary skill and grace in the water. It can tread water, swim on its back, achieve a speed of fifteen knots, dive as deep as 150 fathoms and stay under for twenty minutes. There are no harems, as hair seals are not polygamous. Loose colonies may form around breeding time, when the young are born on secluded beaches and nursed on land until they learn to swim at about four months. Mostly solitary, almost always far out at sea, feeding only on small fish and shellfish, the harmless, appealing little seals have no serious enemies but man. When they follow the schools of fish that the commercial fishermen consider their personal property they are shot out of hand. This represents a far greater danger to the hair seals than the only two animals which are swift and agile enough to catch them, killer whales and polar bears. Neither of these animals kills for anything but food, and until recently the seals were so numerous that they could afford to lose a few to their far less populous predators.

We cross the Breidamerkur Sands, an eleven-mile stretch of gravel plain grooved with slow-meandering water courses. Though at first sight the sands are barren as recent ocean bottom, and resemble it, ridged and rippled by wind and water, the long plain is not quite desert. The skua colony is arriving, and the big dark birds follow one another in courting play, twisting and diving in midair, or perch on the low mounds that soon will be the sites of their shallow nests. There are patches of last year's grass, sparse and wispy like an old man's hair, and fat clumps of moss campion dot the dun gravel with pink and green, brilliant in the rain.

The Breidamerkur Sands peter out in a narrow trickle of muddy lagoon between the frowning Öraefajökull and the low, surf-washed barrier islands. Before us is only emptiness, the eighteen miles of the Skeidararsandur, where no one can live and until recently no road built could withstand the slow, continuous, everyday flow of mud, sand and water from ice-covered mountains to the sea, and the periodic floods produced by glacial bursts. The rain has become a slanting downpour driven by a cruel, cold east wind. The murk of the sky merges with the dull brown of the sands, and there is nothing else. The lagoon, its water flattened and darkened by rain, widens, and far offshore appears a landmark, the barrier island of Ingolfshöfdi. It is lonely and dark and high,

93

and white spume from wind-driven surf flies over its rocks. On a day like this it would have made a grim welcome to the ocean-weary travelers.

But Ingolf found it a landfall of singular grace. When he came ashore, the lagoon was a fine quiet harbor beyond the grass-topped bluff. The rolling fields of the mainland stretched back to mountain and glacier, black rock sharp against white ice. Now those fields are flattened gravel and the harbor is silted to wet sand braided with muddy rivulets. No one lives on Ingolf's headland today, and no trace remains of his landing. Early settlers built, as did later comers — in fact all Icelanders until a generation ago — of mud, turf and driftwood, and most houses disappeared into the scenery within twenty years. The only human signs on Ingolfshöfdi are an automatic lighthouse and a refuge hut for wrecked seamen. The only life is that of the thousands of fulmars, puffins, murres and razorbills that inhabit the oceanside cliffs.

Eleven hundred years ago, when Ingolf found refuge there, the island was no wilder or more inaccessible than it is today.

The landfall of Ingolf's murdered blood brother is more approachable. But if Hjörleif came back today he would not know it. His headland lies directly south of Katla, the volcano in the Myrdalsjökull. In its many eruptions the ice-buried volcano has produced glacial bursts that leveled the hills and created the Myrdalssandur, a 22-mile-long stretch of desert at the edge of the ocean. Hjörleifshöfdi, once at the mouth of a fjord, is now two miles inland. No surf beats on the sheer rock of its cliff face, though the ocean's signs remain, long gouges in the soft stone. The forests of birch and mountain ash that clothed the once hilly countryside have given way to those small, hardy desert colonizers, moss campion, mouse-ear chickweed, and sea pink. Where ocean waves pounded and forest leaves rustled, a silent waste of black volcanic sand stretches in all directions, and dark blue streams coil slowly across it to the shallow sea. Tall and green, Hjörleifshöfdi rises intact from the barrens, untouched by the destruction all around it.

We walk across sand as flat and rippled as a quiet sea to the base of the bluff. There is no way up from the oceanward side, where long ago waves hollowed the rock into caves and overhangs.

94

A hut of corrugated iron with life-saving insignia on its door stands before one of the deeper caves. Ships have often gone aground in the shallow waters of the south coast. Farms are necessarily set many miles inland and seamen, escaped from wrecked ships, have died of starvation and exposure trying to find their way over the swampy sands in winter snows and summer fogs. Refuges have been set up for them at intervals along the lonely beaches. Each contains food, medical equipment, a stove and a radio. Hjörleifshöfdi's little house looks homely and reassuring under the great water-carved cliff.

Back of the oceanside precipice, rock gives way to earth. The grassy slope is scored by an old watercourse, and double ruts indicate a wagon track through its bed. A strong wind at our backs helps us up the precipitous trail. Partway up, the brown gully widens into a green saddle, which opens to a softly rounded meadow. On three sides it is protected by the uneven ridge of the bluff, and the wind does not reach it. In a hollow are the remains of two shepherds' huts with sod roofs, and low wall of turf-covered stones enclose one-time sheep pens. With the years the huts and the walls have sunk, and all are covered thickly with grass. Probably less than a generation ago sheep were pastured here and shepherds stayed to tend them, but the scene is anciently primitive and the houses look like the round, part-underground dwellings of the Picts. It is not hard to imagine Hjörleif's Vikings here.

Today it is a still, secret place. We cannot see the ocean, only the empty sand. No wind blows and the only sounds are the sharp cries of a pair of oyster catchers we have disturbed. They fly around us, close to our heads, then settle to earth and walk nervously to and fro waiting for us to leave. When we move the cries cease and one of them begins to sing, a bubbling sound like musical gargling. The nest is near, probably in a burrow dug under one of the old sod roofs, but they do not enter it while we are still in sight.

From the shepherd's haven the hill rises abruptly to the summit. The slope is terraced by narrow sheep tracks and we follow these. The summit is bare rock, breaking off sheer on one side, slanting steeply on the other. Close to the edge there are cracks in the rock, raw wounds, and it looks as if it would break off at a touch. It is red lava and very brittle. One can pick sharp-edged pieces out of it, loose as if they had just been shoved in. Fulmars nest on broken ledges below and soar in deliberate circles around us.

The summit is marked by a wooden cross. Near it is a squat stone tower and a raised platform of squared-off lava blocks. The wind has been with us since we left the protected meadow, and here it is so strong that we have to crawl up the steps of the platform and crouch on the top. There are three flat gravestones. They are not those of the murdered Viking and his followers; the dates are 1906, 1919 and 1939. The deceased must have had devoted families to drag the large stones of their burial place up this high hill. They chose well. Mountains and glacier, ocean and sand lie around them in enormous, undisturbed loneliness. A rainstorm is coming fast, a gray curtain falling over the ocean. Under it the water is dark; on either side the sun shines on light green and white waves. Below the summit summer flowers are just starting on the bare red earth: mountain avens, cinquefoil and seaside sandwort. A snow bunting sings strongly from his perch on the stone tower, the wind ruffling him to twice his size.

One reason why the sites of Ingolf's and Hjörleif's settlements, and those of most of the early colonists, are so immutably lonely today is that their building materials were so destructible. It seems strange that a country which at first sight appears to be made entirely of loose stones should contain hardly any stone buildings. Then and now the farmers laboriously extracted mountains of stones from the ground and constructed with them only walls to delineate their fields. Along the bases of these lava walls they piled earth from the frost-created hummocks, which they also had to dig out. Grass grew over the earth, giving Iceland's miles of stone walls the romantically picturesque look of Victorian prints of rustic English gardens. The farmers' intent was purely functional, however. The walls were to keep their sheep in, or out. The early settlers ignored this obvious building substance for the reason that the emigrants from Norway, a country of forests, were exclusively wood-oriented. They had never seen stone used in building, except for the foundations, and they could not imagine their long halls and cattle sheds constructed of anything but wood. Ignoring the rock of which their pastures were largely composed, they collected driftwood along the beaches for the frames, made bricks of peat for the walls, and cut turf for the roofs. The buildings were frail and flammable. Those that did not burn down from the fires that had to be kept going summer and winter disintegrated within a generation.

Until recently the method of building, if not the style, was similar. In the early part of this century corrugated iron began to replace sod. It is a practical and inexpensive material which withstands the damp cold of the climate better than the old-time wood and turf. The buildings, usually painted white, with red or green roofs, are simple of shape and devoid of ornamentation. They are comfortable, airy and easy to keep warm and dry. There is nothing the matter with them at all. But their plainness is excessive in the wild beauty of their settings. The Icelanders, keenly sensitive in their literature, in the old days never developed an esthetic sense in their architecture. This is changing. Concrete is coming into general use in the larger towns, and the new architects, trained abroad, are beginning to discover the imaginative possibilities of that malleable material.

None of the dwellings of the Norse settlers remain, except for foundations. But a few of those built later have been preserved. They are beautiful in a way the iron houses never can be, because they are built of the earth. Their wood is weathered dark and the turf of the roofs has field flowers and dwarf birches growing in it. Low to the ground, as they had to be because of their materials, they look like doors into the hillsides.

A few miles from Ingolfshöfdi, in an oasis under a mountain, is the town of Hof, Temple. It consists of five or six houses and a little church which was built in the fourteenth century over the foundations of a temple for the worship of Thor. The original building was reconstructed in the nineteenth century, but it probably looks much as it did 600 years ago, since neither materials nor styles changed in all that time. The churchyard, surrounded by a low stone wall covered with turf, has mountain ashes in fragrant bloom and birches strongly aromatic in the damp air. The church is not more than ten feet high at its peak, and its grass-covered roof, with buttercups growing on it, slopes down on both sides to the ground. The original wood frame has been covered in the front with the ubiquitous corrugated iron to preserve it, but at the sides, between roof and front face, are rows of peat bricks placed diagonally to one another. Their color is soft red-brown. The small church and its green garden lie at the foot of a terraced escarpment like a grim castle wall, and before it are the dark sands of Skeidar. If anything would have motivated to spiritual meditation either tough Viking adventurer or hard-pressed Christian farmer, it would have been this flower-roofed church whose incense is the scent of trees in bloom, whose music is the ripple of water falling from the high rocks, a gentle sanctuary in a fierce wilderness. The old Icelanders may not have been inspired architects but they knew how to place their buildings.

Bright watery sunlight breaks through the rain and a rainbow touches the Skeidararsandur. We cannot see the other end of its arc; then the wind drives the clouds off the heights and there it is, like Bifröst, the gods' stairway from earth to Asgard, their celestial city, leading directly to Iceland's highest mountain, the nunatak Hvannadalshnukur. A row of black spires, called Kirkjan, Church, breaks through white ice and merges with the ice-capped summit rock. The peak appears suspended in the sky, the torn clouds of the storm flying above and below it, only the rainbow connecting it with earth. It is not hard to see where the writers of the Edda got their vivid picture of the home of the gods.

Hvannadalshnukur is but one of the peaks of Öraefajökull. Before recorded history Öraefajökull was a typical volcanic cone, much taller than it is at present. A particularly violent eruption blew it apart, leaving a vast depression called a *caldera* (cauldron) surrounded by the ragged edges of the collapsed cone, the nunataks that today bristle through the ice. Under the exploded volcano there is still a live core of magma, and no one knows when it will burst forth again through the walls of Hvannadalshnukur or out of the ice-hidden lower slopes.

Soon after the sight of Hvannadalshnukur, the road twists steeply upward from the flat sands into a mountain swathed in green, Skaftafell, Shaft Mountain, which was, when we were last there, the end of the coastal highway. Northward are the icy slopes of Vatnajökull, westward is the Skeidararsandur, eighteen miles of sliding sands and shifting watercourses. Skaftafell, a narrow isthmus between two glaciers, is a wild garden, one of Iceland's few woodlands. To insure its remaining so it was declared in 1967 a National Park, with the help of the World Wildlife Fund. Once these low forests covered most of the coastal regions. Some were cut over by farming settlers, some were used for fuel and building material. The main enemy of the trees, however, has been not man but man's animals. Cows and sheep, especially the latter, nibbled and trampled for centuries, destroying almost the entire ground cover, to such an extent that erosion is today a major agricultural problem.

The trees of Skaftafell are birch, mountain ash and willow, Iceland's only native trees. The land is capable of supporting other varieties, but being an island isolated by several hundred miles of ocean, neither plants nor animals can reach it easily. During the Eocene era, when Iceland was part of the Thulean Province, plants and animals moved freely around the enlarged continent of Europe. The later ice ages destroyed most life that had not been able to move south before their coming. When the Pleistocene ice retreated from the continent between twelve and eight thousand years ago the plants and animals began the slow migration back north. But by that time the Thulean Province was part of the North Atlantic floor and ocean-bound Iceland recovered no more than a handful of her erstwhile population, the flora and fauna that could travel by air or water. The country has only about 500 higher plants and no native mammals other than those that live in the ocean, Arctic foxes which migrated from Greenland over the sea ice and stayed to multiply, mink bred in captivity and escaped and, in the days before the recent warm-up, occasional polar bears which crossed the Greenland Sea in the winters but did not stay because the climate was too tepid for them.

Another conspicuous absence is that of amphibians and reptiles. This was noted with such surprise by a traveling Dane that he devoted a chapter to the anomaly. It reads, in its entirety: "Chapter LXXII, Concerning Snakes. No snakes of any kind are to be met with throughout the whole island."[1] A footnote by an assistant writer, a Mr. Anderson, "Late Burgo-master of Hamburgh," asserts that this is due to the "excessive cold." But Iceland is not as cold as many parts of the world that can support cold-blooded animals. Frogs and snakes, like other European creatures absent from Iceland, cannot navigate the ocean.

Beyond Skaftafell's old farm, where lived the family that owned the mountain for 600 years before it was nationalized, a trail leads upward through the trees along the river Skeidar. This wild stream is one of those tempestuous glacial rivers, careening full course in rapids and cataracts onto the sands below, whose ever-changing flood makes road-building so difficult. Up on Skaftafell mountain it stays perforce in the bed it has created, a steep and narrow rock gorge.

Along the lower reaches of the hills the trees, though small, are plentiful. The birches, *Betula odorata pubescens*, are none over sixteen feet, most barely reaching ten. Like our black birch and yellow birch, their leaves and twigs are fragrant with oil of wintergreen. The mountain ashes, *Pyrus aucuparia*, are a little bigger, sometimes reaching a height of twenty-five feet. The flowers, fruit and leaves of both birch and ash are exceptional delicacies to the grazing animals, and Iceland's tiny remnants of woodland have to be rigorously protected with barbed wire. The willows, of three varieties, *Salix phylicifolia*, or tea-leaved willow, *S. glauca* and *S. lanata*, are all dwarf, only the first-named growing sometimes to seven feet, the others resembling creeping shrubs. But they are unmistakably trees, old and knotty, with long tough roots and furrowed bark.

The small trees do not give deep shade, and many flowers bloom between and beneath them. *Geranium maculatum*, wild geranium, with flowers of deep magenta, grows tall and lush in the open spaces. Alongside it is *Matricia maritima*, scentless camomile, the wild daisy whose Icelandic name, *baldursbra*, goes back to Norse mythology and the young god Baldur, Odin's son, most beautiful and beloved of the gods: "So fair, so dazzling is he in form and feature, that rays of light seem to issue from him, and

---

[1] *Natural History of Iceland*, Niels Horrebow, 1758

thou mayest have some idea of the beauty of his hair, when I tell thee that the whitest of all plants is called Baldur's Brow."[2] In the shadows are *Viola tricolor*, wild pansy, with petals of contrasting purple and yellow. Along the river the tender flowers of forget-me-not contrast with the thick pink and white heads of cow parsnip. In dryer areas grows the carnivorous *Pinguicula vulgaris*, butterwort, a delicate purple blossom nodding at the end of a long stem which in turn rises from a rosette of sticky yellowish leaves. These give it its common name as well as its Latin name, which comes from the word for "fat." The upper surface of the leaves is covered with glandular hairs which secrete a gluey liquid. An insect alighting finds itself unable to rise. The leaf's edges slowly fold over, imprisoning it, after which it is dissolved and digested by an acid fluid. The flower, meanwhile, sways with impersonal grace at the end of its slender stalk.

One flower we looked for but did not find, that exists in Skaftafell and here and there along the south coast, is wild rose. It can grow nowhere else in Iceland. And one bird, the starling, is also restricted to the south. The gentler climate which allows these and a few other European immigrants to live here is due, oddly, to the presence of ice. The slopes of Vatnajökull and its outlets reflect the sun, and the reflected rays cast heightened brightness and warmth over the land below, giving the south an extra measure of summertime. The vegetation gets a further bounty from the inordinate rainfall, for which the glaciers are also responsible. Cold air from the icy heights and warm air off the Gulf Stream meet and clash over the south coast, resulting in eighty-nine inches of rain a year.

Higher on Skaftafell the trees give way to alpine meadows, and there yellow poppies bend under the wet wind, mountain avens, close to the ground, stares at the sky and cinquefoil looks like flashes of golden sunlight through the rain.

A mile up the river is a waterfall called Svartifoss, Black Falls, a remarkably geometric semicircular curtain of pillars. The formation, called organ-pipe lava, comes about when gas explodes through cooling lava whose surface crust has already solidified.

[2] *The Prose Edda*, Snorri Sturleson

The escaping gas makes miniature vents all over the solid surface and new, hot lava forces its way through these small holes as toothpaste is squeezed from a tube, hardening in long regular arrangements of cylinders. The slender vertical lines of the Svartifoss formation inspired the architecture of Reykjavik's new National Theater.

Above Svartifoss the land becomes tundra-like heath: hummocks covered with bilberry and mountain juniper alternate with muddy potholes where swamp cotton waves its white plumes. Heath gives way to the unkempt stony slope of the moraine, and above it Öraefajökull's seamed ice reaches beyond vision into the clouds. Below there is the great dark plain of the Skeidararsandur. Twenty miles away, across the water-patterned sand, the ocean's horizon is peaked by storm winds. The green hill of Skaftafell, with its pretty woods and bright flowers and tumbling river, is very small. And for us it is the end of this road.

Once the entire south coast was like Skaftafell. The settlers whose paths we followed found no barriers on land or sea. Fjords and forests, fields and rivers, offered all they needed for a new life. There were eruptions and glacial bursts then as now, but those who first landed came at a time between holocausts. Nothing in their experience told them that the land they found so gentle and welcoming was not so, that the mountains hidden under the distant ice hid unimaginable danger, that one day their farms would lie under a desert.

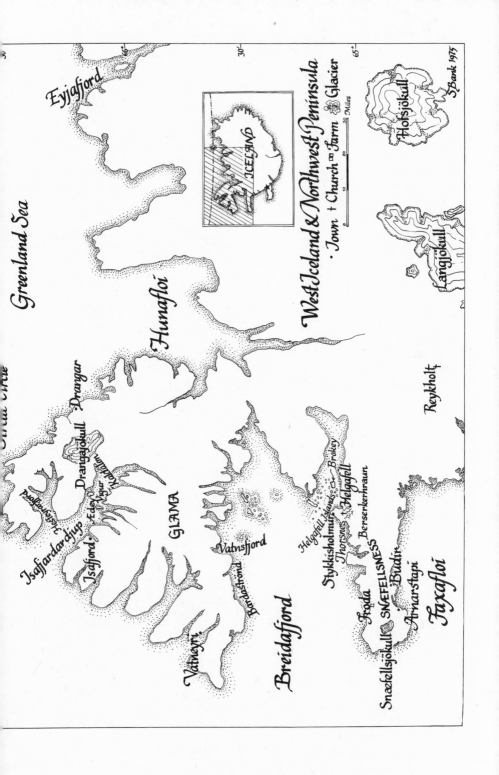

Greenland Sea

Eyjafjord

Arctic Circle

Hunafloi

Drangar

Drangajökull

Pjalfundisigs?

Isafjardardjup

Isafjord

Edey

Vigur

Vatnshorn

Naut-

GLAMA

Vatnsfjord

Vatneyri

Bardastrond

Breidafjord

Snæfellsjökull

SNÆFELLSNESS

Froda

Budir

Arnarstapi

Helgafell · Hjause · Brokey

Stykkisholmur

Thorsnes · Helgafell

Berserkerhraun

Faxafloi

Reykholt

Langjökull

Hofsjökull

West Iceland & Northwest Peninsula

· Town   + Church   ⌂ Farm   ❄ Glacier

Miles

ICELAND

S.Bank 1975

SEVEN

The Proud Republic

THE SETTLEMENT TOOK sixty years. Thousands of immigrants followed the first settlers, colonizing all the coastal regions. By the year 930, 20,000 had arrived and no arable land was left. Iceland could not then, nor can she now, support a large population, as most of the interior is either desert or ice. The early colonists needed a lot of land: fields for sowing barley, pasture for sheep and cattle, access to bog iron (a poor but important commodity), salmon preserves, shore land for fishing and seal-hunting.

Each man, after he had staked out the land his running slave had defined for him, put down the earth he had brought from hallowed ground in Norway and built a temple over it. The head of the family was also the head of the temple. He was called the *hof godi*, the temple priest (the word *godi* is derived from god, in the pagan sense) and, being the chief local landowner, he was chieftain by consent of his community of relatives and friends. The country became in those sixty years a patchwork of independent states, each one but an enlarged farm. Quarrels were frequent and they were settled by immediate violence.

The colonists, most of whom had emigrated as much to escape the continuous bloody bickering at home as to found a nation free of despotism, realized that if their dream were to come true they would have somehow to organize themselves. In 927 a wise and respected *godi*, Ulfljot, devised a code of laws based on

103

a body of Norwegian law. The wealthy *godar*, priest-chiefs, agreed to meet to hear Ulfljot read his code, and in 930 the first *Althing*, Parliament, was held at Thingvellir, Plain of Assembly, thirty miles east of Reykjavik. The code was accepted and the chiefs asked every Icelander to pay Ulfljot a penny. He would not accept the money for himself, and offered it for the building of a temple at Thingvellir.

Most of Ulfljot's Law has been lost; much of the little that remains is religious. It must have been a remarkable document. Iceland's first constitution was based on it, a complex system of equitable laws unlike anything previously known north of the Mediterranean. The rest of Europe was mired in medieval feudalism: abysmal poverty and ignorance went hand in hand with tyranny, and the only thought of despotic rulers was to make war on one another. Yet in Iceland these same Europeans, petty rulers, haughty, quarrelsome, subservient to no one, met willingly, and by free consent founded a republic with a legislative assembly where no man had first place and all (except slaves — and serfdom was abolished in the year 1000) were equal under the law. It was hardly a democracy, and suffrage was less than universal. But it was a consortium of free men, a concept unknown in practice since Greece's Golden Age. In these sixty years medieval Norse raiders, savage and predatory, barbaric to their fingertips, became farmers, fishermen, legislators, patriarchs, founders of a proud new republic.

The law parcelled the country into 39 *godord*, land presided over by a *godi*. There were three *godord* in each *thing*, shire, and the four quarters of the country were divided into thirteen *things*. The men subject to the *godi* were called his *thingmen*. They were not subject in the strict feudal sense, as their relationship was free. Though the *thingmen* promised to accompany and support the *godi* and he in return assured them of his protection, any man could leave if he pleased and "declare himself into the *thing*" of another *godi*. But the farmers had their duty to the *Althing*; every ninth man accompanied his *godi* to the yearly meeting, while the others were subject to a levy to pay the expenses of those who went.

Once a year, in June, the representatives, *godar* and *thingmen*, journeyed to Thingvellir for the two weeks of the *Althing*. There

*hingvellir, where the world's first parliament was held in 930 A.D.,
an ever-widening rift valley over a fault in the earth. In the foreground is the fissure from which the Law-Speaker addressed his
countrymen, massed on the plain below.*

they heard the reading of the law by the Law-Speaker, whom they elected every three years. Before the twelfth century nothing was written down, and the laws had to be preserved orally. The Law-Speaker carried the whole code in his memory and had to recite one-third of it each of his three summers. He spoke in verse; rhythmic alliteration made the code easier to remember. Besides this, every year he had to repeat the laws governing the *Althing*, and he further had the duty of stating the law on any point when consulted. The other main function of the *Althing* was to provide courts of law, with judges chosen by the *godar*, where cases were heard and judgments given.

There was no central administrative authority. Executive privilege lay in the hands of the individual *godar* and its use or abuse depended entirely on a balance of power between them. This was eventually to cause the downfall of the republic. As time passed some *godar* accumulated more land and paid more *thing-men* to join them, creating large private armies. At length most of the wealth was concentrated in the hands of a few families so powerful that they were beyond the law, and the early republicanism deteriorated. Their feuds led to disastrous internal dissension, to the extent that in the thirteenth century the king of Norway found it easy to intervene and finally to take over, ending the Commonwealth.

In the early years, however, the goodwill of the colonists kept the young republic healthy. Each session of the *Althing* was eagerly looked forward to as the most important political event and the most delightful social gathering of the year. Wives and children accompanied the representatives, and every family had its own booth on the wide plain of Thingvellir. During the two weeks of the session old friendships were renewed, new ones made, disputes were settled, marriages arranged. In addition to the social exchange there were sports events and contests: running, jumping, swimming, arrow-shooting, wrestling, spear-throwing. A vital part of Icelandic education was training in the arts of war, and those tall strong young men were physically uncommonly skillful. Some could jump higher than their height, or could leap backwards, forwards and sideways clad in complete armor and carrying weapons. Some could run faster than a horse, others could throw two spears at the same time and catch a spear in flight.

Besides contests in physical skill there were literary events: the recitation of new and old poetry and the telling of the sagas, long family tales that were handed down orally from old to young poets for two centuries before they were first inscribed. Literary education in ancient Iceland was considered of equal importance with athletic. A young aristocrat's ability to compose extraordinarily complicated verse was as highly respected as his prowess with the spear. Regard for poetry lasts into the present: the last sitting of every session of the *Althing* is conducted in verse, in homage to the old-time Law-Speakers.

Justice at the *Althing* was administered by a bench of thirty-six judges chosen by the representatives. Each case was first heard by nine jurors, neighbors of the litigants. Their function was not to give a verdict but to find whether there was a case to answer, and whether each step in the legal procedure had been properly followed. The jurors could be challenged by either side and dismissed for prejudice. After they had weighed the merits of the case it went to the judges, whose function was that of a modern jury, to give a verdict. Every effort was made to arrive at a fair finding in each case, and to follow the law with exactness. But the formality and subtlety of the legal procedure was offset by the fact that execution of the sentence had to be carried out by the litigant. Power and violence came to play a large role in the administration of justice. Men brought large groups, amounting to armies, to support their cases at the *Althing*, and they would stand threateningly, one on each side of the sitting court, glowering at one another across it. "Gunnar rode to the *Althing* accompanied by all the Sigfussons and by Njal and his sons; and they all went about together in a close group, and walked so briskly that people in their path had to be careful not to be knocked over . . . It was said that no other group there looked as formidable."[1]

Sometimes the judgments would be negated by a duel between the contestants, at other times compensation was arranged to fit the seriousness of the crime, and the convicted man would

[1] *Njalssaga*

108

raise it among his friends, the more easily if they were many, rich and strong. If he felt he had been well supported he would present gifts to the friendly chieftains. So justice in the end became mostly a matter of who had the largest number of wealthy friends and relations.

There were three types of punishment: compensation, outlawry and death. Compensation for killing could amount to everything the defendant owned. But in those rough times, when nearly every quarrel was settled with violence, there were nearly always mitigating circumstances. Sometimes one crime would offset another: Gunnar was wounded by the outlaw Otkel and killed him in turn; since the killing of an outlaw was not precisely murder the two misdeeds cancelled each other out. Thorgeir was wounded by the father of a girl he had seduced; the seduction was set against the wound and neither man was sentenced. In a set battle the number and worth of those killed was counterbalanced and compensation set accordingly. Social standing played an important part in compensation. A servant cost less than a householder; a simple farmer's death could not cancel out that of the son of a *godi*. Words were vital: battle over an insult was a matter of honor and was seldom punished. When Gunnar was accidentally wounded and failed to anger, a witness said, "Anyone of lesser birth would be said to have wept."[2] Gunnar avenged the slur on his manliness with his sword, and paid no compensation at all.

In the case of unprovoked or too-frequent murder a convicted man was usually outlawed and his property forfeited to the complainant, a small share of it going to the court. An outlaw could be killed with impunity by those who had won the suit, who also had themselves to carry out the sentence of forfeiture. If an outlaw had powerful friends he was smuggled out of the country and made his way back to Norway, where he recouped his fortunes raiding until his sentence was done. Sometimes, as in the case of Grettir the Strong, who was outlawed for his lifetime, the fugitive stayed on the fringes of society, living off the land, terrorizing his enemies and helping unfortunates in the manner of Robin Hood.

In most cases the death penalty was not invoked for murder,

[2] Ibid.

as the mere taking of life in clean, hand-to-hand combat had no stigma attached to it. The killer, however, must have immediately broadcast his deed to his nearest neighbors. Secret murder was the most heinous of crimes and, along with black magic and common theft, warranted sentence of death. The convicted criminal, if a man, was beheaded on an island in the river Öxara, which flows into the lake at Thingvellir. Women, not considered worthy of death by the sword, were drowned in a deep pool of the same river.

The life-style of the men who founded the *Althing* and followed Ulfljot's Law was based on the heroic idealism of the Norse religion. In the pantheon of the gods Odin and Thor held first place. Odin, called the All-Father, was the wisest of all, and worship of him was mystical. In a barbaric cult of strength and primitive wisdom he symbolized the three prime attributes of life — war, death and poetry — and he was specially revered in the early days by kings and princes and the poets who served them. Later on, particularly in Iceland, founded in defiance of kings and princes, where every chieftain, no matter how noble his birth, was a farmer and life did not include a constant necessity for doing battle with one's neighbors, Thor became the favored god. He belonged to the people. He was the god of the storms, quick to anger, quick to recover himself, a fighter without guile. When he was angry sparks flew from his red beard and lightning flashed from his eyes. His hammer was thunder. He ruled the wind and weather: in this realm he controlled the growing of the crops, so he was also the god of agriculture and fertility. In all his manifestations he was involved with the everyday life of farmers, blacksmiths, fishermen and sailors. He was an amiable companion and had a sense of humor, both traits notably lacking in Odin. Lesser gods and dwarfs easily outwitted him because he had no cunning. But he always won in the end through strength and honest, simple-minded courage. While Odin remained the Norseman's dream of spiritual perfection, Thor had more immediacy as the embodiment of his worldly life. The practical Icelanders considered him their own. Nearly every homestead had its temple to Thor. His hammer was a sacred symbol; people made the sign of the hammer to ward off evil influences, and the same sign was made over a newly born infant, along with water sprinkled on its head, to bring blessings. Many were the children named for him (but never in the genealogies does one find the name of Odin, too ethereal for domestic familiarity). The *Althing* still opens its sessions on Thor's Day, Thursday.

"Far to the east of the River Tanaïs [Don] in Asia," wrote Snorri Sturleson in the thirteenth century, in the prologue to his long poem, *The Beguiling of Gylfi*, "is a land called Asaland, whose chief city is called Asgard. In that city was a chief called Odin. It was a great center for sacrifice. Twelve priests of the temple . . . directed the sacrifices and judged between them. They were called gods, or lords; everyone paid them service and veneration . . . Odin was wise and skilled in magic and people called him when in trouble."[3]

Snorri was alluding to the belief, held all through the Scandinavian countries and recorded as early as the fifth century, that the Norse people originated in Asia and Asia Minor and were of Trojan and Greek descent. The fifth generation descendant of Dardanus, a son of Zeus, was Priam, king of Troy. Under Priam were twelve tributary kings of Tyrkland (Asia Minor), of which Troy was the chief city. One of the twelve was named Munon or Mennon. He married a daughter of Priam, and their son was Thor, a handsome youth of extraordinary strength, a slayer of giants and destroyer of the greatest dragon on earth.

After the fall of Troy the Trojans emigrated, splitting into two main groups. Aeneas and his followers went to Italy and founded Rome. The other party, led by Thor's son, Loride, crossed the great mountain range (the Caucasus) that divides Europe and Asia to Asaland (Asia-land) where they founded the city of Asgard on the river Tanaïs where it empties into the Black Sea, and there preserved the Trojan customs and language. A direct descendant of Thor in the twentieth generation was Odin, a wise and well-informed man who became ruler of Asaland in the first century B.C. He also had large possessions in Tyrkland.

There had been no contact between the closely related peo-

---

[3] *The Prose Edda* of Snorri Sturleson

ple of Rome and Asgard, though both capitals kept up Trojan traditions. At the time of Odin's rule Rome, which had grown into a mighty power, sent an army into Tyrkland under the command of Pompey. Though the land across the mountains was not yet threatened Odin lost his Tyrkland holdings and decided to emigrate before his own country should be invaded. With many followers he moved slowly northward, stopping in Germany, France and the Scandinavian countries. He was welcome everywhere because he seemed to bring good luck to the crops, and he came to be regarded as a man of magical skill and superhuman wisdom. He stopped finally to found a new Asgard in the north, some say in Sweden. Such was his renown that he was able to set his sons to rule in many of the lands they had passed through: Westphalia, France (where they founded the Volsung clan, Siegfried's family), Denmark and Norway. Poetry and the other arts came with him from the south, as well as the memory of the old Asgard and the fall of Troy.

All the later events recorded by Snorri in *The Beguiling of Gylfi*, the complex web of tales of which the Norse polytheism consisted, were related by him as true happenings that followed the northward migration of Odin and his people, and he presented the gods as the mortal heroes of that earlier age. Even Loki, the perfidious, whose black deeds were to bring ultimate destruction to the northern Asgard, had another name. He was Ulysses, the most cunning of the foes of Troy, who brought about its final storming and the fall of its kings. Through Priam, is Snorri's conclusion, the Greek gods are the direct ancestors of the Norse gods. The similarities in many of the legends are too striking for these early accounts to be based altogether on scholarly invention.

Snorri was a scholar well versed in classical history, able to read Latin and Greek easily. He was also a Christian priest and teacher. How much of his retelling of the legends is historic fact and how much was due to his wish to play down the pagan religious aspect and reduce the gods to the status of mortal men, we cannot now determine. Whatever his motives, however, the stories are deep in the Teutonic past. Centuries before the Icelandic scholars first recorded them they had hardened into the formal and fantastic body of Norse mythology, the religion that governed thought and behavior over all the non-Christian northern countries for about a thousand years.

It is written in *Völuspa*, the Seeress's Prophecy, a pre-Christian song of the creation:

> 'Twas time's first dawn,
> When nought yet was,
> Nor sand nor sea,
> Nor cooling wave;
> Earth was not there,
> Nor heaven above,
> Nought save a void
> And yawning gulf.
> But verdure none.[4]

Around this tenantless space of gray twilight were Niflheim, Abode of Fog, and Muspellheim, Abode of Fire. Guarding the border of Muspellheim was Surtur, the First Spirit. When the hot smoke from Muspellheim met the ice clouds of Niflheim, water drops formed over the empty gap between them. By the power of Surtur the drops quickened into life in the shape of a human, a being called Ymir. From Ymir was descended the race of frost giants, the first one born out of the sweat of his armpit. They were the forerunners of the gods, but they were evil.

Out of the same clash of fire and ice Surtur caused a cow to be formed, Audhumla, the Nourisher, on whose milk Ymir lived. Audhumla herself existed by licking the stones (legend does not specify by whom they were created), which were covered with salt and frost. As she licked there sprang from them the hairs of a man, then a head, and on the third day an entire man, beautiful and strong. His name was Bur, the Producer, and he was the father of Bor, who took for wife a giantess, Besla. Their sons were three, Odin, Vili and Ve, Spirit, Will and Holy One, the first gods and the creators of the world.

The sons of Bor killed Ymir. They pushed his body into the great twilit gap. Of his flesh they made the earth, his blood was the

---

[4] *The Poetic Edda* of Sæmund Sigfusson

113

ocean that encircled it, his bones the mountains, his teeth the cliffs
and his hair the trees. His skull became the heavens and his brain
the clouds therein. Out of his eyebrows the gods made a rampart
to surround the earth and protect it from the frost giants. This
walled sanctuary they called Midgard, the middle garden: the middle of the universe, bordered by mountains and surrounded by the
deep ocean. To bring light to Midgard they took sparks from
Muspellheim for the stars, sun and moon.

The gods lived in Asgard, Holy Garden, and the frost giants
in Utgard, Outer Garden, beyond the sea, but no one lived in Midgard. One day Odin, Vili and Ve walked along the sea beach in
empty Midgard and found two lifeless trees twisted by wind and
water into rough human shape. They fashioned from them a man
and a woman, Ask, the ash, and Embla, the elm. Odin gave them
spirit, Vili gave them the five senses, and Ve gave them blood and
color.

In time Vili and Ve faded from the Norse cosmos and Odin
became the most mighty of the gods, the All-Father, who sat in
Asgard on his high throne and saw all the actions of men and
understood all that he saw. He gained his wisdom through sacrifice. The great ash, Yggdrasil, whose branches spread over the
whole world, had three roots. Under the root that stretched through
Jötunheim, the mountains of Utgard where the frost giants lived,
was the well of wisdom and wit, guarded by a giant, Mimir, Memory. Odin journeyed there to partake of the waters, and Mimir
gave him a draft, demanding in payment one of his eyes. In a
further trial, to learn the runes and the skills of magic, Odin under-
went a ritual self-immolation the explanation of which is lost in
the darkness of time:

"I know that I hung on a wind-rocked tree, nine whole nights,
with a spear wounded, and Odin offered, myself to myself; on that
tree, of which no one knows from what root it springs.

"Bread no one gave me, nor a horn of drink; downward I
peered, to runes applied myself, wailing learnt them, then fell
down thence."[5]

As Odin was the apotheosis of the high Norse quality of life,

[5] Ibid.

114

Loki was its evil genius. He was a foster brother of Odin, the son of a giant, and was the most frequent companion of Thor and Odin, often appearing in the guise of fire. Possessing a cunning neither of them had, he was invariably useful in dealings with the Svartalfa, Black Dwarfs (maggots in the flesh of Ymir), who lived in underground caves, banished by Odin from the light of day; and with the frost giants confined to the icy mountains of Jötunheim. Both these races smarted under the sovereignty of the gods, aspiring to rule or destroy the world, and they had to be continually assuaged, tricked or bought off.

While Loki's cleverness was convenient to the gods it went hand in hand with malice. He was a liar, a deceiver and a breaker of faith, and the dark vein of his mischievous transactions runs through all the legends. His final act was to accomplish the death of Baldur. The young god, second son of Odin, "so fair and dazzling that rays of light seemed to issue from him,"[6] was the most beloved of all the gods. In a terrible dream he foresaw his death by violence, and his mother, Frigga, exacted an oath from fire and water, from iron and all other metals, also stones, earths, diseases, beasts, birds, poisons and creeping things, that none of them would harm Baldur. He would stand before the assembled gods and they would entertain one another by throwing darts and stones at him and attacking him with swords and battle-axes, and watching him laugh, unhurt. Loki, bitterly jealous of the beautiful young god, discovered that only the mistletoe had not been asked to give oath, as it was thought too small and feeble to hurt anyone. He cut a twig of the vine and gave it to Hodur, Baldur's blind brother, who was unable to join in the sport. "Show honor to Baldur," said Loki, "by throwing this twig at him, and I will direct thy arm toward the place where he stands."[7] Hodur did as he was directed and his brother fell dead. Loki fled to the mountains, where he built a house with four doors so he could see in every direction. When he saw the gods coming he turned into a salmon and hid under a cascade. The gods tried to catch him in a net but he swam under it. Then he leaped out of the water, and Thor

[6] *The Prose Edda* of Snorri Sturleson
[7] Ibid.

caught him in the air with his hand. He held him by the tail because he was so slippery; this is the reason for the thinness of the salmon's tail. They dragged him into a cavern and bound him with iron chains to three pointed rocks. Above his head they suspended a serpent so the venom should drip on his face drop by drop. His wife stood by him and caught the venom in a cup, but some reached him. Every time a drop fell on him he howled, and twisted his body so violently that the earth shook, and this is what earthquakes are. Here he was to stay, suffering in pain and horror, until *Ragnarök*, World Doom, the day of the death of the gods and the destruction of the world.

But Loki's revenge had been planned long before. As one of the race of giants he had always deeply resented the younger gods, feigning friendship only to mask his perfidy. His wife was a giantess, Augurbodi. Their children were Fenrir, Dweller in the Abyss, a wolf, Jörmungard, Vast Monster, a serpent, and Hela, Death. The gods threw Hela into Niflheim and she was given power over the nine lower realms of death, where she distributed those sent to her, all of whom had died of sickness or old age. "Hunger is her table; Starvation her knife; Delay her man; Slowness her maid; Precipice her threshold; Care her bed, and Burning Anguish forms the hangings of her apartments."[8]

The gods threw Jörmungard into the ocean but he had grown so big that, holding his tail in his mouth, he encircled the earth. On the day of Ragnarök he rose from the depths to advance on Asgard and engage in battle with Thor, who killed him and was killed in turn by the venom vomited on him by the dying monster. Fenrir, the wolf, was chained with a magic chain, as he was so strong he could break iron fetters. On the day of doom he succeeded in breaking his bonds and leaped to the attack, "his lower jaw reaching to the earth, and the upper one to heaven,"[9] to devour, first the sun, then Odin. Loki himself, freed on that day, joined in the forces of destruction as "heaven was cleft in twain, the stars were hurled from the heavens, the sea rushed over the

[8] Ibid.
[9] Ibid.

116

earth and the tottering mountains tumbled headlong from their foundations."[10]

In the ten centuries of its existence the Norse pantheon of gods and goddesses grew into a complicated body of legend resembling an enormous, rambling family saga. The Shining Ones bickered like brothers and sisters, were envious or amiable, weak or strong, stupid or clever. They mixed into the affairs of men, frequently descending Bïfrost, the rainbow, built of fire, water and air, the bridge from Asgard to Midgard, to make a gift, punish a wrong-doer, snatch a warrior to Valhalla. Men were familiar with the sight of Odin in a wide blue cloak flecked with gray, emblem of sky and clouds, a broad-brimmed hat low over his forehead to hide his blind eye, sometimes with a raven perched on his shoulder, appearing at feasts or in the midst of battle, to dispense justice. All-Father he might be, but he was never above mixing into petty family squabbles and settling things to suit himself in ways hardly consonant with celestial wisdom. Impartiality was not a quality of the Norse gods. In fact the multiplicity of their designs and the capriciousness of their favors confused their worshippers to the point where the monolithic simplicity of Christianity came as a positive relief.

Christianity, however, did obeisance to an invisible, imperturbable God. The accessibility and humanness of the old gods kept them alive for many years alongside the new religion. The Shining Ones were dear to the hearts of the converts, like old toys no longer needed by a growing-up child.

The Norsemen of the year 1000, when Christianity came to Iceland, were shaped by their religion which, in turn, they had shaped over the centuries around their particular spiritual bent and material situation. Implicit in the tales of the gods were the lessons to mankind. Every important facet of a brave man's character was developed in imitation of his gods.

They were proud and sensitive and poetic. Their pride was such that the smallest insult was as vital as an attack on life or

[10] Ibid.

property, and drew immediate retribution. Njal Thorgeirsson was referred to in a malicious verse as "a beardless old man," and his sons as "dung-beardlings,"[11] and they retaliated the same night by killing the versifier.

Their isolation in cold, wild countries had developed self-reliance; they were reserved and strong-willed to an extreme degree. Blood ties were all-important, and so was loyalty to one's oath. The two most honored qualities were faithfulness and the courage not only to fight but to bear suffering without complaint. They believed in a harsh and inexorable fate. This did not make them weaker but rather more courageous. A man could defy death and laugh; he would not die before the thread of his life was broken by the Norns. The ladies of fate were three: Urd, the Past, old and decrepit, Verdandi, the Present, young and active, and Skuld, the Future, veiled, faced away from her sisters holding an unopened book. When a child was born they wove the web of its life, not according to their wishes but blindly. The web was of many colors, with a black thread, tending from north to south, for death. Urd and Verdandi were benevolent but Skuld often, when the work was nearly finished, captiously ripped it and scattered the broken threads to the winds. No one, not even her sisters, could know what the future would decide. A death-fated man could not be saved. But he was not to care. As the gods were to fight final destruction even though they knew it was inevitable, so must the heroes of the earth face their fate without giving in to despair.

They often faced it with acerbic humor. Thormod was struck in the heart by an iron-tipped arrow. A woman skilled in leech-craft tried to pull it out but the wound had become so swollen that she could not dislodge it. Thormod asked her to cut away the flesh, then pulled it out himself. Shreds of the heart clung to it, some red, others white, yellow and green, and Thormod said, "The king has fed us well; there is fat around the roots of my heart."[12] He then spoke eight lines of poetry and died, leaning against a wall.

[11] *Njalssaga*
[12] *Fostbrædra Saga*

When Gunnar's house was attacked, Thorgrim, one of the attackers, started to climb to the roof-loft to see if Gunnar was at home. Gunnar, seeing him pass the window, lunged outward with his halberd and struck him in the belly. "Is Gunnar at home?" asked one of his companions as he tumbled down. "That you will find out for yourself. But I know that his halberd certainly is," said Thorgrim, and fell dead.[13]

It was a world for men. All the important facets of their religion, the obsessions with strength, courage and loyalty, the insouciant obeisance to fate, were peculiarly masculine. Heroes of earth were translated to Valhalla, Hall of the Slain, by the Valkyrs, Choosers of the Slain, daughters of Odin, who rode through the sky clad in armor and swooped to earth in battle. Not all men were chosen; only the bravest and the best were brought before Odin's throne to receive praise, then taken to the great hall, where they were waited on by the Valkyrs, now clothed in white robes. There they feasted, drinking toasts from the skulls of their enemies, and fought, giving and receiving mortal wounds that were immediately healed.

Women had no place in these affairs. Upon their deaths they went straight to Hela, the goddess of the underworld, who might or might not be kind to them. In life they counted for little. Divorce and death in childbirth were frequent, and new women were continuously available from raids to take the place of those dead or cast off. Female infants were often exposed at birth.

As the importance of raiding and battle declined the position of women improved. Icelandic women, whatever might be their fate in the next world, were in this one equal in most ways with men. In the daily life of the farm they were quite as necessary as their husbands, and many women owned property. They possessed to an even greater degree the oversensitive pride of the Norse. "Illugi the Red . . . was married to Sigrid . . . Illugi went to live at Outer-Holm on Akraness, when he and Holm-Starri exchanged their property, farms, wives, livestock and all. Then Illugi married Jorunn . . . but Sigrid hanged herself in the temple because she could not bear the change of husbands."[14]

[13] *Njalssaga*
[14] *Landnamabok*

Though women did not personally engage in the blood feuds that plagued the new country almost from its beginning, they were often instigators, some far more bloodthirsty than their men. The wife of Vigfus dug up her husband's murdered body, cut off his head and took it to Arnkel, her kinsman, who had refused to go to court for her, saying: "Here is the head that would not have excused itself from taking up the prosecution for you if that had been necessary."[15]

In another tale Thurid, a combative Icelandic mother, cut an ox shoulder in three pieces and served it to her three sons. "Hugely is it carved, Mother," said one. She answered, "Bigger was Hall, thy brother carven, and I heard ye tell nought thereof that any wonder was in that." When they still failed to avenge their brother she gave them stones instead of meat, saying, in effect: "Your manhood is worth just as little to give you courage as these stones are to give you food."[16]

When a child was born he was left untouched by anyone until his father, acknowledging that the child was his, picked him up and enfolded him in his cloak. After being claimed he was sprinkled with water for luck, and named. The name was that of a kinsman or of a respected old man. A boy was never given his father's name unless the father was dead. If he were not claimed the child was exposed; but after acknowledgment and the sprinkling of water exposure was considered murder. None of this applied to the children of slaves. Exposure of slave offspring was commonplace, and this practice went on beyond the conversion to Christianity.

Into the lives of these fierce and high-mettled people came the new religion preaching meekness in place of belligerent pride, telling the truth rather than keeping one's oath, forgiveness instead of generations-long family feuds. It did not come gently, because the northern Christians had not had time to change their characters along with their gods.

The Settlement had brought some Christians, Norsemen who

[15] *Eyrbyggja Saga*
[16] *Heidarviga Saga*

had come from Celtic colonies or married Celtic women. But Christianity was not taken seriously by anyone of importance. Only women and slaves liked the new, milder religion. The few Christian warriors did not quite forsake the old gods. "Helgi's faith was very much mixed: he believed in Christ but invoked Thor when it came to voyages and difficult times."[17] When these part-time Christians died their families usually reverted to paganism. A few men became converted because it was safer and more profitable when they went abroad as traders or envoys to own to the prevailing religion of the countries they visited. Here and there was a respected man who had a Christian spirit though he still worshipped the old gods. "Thorkel Mane [Moon] was a man of very upright life though not a Christian. A little before the agony of death he caused himself to be set forth over against the sun; and openly admiring the workmanship of Heaven, and the whole world, commended his soul departing when he was ready to die, to that God who created the sun and the rest of the stars."[18] The prospects of neither Valhalla nor Hela evidently disturbed the last meditations of this good man.

The barbaric old warriors' religion came to have less and less relevance in the day-to-day lives of hard-working farmers. They became more superstitious than religious, clinging to the trappings rather than the beliefs. The temple was often very elaborate. "Thorgrim was a great sacrificer. He had a large temple reared in his home field, one hundred feet long and sixty feet wide, whereunto all men [all his *thingmen*] should pay temple-toll. There Thor was held in highest honor. From the inner end thereof there was a building in the shape of a cap [this corresponded to the apse of a church]. The temple was arrayed with hangings and had windows all round. There Thor stood in the middle, and on either hand the other gods. In front of them was a stall wrought with great cunning, and lined at the top with iron, whereon there should burn a fire that must never go out; that they called a hallowed fire . . . On the stall should lie a stout ring made of silver,

[17] *Landnamabok*
[18] Ibid.

which the priest should wear on his arm at all man-motes; thereon should all oaths be taken in matters relating to ordeal cases. On that stall too should stand a bowl of copper . . . wherein should be poured all the blood which flowed from animals given to Thor . . . Blood should be sprinkled over the folk and the beasts; but the wealth which was paid to the temple should be used for the entertainment of men when sacrificial feasts were held."[19]

The sacrifice, of cattle or sheep, took place in a pit called the *blotkelda*, well of sacrifice, before the door of the temple. In two places only were there known to have been human sacrifices in Iceland. At one of them, on Snaefellsnes, can be seen the *blotstein*, sacrificial stone, against which the human victim was dashed — still red, it is said, from the blood that no rain can ever wash away.

When the *godi* put the ring on his arm, having first smeared it with the blood of a bull he himself had sacrificed, he delivered an oath, saying: "I call witnesses thereunto that I take oath on ring, a lawful oath, so help me Frey and Niord, as I shall this case plead or defend, or witness bear, or verdicts give, or dooms deliver, according as I know rightest and truest and ratherest lawful, to all lawful deeds out of hand such as unto my share fall while I be at this Thing . . ."[20] The ring and the oath served as symbols of the unity of religion and law in the person of the *godi*.

After delivering the oath the *godi* and his court sat within a circle of heavy stones, the *Domringr*, Ring of Judgment, in the temple field. No evildoer might enter this hallowed circle, but must stand outside it, awaiting judgment.

The *godar* clung to their double prerogatives long after ordinary people were ready to embrace the new religion. Violence was inevitable, many of the missionaries being just as bellicose as those they intended to convert. The first ones, however, were as harmless as they were ineffectual. Asolf Alskik, a monk part Irish, part Norse, went to Iceland with twelve Irish monks. They preached mildness and got nowhere. Making no converts, Asolf went away and died a hermit. Later he was made a saint, but not in Iceland.

Thorvald Kodransson was born in Iceland and traveled around

19 *Kjalnesinga Saga*
20 *Islendingabok*

122

*The nineteenth century church at Hof, raised on the site of a temple
to Thor, is of sod, peat brick and wood, the destructible materials of
which Iceland's settlers built*

the country with a Saxon bishop who couldn't speak Icelandic. They were a little more successful than Asolf, starting with the conversion of Thorvald's father and family. In the course of their journeys they made a remarkable impression at a splendid wedding, when two berserkers challenged the Saxon bishop to a trial by fire to see whose deities were the most effective. The bishop sprinkled holy water on the fire while the berserkers said magic incantations over it. The challengers walked into the flames with drawn swords in their hands, according to custom, and were instantly consumed, while the bishop came out with not even his clothes touched. This sort of display produced converts here and there, but when Thorvald built a church in 984 and tried to baptize his handful of the faithful, many people "could not be prevailed upon to suffer themselves to be baptized, as they pretended it would be indecent to go naked into the water like little boys to receive baptism."[21] Most of Thorvald's converts converted themselves back to heathens as soon as he left their neighborhoods, because the priests of the temples threatened them with reprisals for not paying temple dues. When Thorvald tried to preach Christianity at the *Althing* before the assembled *godar* he was nearly stoned to death. He left Iceland and died as a monk in Russia.

Next came Stefni Thorgilsson, born in Iceland and baptized in Denmark. He arrived fresh from the court of Olaf Trygvesson, king of Norway, who had converted Norway and the "western lands"— Shetland, Orkney and the Faeroe Islands — with armies, in the full-blooded tradition of the Viking raiders. In Iceland Stefni broke images of the gods and destroyed temples. He was summoned to appear before the courts for blasphemy, then outlawed and expelled.

King Olaf, who took a fierce interest in spreading the Gospel, not least because he had his eye on the eventual acquisition of Iceland, then called on a bloody-minded priest named Thangbrand. The latest missionary was a German robber who had committed acts of fraud, piracy and manslaughter as priest of Mostr, a Norwegian island. As punishment Olaf sent him to Iceland, purgatory for Christians, reasoning that his violence would find satisfactory

---

[21] *Letters on Iceland*, Uno von Troil, 1780

outlet in conflict with those arrogant heathens. Thangbrand's progress through Iceland was a series of ambushes, duels and set battles. It was also outstandingly successful.

Thangbrand came with an Icelander named Gudleif Arason, a redoubtable warrior. The new priests made a good impression on the common people by displays of strength that seemed magical to them. A farmer named Thorkel, opposing the new faith, challenged Thangbrand to a duel. "Thangbrand defended himself with a crucifix instead of a shield, but even so he managed to defeat Thorkel and kill him."[22] A little later, when Thangbrand was riding westward, the ground suddenly opened under him. His horse and all his gear were swallowed instantly but the priest leaped to safety on the edge of the chasm. Crediting God with his miraculous escape, he gained new converts on the spot.

His companion, meanwhile, was not idle. Gudleif went after a sorcerer who had mocked him, chased him until he was cornered on a river bank, then hurled a spear straight through him. A chief named Thorvald the Ailing ambushed the two holy men with a large body of men. They were warned, but, said Gudleif, "we will not let that deter us from riding to meet him."[23] They saw Thorvald at the head of his men. Thangbrand ran his spear through the would-be attacker while Gudleif hacked his arm off at the shoulder. The rest of the ambush melted away.

At Bardaströnd on the Northwest Peninsula, Thangbrand, with a party of sixty converts, confronted a group of two hundred heathens who had no intention of being saved and were ready for armed conflict. Thangbrand proposed a test of faith, that same trial by fire so dear to the hearts of missionaries, before they should engage in battle. A berserker lived there of whom everyone in the neighborhood was terrified. When the fires were duly hallowed the berserker came rushing in fully armed, dashed straight through the pagan fire but halted before the Christian one, saying that he was burning all over. He then turned on the crowd, ready to slaughter any or all. Thangbrand struck him on the arm with a crucifix and the sword dropped from the berserker's hand. The

[22] *Njalssaga*
[23] Ibid.

priest then ran him through with his own sword while Gudleif slashed off his arm. This display of God-given strength and courage convinced all two hundred of the heathens and they were baptized forthwith.

After a year of traveling, baptizing, fighting and preaching during which Thangbrand made a great many converts and a dangerous number of powerful enemies, he returned to Norway and reported to King Olaf Trygvesson that the Icelanders were unmitigated heathens imbued with evil and steeped in sorcery. The king summarily arrested all the Icelanders then in Norway, had them thrown into dungeons and announced that he was going to put them all to death. Two of the prisoners, Gizur the White and Hjalti Skeggjason, pleaded with the king to spare their compatriots, offering to sail back to Iceland and speak at the *Althing*, to try and persuade their countrymen to accept the faith. The king let them go, temporarily reprieving the other prisoners.

The envoys were met on the Icelandic shore by a large group of Christians, and the band rode to the *Althing* in warlike formation. The heathens had massed their forces to meet them, and in this atmosphere of tension the *Althing* met. It was the year 1000. Both groups went to the Law Rock and both, through spokesmen, denounced the others as criminals. There was no attempt at reason or calm speaking. Such an uproar resulted that no one could hear the speakers, and battle seemed inevitable. The Law-Speaker quickly dispersed the meeting.

The Christians then took the initiative of attempting a peaceable solution. They chose their most respected convert, who in turn went to see a renowned leader named Thorgeir, the priest of Ljosavatn, Lake of Light, in the north. Though Thorgeir was a *godi* and a heathen he was known to be reasonable and wise. He agreed to mediate and retired to his booth, of stone and turf with a roof of sailcloth. There he meditated for a day and a night with a sheepskin over his head to keep out the light.

Then he spoke: "Let us all have one law and one faith, for it will prove to be true that if we divide the law, we also destroy the peace . . . All men in this land shall be Christian and believe in the one God — Father, Son and Holy Ghost — and renounce all worship of idols. They shall not expose children at birth nor eat horse-

127

meat. The penalty for carrying on these practices openly shall be outlawry, but they shall not be punishable if they are done in private."[24] People were also to be permitted to hold pagan sacrificial feasts in secret if they wished to, but under penalty of lesser outlawry if they were discovered. He then dealt with the observance of the Lord's Day, Christmas and Easter and all the important feast days.

Thorgeir's speech initially angered the heathens, who felt he had betrayed them. But upon reflection even those most vehemently opposed to conversion came to see that Thorgeir's speech was basically a compromise. He had succeeded in so diluting the spirit of Christianity with the dictates of social necessity and convention that even the most fanatical Thor-worshipper could be a Christian too. Everyone at the *Althing* finally agreed to be baptized. However, even these hardy Norsemen balked at going into the icy water of Thingvallavatn, Lake of the Thing Plain, so baptism was postponed until the journey home, when they all detoured by way of Laugarvatn, Lake of Hot Springs, a few miles west of Thingvellir, and easefully transformed themselves into Christians in its steamy water.

Thorgeir went home to Ljosavatn and threw all his heathen idols over Godafoss, Waterfall of the Gods.

[24] *Islendingabok*

EIGHT

The Good Life,
and a Notorious Volcano

THINGVELLIR, THE HEART of Iceland's early republic, is a rift valley directly on top of the central split down the Mid-Atlantic Ridge, where the earth is spreading as the Eurasian and North American plates move apart. Here you can see it happening. The valley is twenty-five miles long and six miles wide. At least that is its size today. It grows 0.4 inches a year, so when the representatives met at the first *Althing* the surrounding mountains were 34.8 feet closer to them. From the air the inexorable process is strikingly evident. The valley is a long green plain edged with straight lines of hills running from northeast to southwest, Iceland's line of volcanic activity. Fissures cut parallel grooves down the plain in the same direction. The middle fissure is so wide that it is filled with water, the elongated lake Thingvallavatn, the largest in Iceland, fifty square miles. Three other big gashes cleave the plain and many shorter, narrow ones, young fissures, are just starting.

Thingvellir is not only getting wider, it is sinking at the same time. The last major recorded slippage, in 1789, was three or four feet. The fissured rocks, therefore, have become cliffs as the ground subsided around them. From above they look like walls enclosing a moat, black and bottomless along its entire length.

The largest of the fissures besides that hidden under the lake is called Almannagja, Rift Rock of the People, 120 feet high and four and a half miles long. Walking along it, the sense of the earth splitting apart beneath one is very strong. The rock has pulled apart jaggedly; pushed back together again the margins would fit, like pieces of a jigsaw puzzle. If it weren't for chickweed and moss campion growing in the crevices the cliff might have only just fractured.

A road goes from the valley floor up into the fissure of Almannagja and one can drive a car part way. The road narrows as it enters the crack, and one continues on foot, climbing between dark, broken walls. Near the top there is an opening, and the plain is spread out below, rippled green, with the lake an intense, burning sapphire beyond. All around the ranges of folded brown hills enclose the valley, protecting it from the worst of the winter winds. It is fine farmland; all the years that the *Althing* met here it was farmed intensively.

Here at the opening is the Law Rock, a big boulder marked with a flag and a metal plaque. On this rock the Law-Speaker stood and repeated the words of the Law from memory, his voice enormous with the sounding board of Almannagja behind him. The representatives assembled on the grass below, and scattered around them over the plain were the family booths of turf with many-colored roofs of woolen sailcloth, where the friends and relatives walked and talked.

Today the *Althing* meets in Reykjavik. Thingvellir has been made a national park of 6,800 acres and the fertile farmland is enclosed with fencing to keep out the sheep of neighboring farms. A hotel in a grove of newly planted spruces at the edge of the lake serves freshly caught trout, and a small church stands over the foundations of Ulfljot's temple. The valley is melodramatically evocative, and naturally, so near to the capital, it is popular for day holidays. It lacks the south shore's quiet sense of undisturbed past, because around every corner appears a tourist with a camera or a family playing ball. But Thingvellir was ever a populous place. If the gay woolen roofs have given way to picnic baskets, it is but a new style of an old usage.

The homes to which the *Althing* delegates scattered after they left Thingvellir in the year 1000 were large farms set in the midst of vast holdings that included ocean or lake shore for fishing, fields and dales for cultivation and mountains for summer pasture.

Iceland was a generous land, and the farms had within their boundaries nearly every necessity for self-sufficient living. Wild ducks, geese, ptarmigan and seabirds existed in multitudes probably unequalled anywhere in the world, to supply them with eggs, flesh and feathers. In the lakes, rivers and fjords was a seemingly inexhaustible fecundity of every kind of sea animal from shrimps to salmon to whales. Myriads of rivulets streamed from the ice-topped mountains down through the valleys, enriching the soil with glacier-born minerals, so that their grazing animals needed no additional food to the luxuriant grass. Life in the early days of the republic was gracious. In material ways the settlers wanted for little, and spiritually most of them were far better off than they had been in Norway: free, wealthy and at peace. They were willing to travel far to keep things that way.

One of the more distant farms was that at Ljosavatn, Lake of Light, whence had come Thorgeir to mediate in the Christian controversy. The lake is in the far north, at the head of the valley Kaldakinn, Cold Cheeks, which extends from Skjalfandi, the northern fjord where the early explorer Gardar made his final landfall and built his house. The valley is kept fertile by the Skjalfandafljot, Shivering River (*Fljot* means literally "flood," hence a big river), on of Iceland's longest rivers, 105 miles from Vatnajökull north to its outlet in the fjord.

This part of Iceland is old, as Iceland goes. Its fjords and valleys run north and south and are divided by mountain ranges of the black-gray Eocene basalt of fifty million years ago, remains of the Thulean Province. Around Ljosavatn the ancient low mountains are flat-topped, sheared off by the Pleistocene glacier. Their mild inclines are clothed in a dense cover of dwarf birch that looks like fur, and seamed with hundreds of twisting gravel paths where little streams run. A higher mountain is a dusky shape through fog over the lake. It is Storadalsfjall, Mountain of the Big Valley. On the lake shore below it is a large, uneven mound of broken rock and sand with patches of sparse green vegetation on it. Debris from this has spilled into the lake and blanketed its southeast end with gravel. At the end of the Ice Age Storadalsfjall's rock strata burst when the great weight of the ice was removed, and this untidy gravel mound is the remains of the enormous landslip.

Thorgeir's farm of Ljosavatn, the only dwelling visible for

miles, is south of the landslip on an elevation overlooking the ample valley. On one side of it is the lake, with trumpeter swans swimming serenely on its pale surface, on the other the broad flood of Skjalfandafljot. The house is large, white-painted with a red roof and many windows. Around it are clustered five or six outbuildings, also cleanly white. It looks comfortable and prosperous. But a few cattle in the home fields are the only signs of life in the whole lonely valley.

Ljosavatn seems insuperably remote. One wonders how Thorgeir even knew about the *Althing*, let alone got there. His holding was far from the coast, and the mountains and glaciers of Iceland's unfriendly inland plateau lay between him and the south country. Even today it is an impracticable journey. But the farmers of those days thought little of traveling long distances. Most of them had known one another in Norway and many were related by marriage. In Iceland they became more dependent on the old ties as their only link with the mother country. No matter how isolated their holdings, they saw to it that their lives were not isolated. Such was the mildness of the climate that communications were rarely paralyzed by snow, and nature's other manifestations, however inclement, did not daunt them. On their sure-footed little horses they insouciantly traversed swamp, ice or lava field to marry off their sons and daughters in distant farmsteads, to right wrongs and avenge insults, above all to attend the vital yearly convocation at Thingvellir. Thorgeir deemed it just as important to attend to his duties as a representative of his country as to manage his extensive estates. He and the others of those responsible priest-chiefs of the early years saw to it that their new republic justified its independence.

A few miles northeast of Ljosavatn is Thorgeir's waterfall, Godafoss, where he dramatically renounced the old gods. Though Iceland is a country where water is the most plentiful and the most noticeable element, none of her rivers is navigable. The rock is so young that the water has not had time to form drainage systems, and the streams rush headlong down the hills and sluice unevenly, ever changing their courses, through the plains and valleys. The glacial river Skjalfandafljot, reinforced by rivulets off the basalt walls of its valley, winds widely through the Kaldakinn, then narrows to race through the Ljosavatn Pass just beyond

132

Thorgeir's farm, out of the ancient land and straight into one of Iceland's youngest volcanic regions. That is the Bardardal, Border Valley, an eighty-two-mile-long sheet of shield-volcano lava that issued from the mountain Trolladyngur, Bower of Giantesses, 8,000 years ago.[1] Here the river cuts a channel through a desert region of crumbled red volcanic rock with enormous boulders strewn through it, their rough contours softened by a hairy cover of the yellowish moss *Rhacomitrium lanuginosum*, a northern moss that loves rock and is always the first plant to grow on young lava. Off the road smoke rises from the flat ground and the air is full of roaring sound.

You don't see Godafoss until you almost walk into it. The river has slashed into the brittle lava and torn a gorge down which it plunges in a magnificent triple waterfall. As you stand beside it on the gnarled rocks, pockmarked by eighty centuries of water drops, there seems to be nothing in the world to hear, to touch and to see but water, green-white, pulsing and thundering, filling the air with heavy clouds of spray. The land has gone and the sky is invisible. The gorge continues below the falls, and the river, contained by the walls it has made, surges over the dark red rocks in a milky torrent. When Thorgeir threw his heathen idols over Godafoss they were well and truly lost.

The falls and their flume disappear as suddenly as they appeared. Looking back from a few hundred yards down the road there is only a dark space where the river has vanished into the earth as if it had dug a hole in the ground — which it has. All around the chasm floats the gray spume, but the flat land is as dry and bare as if there were no water this side of the Greenland Sea.

One of the most celebrated delegates at the *Althing* of the year 1000 was Njal Thorgeirsson, chief subject of *Njalssaga*, the noblest of the classical sagas. Njal was "wealthy and handsome . . . He was so skilled in law that no one was considered his equal. He was a wise and prescient man. His advice was sound and

[1] A shield volcano starts with a long fissure through which lava fountains, hurling streams hundreds of feet into the air in curtains of fire and sending great floods of molten rock in rivers over the countryside. Repeated eruptions at different points along the fissure create an extended, dome-shaped mass of congealed lava. These large flat lava flows are known, descriptively, as shield volcanoes.

133

benevolent and always turned out well for those who followed it. He was a gentle man of great integrity . . . He solved the problems of any man who came to him for help."[2] Long before he experienced Thangbrand's expert proselytizing, Njal was convinced of the virtues of Christianity. Differing from his neighbors, who thought it heinous to forsake the old beliefs, Njal said, "In my opinion the new faith is much better; happy the man who receives it. And if the men who spread this faith come out to Iceland, I shall do all I can to further it."[3] He was duly baptized by Thangbrand and was one of the strong advocates of the new creed at the *Althing*.

Despite his high character and good intentions Njal's story is one of mounting tragedy with the brooding sense of inescapable fate that pursues the protagonists of Greek drama. It is also, incidentally, a fine broad canvas of Icelandic life at the apex of its pagan civilization. If any one year can be said to be crucially pivotal it was the year 1000, when Christianity was formally adopted. The events of *Njalssaga* took place when the venerable pagan values were still foremost but the new morals, opposed on every count to the old, were already gaining credence. The author of *Njalssaga*, writing nearly three hundred years later, could see the struggle already crumbling the social fabric, and could picture the desperate uncertainty of brave men caught between two worlds.

We visited the country where the complex, tempestuous events of *Njalssaga* unfolded. To get there we went as Njal did in that fateful year, south and east from Thingvellir, past steaming Laugarvatn, the hot springs of Hveragerdi and the ravaged plains around the volcano Hekla.

Laugarvatn, which the *Althing* delegates found a comfortable baptismal font, is a small, shallow lake with gray water, ruffled this day by wind and rain. Steam rises all over it, to mingle with the low clouds, and there is a strong smell of sulphur. On the shore is a cluster of cement buildings with no windows. These house sulphur steam baths and a swimming pool. Behind them are greenhouses full of tall tomato plants. On the bank above the lake

[2] *Njalssaga*
[3] Ibid.

stands a modern concrete building of severely elegant lines. It is a school, one of Iceland's many excellent free boarding schools. Now, in mid-June, school term has finished and the building will soon be turned into a tourist hotel, as most of the country schools are in July and August.

Soon we hit the highway to Hveragerdi, Garden of Hot Springs. This was Iceland's first paved road, built in the 1890s. It is a wonderful road, wide and smooth, cutting straight between hills and lava fields, quite unlike most of Iceland's seven thousand miles of motorways: narrow dirt roads, onetime pony trails following the line of least resistance, at the mercy of rain and frost. From the massive volcanic debris of the mountains outside Reykjavik we descend into a flat alluvial plain, the valley of Hveragerdi. Bare steep mountains hang over it on three sides, so new and so pebbly that even moss cannot cling to their flanks; on the fourth side is the light green water of Eyrarbakkabugur, Bay of the Gravel Banks, named for its shallow, sandy shores. Hveragerdi's grassy plain is so lush against its backdrop of gray and brown hills that it looks almost blue. The steam of hot springs drifts upward from the grass and hangs in the still air. The town is one long, broad street lined with concrete stores and dwellings. Its openness reminds one of a prairie town. All around it are enormous greenhouses. The hot springs have been harnessed to grow vegetables and flowers, from tomatoes to bananas, roses to orchids, and Hveragerdi is indeed a garden.

At the edge of the town, tourists are taken to a square stone with a hole eight or ten inches in diameter in the middle of it. A thin plume of stream rises from the hole and water is visible below. One is handed a packet of green soap and instructed to open it and throw it into the hole. The jelly-like soap covers the water and creates pressure. Soon the water bubbles heavily, looking like a washer with too much detergent in it. After a minute or two it begins to shoot up, exploding again and again like wet fireworks. Eventually the plastic soap container flies up into the air and lands on the stone square along with all the other plastic soap containers. The whole undignified affair lasts about ten minutes.

Far below the little geyser is the reservoir of magma that underlies all of the southwestern part of Iceland. Vapors from this liquid rock heat the underground water. The concentrated heat raises the water temperature higher than its boiling point, due to the pressure of the mass of cooler water above. As the heat builds up the pressure below becomes stronger than that above, and the hot water pushes upward, causing an overflow at the surface at the ground's weakest point, a narrow split or hole in the rock. With the sudden lessening of pressure the overheated water turns abruptly to steam and explodes violently through the vent in a column of mixed water and vapor. When all the pressure below ground is released the geyser subsides and the process starts over again.

As thunderbolts were the gods' weapons, so geysers must have seemed to primitive man evidence of diabolic anger from below. It is probably a throwback impulse in modern man to belittle the unknowable force that threatens him. To reduce this magnificent and relentless display of nature's power to a ten-minute amusement, to control it with soap and laugh at it, may be a healthy sign. In Hveragerdi it does not matter; the geyser is small and provides a diversion for tourists. But the splendid Geysir, Gusher, twenty miles northeast of Hveragerdi, that gave its name to the world, gushes no longer. Too many people have essayed for too many years to stimulate it to more frequent or spectacular activity. Its long pipe down to what early farmers may have considered hell is plugged with pebbles and toys and soap packets. Clear sea-green water still fills its sixty-foot smoothly layered basin, steam still spurts from other holes around it, staining the rocks yellow-brown with sulphur, pale mud bubbles in nearby cauldrons and another, small geyser a hundred feet away, Strokkur, The Churn, throws its water periodically 80 to 150 feet in the air. But Geysir is destroyed.

Southwest of Hveragerdi the rolling fields of grass continue for many miles; then quite suddenly there are no more green hills, but a vast plain. The sky is very light over it and the earth is very dark. Black ash and pumice consume the light. Their source is the volcano Hekla, Cowled Cloak — named for the veil of cloud nearly always around its summit — which rises, a pure, snow-clad pyramid, beyond the wasted fields.

Hekla is Iceland's best-known volcano, not because it is the most active but because sailors on ships passing south along the coast from Europe to the west could not help seeing it. Though thirty-three miles from the sea it is dramatically visible, an almost perfect cone rising above a line of irregularly shaped mountains beyond the coastal plains. Its height today is 4,893 feet, 144 feet higher than in 1947. Every eruption adds a few feet.

The mountain is a mixture of cone and fissure volcanoes. Its line of craters runs diagonal to the coast, and viewed from the northeast (a difficult view, from an almost roadless area of rocky desert and ice) it is a long arched ridge, highest in the middle. Its biggest eruptions have occurred out of a central vent, giving it from other angles the clean-lined elemental mountain shape.

It was this shape that Saint Brendan saw when he was looking for his promised land beyond the sea. His account of the flaming mountain is the first historic mention of Hekla. It is now known that Hekla's eruptions have been more or less regular since it first came up out of the earth after the end of the Ice Age. But when Njal passed that way in A.D. 1000, the mountain looked as it does today, innocently white. The land around it was among the prettiest in Iceland, gentle hills clothed in birch, wide river valleys, green fields nourished by hot springs. The settlers had never seen it erupt. There had been an eruption shortly before they came, early in the ninth century. The Irish monks must have been witnesses but they left no record. The mountain itself records its history in successive, datable layers of tephra and lava, but the settlers could not read it. They homesteaded all around its flanks and along the fertile valley of the Thjorsa, Ship's Beak River, Iceland's longest and largest river, which flows from the ice sheets of the central plateau around Hekla's north flank down to the sea.

In 1104 Hekla erupted again, the second largest tephra explosion ever to occur in Iceland during historic times, covering more than half the country with ash. The fields around the mountain were buried under three feet of ash and pumice, and all the farms were destroyed. This was the end of settlement around Hekla. The farms were never rebuilt.

Some have been excavated, the best preserved being that of Stöng in the Thjorsa Valley, the holding of Gaukur Trandilsson, an early settler and hero of the lost Thjorsadalur Saga. Stöng, where seventy-five people lived and worked, was the largest of sixteen farms in the valley, all buried. Its builders picked a beautiful site. The one building that has been excavated lies on the side of a hill overlooking a winding, tumbling stream called Fossa, Torrent, a tributary of the Thjorsa. The stream pours noisily through a gorge and makes a little waterfall down organ-pipe rocks into a deep stone basin. Sweet-smelling birches hang over the dark water, and bright moss and wildflowers grow on the banks. The pasture land around the farm is thickly verdant, and little green hills on all sides obscure the vacant ash fields beyond. In the distance Hekla's white flanks can be seen but its summit is covered with drifting clouds. Around the sun is a full, bright rainbow ring, with another fading ring in a wider circle. It is hard to imagine that a destructive volcano threatens this idyllic spot. The only reminders are the paths around the house. They are made of pumice stones like crisp little pillows, light and bouncy underfoot.

The main hall is sixty yards long, with walls five feet thick. The foundations are of lava blocks and the walls have been restored with large turf bricks, their original material. Down the length of the hall is a depression where fires were laid. Upright stones stand along the walls, where planks were placed for benches which doubled, after the feasting was done, as beds. Three smaller chambers are in an ell off one end, also enclosed by turf walls. They are thought to have been the women's room, for sewing and weaving, the bathroom, for steam baths, and the dairy, with a round cavity in the middle of it for the vat containing *skyr*, the sour milk concoction that was a year-round staple. On the walls of the dairy hung dried meat and fish. The original roof, about ten feet high, was of turf, like the walls, either thatched or held down with rocks. Now there is a corrugated iron roof, and the rain thumps on it, obliterating the sweet splash of the waterfall. Horsetails grow among the bench stones and ferns sprout from the turf walls. The plants are undersized as they don't get much light from the only two windows, small apertures at either end of the hall, letting almost no daylight through the thick walls. But they grow lushly, and the old hall has the damp, rank smell of a hothouse.

At the time of Njal the prevailing smell, even above that of food and people, would have been smoke from driftwood fires. The feast-fires in the open hearths along the center covered the inside of the hall with soot, their smoke escaping eventually through holes in the roof. The inadequate end windows were closed with opaque membrane from the fetus-covering of an unborn calf. The men sat along the walls on the raised section, out of the way of ashes and food scraps, their swords and shields hung behind them.

The high-seats on either side of the hall, for the chieftain and his most honored guest, were wide enough for two or three, and sometimes a wife sat with her husband in conjugal equality unknown in the mother country. The food was simple: bread and butter, large bowls of *skyr*, meat and fish roasted on the open hearths. The drink was mead, a ferment of honey and malt. The meal was enlivened by the music of harp and one-stringed fiddle, by reciting of poems and telling of sagas and by not-so-occasional fighting. After the long session of hearty eating and drinking the men slept where they were, on straw pallets, under their own cloaks. Stöng, unlike smaller farms, had the luxury of its three extra rooms. It was a very good life for those early farmers. But for us the smell and the discomfort of that low-roofed, airless, much-lived-in hall would have been insupportable.

Hekla erupted fourteen times after 1104, sometimes slightly, sometimes disastrously. In 1300 the fifth eruption produced another great fall of tephra, covering about 30,000 square miles of land. "A fire broke out in Mt. Hekla, so powerful that the mountain split in such a manner that it will be visible in Iceland as long as the country is inhabited. Large rocks moved about in this fire like charcoal in a blacksmith's hearth and crushed together with so much thunder and noise that it was heard as far as the North Land . . . So much pumice stone was cast out . . . that the roofs of the farmhouses were burnt off. No man knew if it was night or day, inside or out, while the falling sand covered the ground completely."[4]

It may have been this tremendous eruption, which lasted for a year, that started the legend that Hekla was the gateway to hell. By the sixteenth century it had gained wide credence, even among scholars. "There is in Iceland," wrote the son-in-law of the German theologist Melanchthon, "Mount Hekla, being of as dreadful a depth as Hell itself, which resoundeth with lamentable and miserable yellings, that the noise of the criers may be heard for the space of a great league about. Great swarms of ugly black Ravens and Vultures lie hovering about this place, which are thought by the inhabitants to nest there. The common people of that country are verily persuaded that there is a descent down into Hell by this gulfe; and therefore when any battles are foughten elsewhere, in

[4] *The Logmanns Annal, circa* 1325

139

whatsoever part of the whole world, or any bloody slaughters are committed, they have learned by long experience, what horrible tumults, what monstrous screeches are heard around this mountain."[5]

A German traveler of the sixteenth century carried the punishment of the damned a step further: "About the beginning of July . . . a great store of ice suddenly floateth to the island about Hekla . . . making a miserable kind of moan . . . The damned souls are tormented in the flame in the mountain, and after in the ice. This ice for three whole months floateth about Hekla."[6]

The mountain became so notorious that it was used in expletive. "Dra åt Häcklefjäll," yelled the Swede — "Go to Hekla." The Scot would consign you to "John Hacklebirnie's House," the German to "Hackelberg."

The people of Iceland set little store by these tales, and rebutted them angrily as demeaning and unfair. The sounds of the earth's fires and the ocean's ice were familiar to them, to be feared but not superstitiously. However, even they caught the fever occasionally. In an account of the eruption of 1341 it was written that "people went to the mountain where the lava was being thrown up, and it sounded to them as if a great boulder were being flung back and forth inside the mountain. It seemed to them that they saw birds, both large and small, flying in the fire with loud cries. These they took to be souls."[7] Thus fancifully did the writer describe the weirdly shaped lava bombs shooting out of the smoke, fizzing as they came.

The superstitions faded but caution remained. Since Hekla's eruptions usually occurred within the span of a generation everyone knew its reputation, and the land remained empty. Hekla's damage was not confined to its immediate lava flow. Every eruption, even the smaller ones, ravaged far beyond the vicinity. One of the worst was that of 1766, lasting two years and carrying tephra not only over the settlements of the south coast but all over the farmlands of the north as well. Ashes and fumes stunted the grass and poisoned the rivers with fluorine so that livestock

---

[5] *De Dimensione Terrae*, Dr. Kaspar Peucer, 1550

[6] *Voyages and Historie of Iceland and Greenland*, Dithmor Blefkens, 1563

[7] *Flateyjarbok*, 1380–90

and fish died and many people starved. "In many places . . . there was heard neither the sound of the churn nor the shout of the shepherd." This was during Iceland's most unhappy period, when famine and disease were added to two of the worst volcanic eruptions ever, when most of the people were wretchedly poor tenant farmers in thrall to the Church and the Danish king, when the weather, progressively colder, hurt the crops and impeded the fishing.

By the time of the 1947 eruption Hekla had been quiet, for the first time since the Settlement, for over a century. But people did not forget. When someone remarked in March of that year to a local farm wife that it was unimaginable that this pretty, snow-covered mountain could erupt, she answered, "Oh, it won't take her long to change appearance, the wretched beast." A few days later came the warning earthquake, then the columns of smoke spreading into an enormous umbrella 30,000 yards high. Ash blackened the snow on the glaciers and turned morning into midnight. The winds in the upper atmosphere carried the ash across the British Isles and the Scandinavian peninsula all the way to Helsinki, even to Russia. Ninety-eight farms suffered damage, 1,200 square miles of land were covered, water supplies were spoiled, trees and grass were injured and sheep showed signs of fluorine poisoning. But such was the immediate response of men and modern machinery that by the end of July all the farms had been cleared of tephra and large areas planted with new grass seed and oats. Floods of water accompanied the beginning of this eruption, estimated at about four million cubic yards, due to the melting of the year-round glacial ice on the slopes of the mountain. The water carried lava bombs that raised it to the boiling point as it rushed down the mountain and spread steaming over the fields. The lava flow started almost at the beginning, and by the end of the eruption thirteen months later had covered an area of about a thousand acres with a volume of about one billion cubic yards.

To no one's surprise Hekla erupted again in 1970. The lava did not flow far, but 45 million tons of tephra were thrown out, to cover and poison all the newly planted farmland and to drift by air or sea to every part of Iceland. These two latest eruptions have not been among Hekla's worst. But as we drive southward, away from the green Thjorsa Valley, the country, devastated by the volcano, looks sad. We cross the Merkurhraun, Boundary Field of Burnt Lava, and the Krokahraun, Winding Field of Burnt Lava.[8] It is flat land with no mountain but Hekla in view. The ash is black, covered with a thin sprinkling of gray-brown pumice stones and strewn with ragged lava boulders. Sometimes there is a meadow planted with new coarse grass, the ruined earth showing through the sparse blades. (This planting, which we have seen in other volcanic areas, is not so much to reclaim the pasture as to keep the fine ash from blowing in the high winds of winter and covering the farmlands anew.) Incredibly, there are sheep on the infertile fields, nibbling at the thin grass cover, nosing the moss that has gathered on the lava. We come on a surprising small woodland surrounded by lava fields. It is of dwarf birch left over from pre-Settlement days, and somehow all fifteen eruptions have missed it. A high fence keeps the sheep out; they would eat not only leaves but bark, destroying the brave little copse.

In front of us a hillside streaked yellow and orange rises from the blackened plain. Beyond its curve is a swimming pool, all alone in the desert. It is painted bright green and new grass hardly less green has been planted thickly around it. Beds of begonias and two-feet-high larches are arranged formally within its low concrete wall. Steam, slightly sulphur-scented, rises from the pool, which feels about 90°F., into the dank, chilly air, which is around 50°. The stream that feeds the pool comes steaming from a spring on the sulphur-stained hillside, a *solfatara*, hot spring area. There is no house within sight of the pool, which looks out of place and garish. Icelanders will go a long way to swim, and they do so outdoors in winter as well as in summer.

The country begins to change as we come to Rangarvellir, Crooked River Fields. The Ranga, Wrong or Crooked River, is so-called because its original bed was twisted by storms and sands, and by another great river, and it now makes a right-angle turn just before the place where it once emptied into the ocean. Here the flattened plains gradually give way to rounded hills and long green valleys with slow rivers winding through them.

The Rangarvellir is the beginning of Njal's country. It acquires an extra dimension when one knows the story.

[8] *Hraun*, originally meaning wilderness, is the Icelandic word for a volcanic field when the lava has grown cold, a burnt place.

NINE

Njal's Country

IT IS POSSIBLE in the confines of these pages to retell the Saga of Njal only in the barest outline, thus losing the sharpness of the dialogue, the drama of minute-by-minute action, the spare and trenchant delineations of character, above all the inevitable sweep of tragedy built up by cumulative detail. It is the longest and noblest of the sagas, and having read it one knows more about the philosophical and moral dilemma of the tenth-century Icelander, trapped in the clash of opposing rationales, than any history can tell.

As to its historical truth, the author, whose identity is unknown, evidently used a number of written records. Most of the characters were real people, and many of the events are known fact, somewhat embellished by time and the historian's sense of drama. Even *Landnamabok*, the bible of Icelandic genealogy, which is one of the author's sources, has been shown to be not always scrupulously accurate. Many of the happenings of *Njalssaga* come not from written sources but from oral narrative, tales told and retold before men began to write things down, and changed in the telling. The known chronology is mixed up here and there, and some episodes sound more like the thirteenth century, when it was written, than the tenth. The author's intention, it seems, was not bare history but a serious entertainment based broadly on historical facts; and where story line and character development demanded he twisted history to suit his tale. In his idea of entertainment he was true to the concept of saga-telling in his day. "With sagas," wrote a contemporary, "one man can gladden many an hour, whereas most entertainments are difficult to arrange; some are very costly, some cannot be enjoyed without large numbers of people . . . But saga entertainment . . . costs nothing . . . and one man can entertain as many or as few as wish to listen; it is equally practicable night or day, by light or in darkness."[1] It was also thought that the telling or reading of sagas was morally uplifting, showing "noble deeds and brave feats, whereas ill deeds are manifestations of indolence; thus, such sagas point the distinction between good and evil . . ."[2] Whether the author of *Njalssaga* meant to teach, uplift, entertain or a blend of these, his story is high drama.

Hrut and Unn were betrothed. Hrut delayed the marriage so that he could go to Norway and collect an inheritance. To improve his position at the court of King Harald Gray-Cloak he allowed himself to be seduced by Harald's mother, Gunnhild. When he returned to claim his bride, Gunnhild put a curse on him so that he could not consummate his marriage. Unn divorced him and her father claimed the dowry back. Hrut, deeply hurt and insulted, refused.

Unn inherited her father's estate and squandered it all within a few years. She went to Gunnar, her cousin, to ask his help in getting her dowry back from Hrut. Gunnar was a handsome man of great strength and outstanding physical skill, with a streak of gentleness in him which made it difficult for him to become angry enough to kill. He became, however unwillingly, the attraction center of most of the violence of this tale. When Unn appealed to him he went to his friend Njal, the wise and benevolent, to ask advice on how to regain the dowry. Njal advised him sagely, and the money was recovered. Unn then married a vicious man named Valgard who turned her against her benefactor. She brought up their son, Mord Valgardsson, to hate Gunnar. This was easy

[1] Anonymous scribe, 13th century
[2] Ibid.

because Mord was from the beginning a force of evil, one of the two malevolent spirits of the story, consumed with envy and feeding on vengeance, his life dedicated to plotting others' downfall.

Gunnar left the country to go to Norway and make a fortune. He attacked and defeated a force of pirates much larger than his party, found their treasure, and returned home a wealthy hero. At the *Althing* he met twice-widowed Hallgerd, Hrut's niece, a woman of mischief who was to become the story's second malignant genius. As a girl Hallgerd had had "thief's eyes."[3] She had grown up to be "a woman of great beauty . . . very tall . . . her lovely hair so long that it could veil her whole body. She was impetuous and wilful." Her first two husbands had been murdered by her jealous foster-father, Thjostolf, with her implicit approval, after they had slapped her in attempts to curb her arrogance. Thjostolf, a man of unpredictable black tempers, was wont, at the *Althing*, to "stalk about brandishing his axe in a sinister way." When Gunnar met Hallgerd she wore "a red, richly-decorated tunic under a scarlet cloak trimmed all the way down with lace. Her beautiful thick hair flowed down over her bosom." They fell in love and were betrothed on the spot, against the strong advice of Njal as well as of Hallgerd's father and uncle, who knew her propensity for making trouble. She immediately started quarreling with Bergthora, Njal's wife, herself a high-tempered woman, and their feud led to the deaths of seven men. One of them was the foster-father of Njal's sons, and the three boys never forgave the murderer, a man named Thrain Sigfusson, Hallgerd's son-in-law. Hallgerd continued to make trouble, blackmailing a slave to steal food from a fractious farmer who then refused Gunnar's generous offer of compensation. This was only one of a series of vexatious events making good-natured Gunnar, a hero against his will, the prey of all the malicious forces around him. These forces were led by Mord, the son of Unn, ever scheming in the background, twisting events to confound men of good faith. Njal, faithful to his friend despite the enmity of their wives, continually helped Gunnar to escape with honor the snares set for him. But even wise and

[3] All further quotations in this chapter are from *Njalssaga*.

145

loyal Njal could not avert final tragedy. Gunnar was outlawed and ordered to leave the country. As he was on his way down to the sea his horse stumbled and he had to leap from the saddle. He glanced back at his home hillside. "How lovely the slopes are," he said. "More lovely than they have ever seemed to me before, golden cornfields and new-mown hay. I am going back home, and I will not go away." There he was at last cornered by his enemies. Alone he stood off a large band of men, wounding many of them. Running out of weapons he shot his enemies with their own arrows and finally was left defenseless. "Let me have two locks of your hair," he said to Hallgerd, his wife, "and help my mother plait them into a bowstring for me." "Does anything depend on it?" she asked. "My life depends on it . . ." "In that case," said Hallgerd, "I shall now remind you of the slap you once gave me." "To each his own way of earning fame," answered Gunnar. "You shall not be asked again." Still his enemies had a hard time. Gunnar fought with his hands alone until he was exhausted from his wounds and they could finally kill him. But not before he had wounded sixteen and killed two.

Gunnar's death was avenged by his son, with Njal's oldest, a formidable warrior named Skarp-Hedin. This turned the smoldering bitterness in a new direction, as Njal's sons became involved in continuing the blood feuds of their friends. Njal, always a peacemaker, tried to still the passions of hate by adopting Hoskuld, a gentle child, the son of Thrain, the murderer of his sons' fosterfather. Hoskuld grew up in the household and received extra signs of Njal's favor, to the extent that Njal intervened at the *Althing* to have him made a chieftain. Mord worked on the jealousy of Njal's true sons for this favored youth, and they murdered Hoskuld in his own cornfield. As Skarp-Hedin struck him on the head the young man, a Christian too saintly to fight back, fell to his knees. "May God help me and forgive you all," he cried just before they cut him down. His wife, Hildigunn, another of the strong, vengeful women who play such a large part in this saga, goaded her uncle to revenge.

After a long, futile effort by Njal to see justice done at the *Althing* in the case of his sons, a group of one hundred men intent

146

on vengeance gathered outside his house. Unable to defeat Njal and his redoubtable sons in open warfare, they set the house on fire. Njal, at the end more Christian than Viking, surrendered to his fate and refused to fight any longer, preferring death as a merciful providence. Though their enemies allowed the women to leave the burning house, Bergthora, Njal's wife, elected to stay. "I was given to Njal in marriage when young, and I have promised him that we would share the same fate." When she told her small grandson to leave he answered, "But that's not what you promised me, grandmother. You said that we would never be parted; and so it shall be, for I would much prefer to die beside you both." The three then lay down on their bed, crossed themselves and commended their souls to God. "Father is going to bed early," said Skarp-Hedin, "and that is only natural, for he is an old man." Skarp-Hedin, his weapons gone, began throwing burning brands out of the house at the attackers. One man he killed with the jawbone he had hacked out of the mouth of Thrain, who had killed his foster-father. At the end he too, with his brothers, was pinned under the wreckage of the burning house. His body was found, still defiantly upright against the wall, though his legs were almost burned off below the knees. The bodies of Njal, his wife and grandchild were unmarked by the flames. Njal's features, said one of those who found him, "appear to have a radiance which I have never seen on a dead man before."

Njal was avenged by his son-in-law Kari the Lucky, the only one to escape the burning. He killed the attackers with true Viking fury, one by one, until finally his need for revenge was sated, all the evil forces had burned themselves out and the erstwhile enemies came at last to peace with another.

It is easy to imagine the horsemen of *Njalssaga* galloping over the fields, ambushing one another at crossings of the wide rivers, visiting with either friendly or malicious intent between the farms, many of which still have the old names. It is now, as it was then, country attuned to a small population of prosperous farmers. The neat white red-roofed farm buildings are dotted, widely spaced across the meadows. The holdings, now as then, are large, to

147

accommodate big flocks of sheep; the more promising fields are cleared of the ubiquitous lumps and kept for haying, and for grazing milch cows and horses.

As we go south, following Njal's path homeward from the *Althing*, the ashy plains of Hekla gradually merge with the fertile Rangarvellir. The first of the *Njalssaga* farms that we come to is at the edge of the changing land, a hilly oasis in the dusty desert. Its name is Keldur, Well-Spring, and it is the only one built at the time of Njal which still stands because, unlike most, it was built of stone. Keldur belonged to Ingjald, uncle of the saintly Hoskuld, Njal's foster son killed by his blood sons. Ingjald was torn between the need for revenge and his loyalty to Njal, a staunch friend who had saved him three times from outlawry. At the end he cast in his lot with Njal, refusing to go with the burners.

There are three farms at Keldur, dating from the eleventh, the nineteenth and the twentieth centuries. The oldest differs from Stöng, the old-country Viking dwelling, in being a passage house — a collection of five attached buildings — a style new in the eleventh century, and better fitted to Iceland's climate than the long drafty halls. From the outside it looks like five lumpy hills in the middle of a field. Most of it is underground, the roofs, barely protruding from the earth around them, being covered with grass-grown sod. One bends almost double to go through the door, down stone steps into the house. The floor, the walls and the roof are of stone two or three feet thick. Light and air, but not much of either, come through the small door and through a hole above the raised fireplace. There are no windows. The first house of the row was the dwelling place of the family. Here there was a kitchen, a storage room for milk and curds, and a living and sleeping room. The other houses, connected by narrow passages, were for animals and their food, and for meat and bread. They are all low-ceilinged, and exceedingly dark and damp.

But when the houses were alive warmth flowed from one to the other, and was preserved by the heavy walls and roofs, chinked and covered with sod. The people probably bathed in the kitchen, as it was the only room with a fireplace; they also must have done much of their living and working there in the winters. The other really warm place was the house in the row that served as cow stable. Mothers took their children out of bed in the mornings and put them with the cows to warm up.

One can go straight from the eleventh-century passage house into the nineteenth-century farm, which is not much less primitive. Much of it is also underground; when one walks upstairs to the bedroom floor one is at last on a level with the ground on one side, one-half story up on the other. A large square stone chimney goes through the middle of the house, keeping all of it warm. The bedrooms are finished with wood, and the furniture, made by the farmer who built the house, great-grandfather of the present owner, is simply carved and beautifully proportioned.

The third dwelling is the modern house, built in 1946 by the son of the couple who last lived in the nineteenth-century building. It is of the usual corrugated iron, simple, comfortable and airy, with many windows. Its young owner, when his father died, asked his mother to move in with him but she preferred the small dark nineteenth-century house where she had lived as wife and mother. Now both the old people, along with their parents and grandparents, are buried in the churchyard right beside the farms. The church itself is modern, built over a fifteenth-century church which in turn was built over an eleventh-century monastery. Such is the continuity of Icelandic life and the attachment of her children to their homes that it is probable that the present owner, a personable young man with a charming, friendly wife and two small children, can trace his family back to Ingjald, who saved his honor and his life by being loyal to his friend.

On the peak of a green hill behind the farm is a tall rounded cairn built of rough lava stones carefully fitted together. When you stand beside it you can see another one on a distant hill. If you stood on that hill you would see still another, and so on all through this country. They are Viking beacons, used to relay messages from farm to farm over the thinly settled land. The farmers keep them up. Whenever a stone has fallen out, through the centuries, it has been replaced.

Keldur's arable land is small compared with many farms. The Rang River winds quietly through it. Its steep hills and valleys are

149

a little world to themselves in the middle of a vast desert of dust and lava. In the distance is the cause of this, Hekla, rising from the dark plain. There is no sun, and the cone of the mountain shines as if it had light inside it.

Njal's farm, Bergthorshvoll, Bergthora's Hillock, is a handsome house on a little dome-shaped hill in a broad plain, Landeyjar, Land Isles. It is thought that the original farm stood on or near the same spot. Excavations close by have disclosed evidence that buildings, probably outbuildings of the farm, were burned there many hundreds of years ago, the exact date unknown.

Landeyjar is barely above sea level, and marshy in places. Drainage ditches cross it at right angles to one another, marking off squares and rectangles with lines of grass-covered sod humps. Marsh marigolds shine bright yellow against the dark wet earth of the ditches. The land is too low for the ocean, two and a half miles away, to be visible, but across it the rocks of the Westmann Islands rise, enormous and dusky. A plume of smoke pushes out of the side of Heimaey, growing bigger until it is a gray shadow obscuring all the islands. Back of the farm the plains stretch into misty distance. The only elevations to be seen are the distant pyramid of Hekla and the nearer heights of sharp-peaked Tindfjallajökull, Spike Mountain Glacier, and Eyjafjallajökull, Island Mountain Glacier, a great rounded dome 5,468 feet high. Around the farm all is quiet; men and women are all off in the fields. Arctic terns dive again and again into the long grass, seeking insects. Small fish and crustaceans are their usual food; today the ocean must be too rough for hunting.

Gunnar's farm, Hlidarendi, Farm at the End of the Hillside, is, as its name says, on the last hill of a low range before the marshy plain called Teigsaurer, Meadow Swamp. It nestles in a hollow of the hillside. Near it a waterfall drops into a fern-bordered basin. Its surrounding slopes fall gracefully away to the green marshes below. It has a long view over the flats and the river to the towering Eyjafjall Glacier beyond. A rainstorm is coming over the plain, dark and slanting in the wind, but where we stand the sun shines. One can see how Gunnar's heart was torn as he rode away into exile.

The farm itself exists no longer. On its site is a sad little corrugated iron house, its paint discolored and peeling. It looks abandoned; it may only be poor. A town has grown up on Gunnar's "golden cornfields," built into the side of his hill. Above the plain houses of painted concrete and iron is a little white church, highplaced as churches usually are in Iceland. It has the classic shape of small churches, a rectangular box with a tapered steeple. Inside it is as severe as outside, with straight wooden pews, an altar adorned only with a white embroidered cloth probably made by a local farm wife, and narrow windows too high above the pews for the congregation to be able to see out. Within its fenced yard trees have been planted, larch and mountain ash. This is the only attempt to beautify. But the site itself is so beautiful that the church needs no decoration. Its stark simplicity is its best asset.

Below the town a farmer with a tractor is digging lumps out of a field. The tractor has rotary blades attached, which chew up the soil into a rough evenness. All Iceland's fields are full of lumps, which are caused by frost action. A willow shrub or a clump of hardy flowers, moss campion or mountain avens, gather moisture around its dense roots. The water attracts fine sand or silt, which adheres in a wet hump around the plant. When the earth freezes in winter the moisture-laden silt expands, pushing the soil upward in a bubble. The farmer has to contend not only with earth lumps but with stones. He will clear a field one spring, and the next spring rocks have mysteriously appeared again. This is also a phenomenon of frost action, the expanding earth pushing out hard objects. In the next field a farmer, having dealt with his lumps, is dragging an outsized snowplow across it, pulled behind a tractor. When he has finished this he will apply an iron roller like a gigantic tennis-court roller. Only then can he begin to plant his hay crop.

The swamp, Teigsaurar, has the intense greenness of grass whose roots are in water. A road crosses it, solid and important on the map. In reality, as with most Icelandic roads, it makes no concessions to automobiles, having been created by horses. The rain has added to the native wetness of the ground, and every few

151

hundred yards we drive through unbridged streams of varying depth and swiftness. They have rocks in their beds, brought down from the cliffs we can barely see through cloud off to the east. There is no habitation here, and it would not be a good place to get stuck in the middle of a river with a hole in a tire. This time we are lucky; the tires are intact and only our brakes have given way. Teigsaurar, like much of the country, is no place for an automobile. It was easier to travel in Njal's time.

The cliffs approach, high and dark. Down them course innumerable long, thin cataracts. Between us and them is the Markarfljot, Border River. It is a fast, wide, imposing river, an obvious boundary line demarcating the flat sea-level plains to its west from the high cliffy ridges, continuation of the mountainous inland glaciers, that come almost down to the sea on its east. Its western shore is all swamp, and the river spreads through it in broad low arms. Its main flow is to the east, under the shadow of the rock walls. An iron bridge about half a mile long crosses the whole thing, from swamp to precipice. Upstream is a flat pattern of black and silver in the rain, water and islands. Here Skarp-Hedin, Njal's combative son, killed Thrain, the murderer of his foster-father, in a colorful battle: "Skarp-Hedin was in the lead, dressed in a blue jacket and carrying a round shield, with his axe hoisted on his shoulder. Next to him was Kari, wearing a silk jacket and a gilded helmet; there was a lion painted on his shield. Behind him walked Helgi, wearing a red tunic and a helmet, and carrying a red shield decorated with a hart . . . Skarp-Hedin raced down towards the river . . . A huge sheet of ice had formed a low hump on the other side of the channel. It was as smooth as glass, and Thrain and his men had stopped on the middle of this hump. Skarp-Hedin made a leap and cleared the channel between the ice banks, steadied himself, and at once went into a slide: the ice was glassy-smooth, and he skimmed along as fast as a bird.

"Thrain was then about to put on his helmet. Skarp-Hedin came swooping down on him and swung at him with his axe. The axe crashed down on his head and split it down to the jaw-bone, spilling the back-teeth on to the ice . . . No one had time to land a blow on Skarp-Hedin as he skimmed past at great speed. Tjorvi

152

threw a shield into his path, but Skarp-Hedin cleared it with a jump without losing his balance . . ."

After we have crossed the Markarfljot we are on the coast headed for Dyrholaey, Island with a Door in the Hill, where Njal's son-in-law Kari had his farm. Dyrholaey is an island, not in the sea but on the sand. It is a sheer-sided butte about one and a half miles long and 350 feet high, rising spectacularly on the edge of the ocean across a waste of charcoal-gray sand. Its grass-grown table top is inaccessible on all sides except for a narrow space on the east where a dirt road winds up to a lighthouse on the highest point. There is no indication of where Kari's farm was. It was clearly not on this rock, which can support nothing but a few sheep. Some fertile acreage inland has taken the name of the rock, the dominating feature of the land for many miles. Kari's farm was probably there, across the sands, where today are the farms of Dyrholhverfi, Door Hill Village, long flat fields between the ocean and the coastal ridge, protected by high escarpments and well-watered by glacial run-off from Myrdalsjökull.

The sand around Dyrholaey is scored by the wind and looks like the bottom of the sea. It is thick and soft, hard to walk on, and the two miles from the road to the rock seem long. A dull, steady roar accompanies us. As we come under the shadow of Dyrholaey a cloud flies up in the air ahead of us and quickly subsides. We cannot see the ocean, and had not expected it so soon. Then suddenly it is there, thirty-foot breakers crashing with the sound of thunder at the bottom of a steep beach. The spume cloud we saw comes from waves breaking on an offshore rock. All of Dyrholaey's outer coast is lined with these rocks, split off from the main bulk by wave action. Erosion is carried to its relentless conclusion on the beach, which is made of black pebbles smooth as wax and glistening with spray, all the same size, about a half inch long. They are the last stage before sand. Once this shining beach was part of the cliff; then it was offshore rock; tomorrow the black rocks now scattering the water into spindrift will themselves be scattered into sand.

It is hard to know how birds manage to live in this climate of

153

breaking, tearing water. But the rocks are covered with murres perched on slanting ledges. Puffins fly straight across the roiled waves to their burrows high on Dyrholaey, glaucous gulls hunt through the offshore eddies, ghostly pale against the dark water, and fulmars glide close to the sea, lifting easily over the massive swell.

As we walk on, the beach narrows, and at last the ocean pounds at the very edge of the cliff. We turn back without having been able to see the great door which gives Dyrholaey its name.

Another day we approach Dyrholaey from the east, where the lighthouse road climbs from a sandbar between ocean and lagoon. On its inland side the sandbar slopes gently into the lagoon. There Arctic terns nest and flowers bloom: *Lathyrus japonicus*, beach pea, and *Potentilla anserina*, silverweed. Silverweed (the first part of whose Latin name means "little potent one" because in medieval times it was used as a medicine) has a thick rootstock bearing runner roots from which rise leaf fronds covered with fine silver hairs to protect it against wind and spray. Its large five-petaled single blossoms are light yellow with deeper yellow centers. Beach pea has gaudy, convoluted mauve and purple flowers and long flexible leaf stems lying supine, not resistant to wind and blowing sand but giving easily before them. Among the flowers are clumps of sea lyme grass, *Elymus arenarius*, Iceland's wild wheat, pale gold heads lifted above the hard, sharp-pointed leaves that sketch circles in the sand. All the spare vegetation of the beach has a special glint against the black sand.

The terns are hunting in the lagoon, as the ocean is too high for them this day. They circle, heads down, then hover in one place with rapid wingbeats, before closing their wings and dropping like stones in brief underwater dives, to pick out the small marine animals they have spotted. No species of tern can stay underwater for long, some not at all, and none of them are good swimmers. This early in June they have not started laying their eggs, but territories have been defined and they dive at us repeatedly with hoarse cries. The nests will be scant scrapings in the sand, perhaps lined with a few blades of grass or dry seaweed, perhaps bare. The two or three eggs will be exposed not only to predators but to shifting sand. Sometimes, in competition with other species of terns, Arctic terns have to nest so close to the water line that an exceptionally high tide may inundate the nest. The reason this species is confined to beaches is that the birds' legs are so short that they cannot navigate in thick vegetation; in fact they can hardly walk at all. Arctic terns have adapted to their precarious, sliding environment: they are able to find and recognize their nests when wind and water have moved them, even if the eggs have been disguised with jetsam.

Pursued by predatory gulls and skuas, confined to exposed beaches as breeding areas, unable to swim, to walk or to stay underwater, condemned to a 25,000-mile yearly migration from Arctic to Antarctic and back — it seems as if the Arctic terns are ill-fitted for life in their exceptionally harsh world. Yet they live and multiply, being adaptable to an extremely wide range, unlike their predators. If harassed beyond endurance they can establish new territories anywhere in the circumpolar regions where there are beaches, and even south of it, from uninhabited coasts of Norway to Iceland and Greenland, from Massachusetts to Resolute Bay, from the islands of the Sea of Okhotsk to northern Siberia. These swift and graceful fliers, who live more in the sunlight than any other animal, are a bright example that the conditions of survival need not all be uncompromisingly functional.

At the other end of the sandbar, out in the ocean, is Reynisdrangar, the Rowan Stacks. The name Rowan comes from the farm village inland of the stacks, where there must have been a grove of rowan, or mountain ash, at the time of the Settlement. The stacks, four pillars of black rock, were once thought to be giants turned to stone. They have a resemblance to stark modern sculpture, one of them exactly resembling a gnarled thumb. The wild ocean breaks over them, and a sudden heavy fall of rain veils them. We take shelter in a cave that also could have been cut by man. Its entrance is framed with organ-pipe rocks sharply cut off at bottom and top, and inside the big blocks of its walls are straight-edged. All along the front there have been showers of broken rock, thin as roof slates and looking like them, any one of which could cleave a skull. We stay well back.

155

When the rain has stopped we walk down the beach toward Dyrholaey. The broad sweep of black sand glitters with wetness in the sunlight. The thundering waves break high, their hollow undersides green-white and glassy. From their torn heads comes a perpetual spray that fills the air with light mist, so that our faces are wet and we breathe in salty air. The sun shines through the mist and distant Dyrholaey is huge and mysterious, wrapped in gold clouds.

The lighthouse on Dyrholaey is an attractive square beige-pink building of concrete set just back from the edge of the highest cliff. A fence encloses its grass-grown plot and below the fence the rock falls precipitately to a sort of anteroom of the ocean 360 feet below. The anteroom has three walls, the one we stand on and another where the cliff makes an abrupt right-angle turn. The third is Dyrholaey's door. It is an immense square block of stone with a rounded arch in it, through which the water sucks and swirls in ponderous eddies. The enclosure is full of noise; over the solid boom of ocean waves echoing through caves far down the walls is the continuous husky chuckling of hundreds of fulmars. They sit, one pair next to the other, on their infinitesimal ledges; they cross and recross down to the sea and up over the tops of the cliffs, alternately flapping and soaring. A pair on a narrow shelf near us is performing a courtship play, clashing their beaks together, then opening and shutting them as if feeding one another. A single fulmar flies straight toward us and comes down on the rock about five years away. It uses only its wings and tail in landing, the large weak webbed feet folding under it so that it lies belly down. It eyes us worriedly as we step closer, turning its head all the way around to watch us. It tries to get to its feet, but they are limp, looking as if made of pink-gray oilcloth. Unable to support itself upright, it slides to the edge of the rock and falls off, instantly becoming airborne.

Away from the lighthouse on the western side, Dyrholaey's crest slopes gradually downward in a series of hummocky terraces where sheep graze on the rough grass and alpine flowers. A female eider flies up almost beneath our feet, leaving three large eggs colored dull chartreuse in a shallow depression lined with dead

On the south shore eroded cliffs rise from black volcanic beaches. The Rowan Stacks, near Dyrholaey, products of water erosion, were once thought to be giants turned to stone.

157

grass and gray down. We have surprised her and she had no time to cover her nest. We leave at once to allow her to return.

Eiders must be nesting all over Dyrholaey. Many dozens of them pass us, in pairs or groups of single males or females flying straight and fast over the summit down toward the lagoon, where they will feed on crabs and mussels. The big ducks have been a prime resource for farmers since the Settlement, providing not only meat and eggs but the down of the brooding female. Kari's farm, besides encompassing the flat, well-irrigated fields below the coastal hills, contained an excellent supplementary source of wealth on Dyrholaey.

Kirkjubærklaustur, Church Farm Cloister, was the site of the first Irish settlement, on which lay a curse after the monks were frightened or driven away by the Norse newcomers. Though the haunted property lay empty for many years, eventually the ghosts were laid. By the time of Njal the owner was Otkel Skarfsson. He was close kinsman to Gizur the White, one of the two who saved their countrymen condemned to death by King Olaf, by promising to bring Christianity to Iceland at the *Althing* of the year 1000. All of Gizur's clan were Christians, and that is why Otkel was able to live unscathed at Kirkjubær (it was not until the fifteenth century that a monastery was founded there and *klaustur* was added to the name). Christian though he was, Otkel was one of the less pleasant characters of the story. In an un-Christian manner he refused to sell food to Gunnar in a time of famine. Gunnar's wife, the scheming Hallgerd, angry at this, retaliated in a typically malicious manner. She blackmailed an Irish slave into stealing some butter and cheese from Otkel, then burning down his storehouse. When Gunnar found out what she had done he slapped her face. That slap was the cause of her refusing to give him a lock of her hair for a bowstring when he was fighting the last battle of his life. The quarrel over the stolen food became enormously magnified through the intrigue of those who wished ill to Gunnar and Njal, and by the sensitivity to insult of all the parties concerned. It was not easy to arouse Gunnar, but when the unforgivable gibe came that he had wept at receiving a slight wound on the ear, he finally took fire. There ensued a splendidly bloody battle on the Rang River. "Now you shall see if you can make me weep," cried Gunnar, single-handedly taking on eight. He killed four of them before he received the help of his brother, when they finished them off together. "Audolf the Easterner," runs the account, "snatched up a spear and threw it at Gunnar, who caught it in flight and hurled it back. It passed right through the shield and Audolf behind it . . . Gunnar lunged with the halberd; he speared Skamkel on the point, heaved him up into the air and dashed him head-first down on the path . . . Otkel swung his sword at Gunnar, aiming just below the knee. Gunnar leaped high and the blow passed underneath him. Gunnar thrust with his halberd and drove it through him." At the end Gunnar the gentle, always loath to kill, remarked to his brother, presumably dusting his hands: "I wish I knew whether I am any the less manly than other men, for being so much more reluctant to kill."

To get to Kirkjubærklaustur from Dyrholaey we cross the Myrdalssandur, a fifteen-mile desert dotted with boulders. The wind blows the sand into dust clouds to the north. Behind the brown clouds the Myrdal Glacier sometimes appears, gleaming white and peaked in many places, a range of ice mountains. One of the peaks belongs to Katla, the ice-hidden volcano which in 1918 created the desert over which we drive. It is not a lava desert — Katla's lava production is relatively small — but a titanic flood of mud and gravel brought down in a glacial burst.

The Myrdalssandur has little life. The sand is so fine and loose that few plants can keep their roots. The boulders cannot accumulate moss because of the abrasiveness of wind-blown sand. Bridges cross dry washes that were destructive torrents of mud-filled water in early spring. Curious sharp-edged dunes dot the landscape where the near-constant wind has buried rocks in sand. The dunes are rows of jagged crests that look like teeth.

At the far side of the Myrdalssandur the green fields gradually reassert themselves. They have grown up or been planted over and around a lava flow. There are fields of red and black cinders where the farmers have not yet reclaimed the land; even in the meadows lava rocks rise from the grass, wrinkled and holey like petrified sponges. In the midst of the regenerated fields, beside a wide, marshy river, the Kudafljot, Salmon Fry River, is a dairy village named Thykkvabæjarklaustur, Cloister of the Copse Farm. The copse has long since vanished. But one farmer is making a brave if pathetic effort to bring it back. In the grass before his house is a single row of larches a few inches high, each one protected by a white paper bag. If the frail trees live to outgrow their paper walls the cruel wind of the sandy plains will surely destroy them. The little church on the site of the cloister is in the middle of a pasture. No road leads to it. We walk through a field of cows and climb a fence to reach it. Around it are the grass mounds of old graves, dominated by a tall slab of rough-hewn rock commemorating the cloister that was in this place from 1168 to 1550.

We stop to ask directions at the farm near the church, to which the cows belong. Our faltering efforts with map and dictionary bring three generations into the yard. The faces of the old man, the young farmer and four little boys are exactly alike, long and bony, red and wind-bitten. Their somewhat squinted blue eyes are very bright, and they all laugh all the time, unconquerably amused in the face of a life even harder than that of most Icelandic farmers. The name of their farm is Hraungerdi, Pasture in the Burnt Field. It is an exact description. On one side of the house is a stretch of flat meadow with rows of high-piled sod on its edges, on the other a field of lava cinders. When we came the farmer had been digging squares of sod from one of the rows and carting them with a small stout horse and wagon over to the lava field, where he piled them. Later he will lay them side by side, then fertilize and sow the new field. In a year he will have a stand of thin grass there, in two years a cow pasture.

Our way parallels the Kudafljot to Flagavöllir, which means the field where they cut turf for building. Between the road and the river is a little hill densely covered with birches and willows as high as our knees. The miniature forest is fresh and fragrant, and alive with birds. The birch leaves shine from recent rain and the willows' furry blossoms gleam with water drops. Redwings, small thrushes, fly up before us and land on treetops to scold in fluty tones. Meadow pipits dart from branch to branch, then fly

161

into the air, to drift slowly to earth with thin, piping songs ending in musical trills. A surprised snipe runs almost under our feet and disappears in a thicket of willows. Another circles rapidly in the air, diving and twisting, with repeated sharp calls like the loud ticking of a clock. Snipe need soft, swampy ground in which to dig for worms, insect larvae and small crustaceans with their long bills, and high grass or brush for their well-hidden nests. Flagavöllir, with its luxuriant dwarf woodland and its marshy river banks, is made for them.

A pair of gray lag geese flies up from the river followed by a black-headed gull. They circle round and round, honking, the gull still after them. At last the gull gives up and the geese return to the slow, shallow river, where they have been feeding on the roots of aquatic plants. Near them stands a golden plover alone, crying its thin, sad cry.

The road beyond Flagavöllir rises and dips through rounded hills with red patches of willows not yet in leaf on their soft green sides. Shortly before Kirkjubærklaustur the hills end abruptly and the road straightens, built up over a stretch of twisted lava, its catastrophic appearance slightly modified by moss. This kind of lava, knotty and porous due to the sudden explosive escape of gases from liquid rock, is called in Iceland *apalgryti*, apple stones, and its chief characteristic aside from extreme unattractiveness is its impassability. The technical name by which it is generally known is *aa* lava, a Hawaiian word. The field we traverse is called Nyja Eldhraun, New Fire-Field. It was the main stream that flooded out of the fissure volcano Laki, Maw, in 1784, in the biggest eruption that has happened anywhere in the world within recorded time.

Laki's eruption was similar to the basalt floods that welled up out of the ocean to form the Thulean Province fifty million years ago. Instead of pouring out of a central vent and forming a cone, tongues of lava burst through about a hundred small craters along a ten-mile fissure and spread flatly over the countryside, creating plateaus where there had been hills and valleys. One river valley was filled four to six hundred feet deep, another was flooded with a forty-mile flow seven miles at its widest. In the eight months' duration of the eruption lava spread over 350 square miles of land with an estimated volume of sixteen billion cubic yards. Rivers flooded by the melting of glaciers and the damming of lava-blocked streams added to the destruction. Lava engulfed two churches and thirteen farmsteads. Thirty other farms were damaged beyond repair. The havoc wrought all over Iceland by dust and poisonous gases lasted for several years and nearly caused the entire evacuation of the country.

The two great lava flows from Laki, the Nyja Eldhraun to the west, and the Brunahraun, Burnt Fields, to the east, left untouched between them a long narrow island called Landbrot, which means land desolated by sea or rivers. We expected a bog, but Landbrot, while very wet, is hilly and fertile. It must today be much as it was when the wandering Irish monks found their place of peace and when, a century or so later, times having violently changed, Hall-gerd's slave rode over to steal Otkel's food and burn his store-house. Its village, Kirkjubærklaustur, lies by the edge of a quiet fork of the Skafta, Shaft River, beneath a tall hill covered with trees, native birch and mountain ash interspersed with imported spruce and larch. The hill has a sunny southern exposure and is protected by a wall of cliff at the top from the north wind off the glaciers, so the trees have grown tall and their branches spread wide. When we arrived, in mid-June, snow was falling, big soft wet flakes, in one of Iceland's freakish weather turnabouts. The severe iron and cement houses of the village were clothed in white, and tufts of snow were held in the broad-flung branches of the forest trees behind it. The scene had a softened New England quality at extreme variance with the fierce landscape at its gates.

At the edge of the town, where its last houses touch the Bruna-sandur, a new church is going up, a beautiful modern structure of molded concrete and wood, to commemorate the preacher Jon Steingrimsson, pastor of the church that stood at the time of the Laki eruption. Laki started to erupt on a Sunday, so goes the story, and the stream of lava was approaching the church when the congregation was assembled. The people begged their preacher to open the doors in case they had to escape. He told them to take heart and listen to him. With doors closed he preached a "sermon of fire," and at the end, when the people went outside, they found the flow had stopped at the door of the church. The lava is not quite that close, actually, but a short walk away it starts, a flood to the horizon of the worst imaginable rock, torn and scoriated. Pastor Steingrimsson is remembered with gratitude not only for his defiance of the fiery tide but because he kept the only written records of all the people who had farms in the neighborhood which were buried or burned in the holocaust.

Around Kirkjubærklaustur is fine farmland, of mild hills and saturated valleys. Each hill has a pond at its base where trumpeter swans and tufted ducks float. Rivers flow in every direction, some harnessed for generators just big enough to run individual farms. Cattle and sheep graze in unfenced fields and the farmhouses are small, comfortable and well-kept. Here and there one is deserted. Even in this easeful place farming is hard and, as in nearly every country in the world today, there is a cityward trend away from agricultural pursuits. But Icelanders are loath to leave their home farms forever. Many return, successful in the city, to visit their still-farming parents and build their own vacation cottages on the land where they grew up. So Landbrot's empty farms are being reclaimed and pretty new houses, often of wood, an imported luxury affordable by the newly rich businessmen, are set beside winding rivers stocked yearly with trout and salmon fry.

From Kirkjubærklaustur we followed the route of the Burners of Njal as they fled eastward to the farm of their leader, Flosi Thordarson, at Svinafell across the Sands of Skeidar.

Flosi was not a bad man. He was "a powerful chieftain, tall and strong and . . . forceful," and he was one of the earliest of Thangbrand's Christian converts. He had a friendly relationship with Njal through the marriage of his niece, Hildigunn, to Njal's foster-son, the saintly Hoskuld. But he, like others, was caught up in the relentless tide of insult, murder and revenge that swept to the climax of the burning, and, almost against his will, found himself the leader of Njal's enemies. In the first place he was viciously goaded by his niece Hildigunn, "a woman of great beauty and spirit . . . harsh-natured and ruthless," who demanded vengeance

for the slaying of her husband by Njal's sons (who had been persuaded to the deed by the evil Mord Valgardsson). She took the
cloak in which Hoskuld had been killed, and threw it around
Flosi's shoulders, "and the clotted blood rained down all over him.
'This is the cloak you gave to Hoskuld,' she said, 'and now I give it
back to you . . . I charge you in the name of all the powers of your
Christ . . . to avenge every one of the wounds that marked his
body — or be an object of contempt to all men.' " Flosi was so
agitated that "his face changed color rapidly; one moment it was
red as blood, then pale as withered grass, then black as death . . .
'Monster,' he cried, 'You want us to take the course which will
turn out worst for all of us. Cold are the counsels of women.' " He
stayed true to his friendship with Njal, and agreed to a financial
settlement of the killing. The two chieftains shook hands and
vowed the end of the quarrel. But Njal's unquenchably combative
son Skarp-Hedin refused to be party to this mild solution and
gratuitously insulted Flosi. He threw on top of the pile of compensation money a pair of trousers, saying Flosi would have use for
them. When asked why he replied, "You will need them if you are,
as I have heard, the mistress of the Svinafell Troll, who uses you
as a woman every ninth night." The hint of perversion was the one
entirely unforgivable taunt. Flosi kicked away the silver and rode
off to Svinafell in a fury, intent on full blood vengeance. He
gathered his kinsmen and followers together and they vowed "to
attack the Njalssons with fire and sword and not withdraw until
they are all dead."

The way east led past a great swamp between the last of the
Laki floods and the beginning of the Sands of Skeidar, the product
of another kind of underground eruption, glacial bursts from the
hot lake Grimsvötn under the ice of Vatnajökull. A two-rutted
wagon road traversed this and we left the main road to follow it,
hoping to reach the sea eleven miles to the south. The flat green
land was alive with birds: whimbrels, phalaropes, swans, geese,
skuas, all apparently sharing the rich habitat with some degree of
uneasy tolerance. Five miles down the road the land rose infinitesi-
mally, just enough to get it out of the water. There, as always in
Iceland where there are a few acres of land in whatever inhospita-

ble environment that can be tilled or grazed or built upon, was a little farm named Slettabol, Farm in the Plain. It had the loneliest situation imaginable, hung in a limbo between earth and water, neither by the sea nor quite on the land. Nothing was visible in any direction but water-soaked swamp, green and brown and dull blue. But the elderly farmer, who approached us across the marsh riding a lively young piebald horse and leading another, was cheerful, greeting us with waves and smiles and a lot of incomprehensible talk. He and his wife lived in one of the two dwellings, a two-story four-room house of corrugated iron, newly painted. The other house, directly behind the modern one, was double and built into the ground, its two peaked roofs covered with grass-grown sod, its small windows at ground level. Here the couple had lived until ten or fifteen years ago, when they were persuaded to replace with metal their attractive but dark and damp ancestral home.

For all reasonable travel the road ended at Slettabol. We continued farther, dipping into shallow lakes, skirting quaking bogs, the ruts of the wagon road alternately filled with water or slippery with black mud. At last we were forced to turn back, unable to reach the place where ocean blended into land, the tides creeping over the muddy sands, replacing the green of bog growth with stranded algae.

Back on the main road again, we crossed the terrible lava of the Brunahraun, then for a little while traversed a pretty stretch of farmland with high cliffs on the inland side. At one farm a dog was chasing a little lamb round and round a field. The terrified lamb tore through a barbed-wire fence, tangled its legs in the wire and fell, hanging head down in a water-filled ditch. After the two raced a farmer and a boy, probably his son. Before they could catch up with the first dog, a second started chasing another lamb in circles and the boy veered away to head it off. The two dogs barked happily, eluding pursuers, while the lambs bleated in panic, the farmer yelled and the mother ewes stood in the middle of the field baaing miserably, unable to help anyone. The two lambs were rescued, but the dogs continued to leap around the field in an excess of joyful mischief, scattering the whole flock. What, we wondered, did the farmers keep dogs for? Most farms had dogs,

166

relatives of the border collies so swift and clever on Scottish sheep farms. But these Icelandic dogs sat in the yards barking at strangers, ran away tail down when one approached, chased cars, teased lambs, were frightened of full-grown sheep. Dogs are mentioned a few times in the sagas, as companions and guards, not as farm workers, and this seems to be the tradition of today. But one would think that the least requirement of man's best friend would be to refrain from interfering with the family livelihood. The real heroes of the farms are horses. They can go where a dog would not run and a man could not walk, into the tumbled lava fields, through snow-filled gullies, across spring torrents, along rocky rims. Their owners ride them after lost animals and use them for everyday herding and periodic roundups, where they excel even the finely trained cow ponies of the American West.

The last farm before the Skeidararsandur was named Nupsstadur. *Nup*, or *gnupr*, is a peak, and *stadur* dates back to the thirteenth century when the struggle between church and laity over ownership of churches and church lands was settled in favor of the laity. The *stadamenn* were lay proprietors of church estates. The church of Nupsstadur, ancient but not as old as the litigation over it, was of black wood, its roof heavily sodded. It had two attendant farmhouses, the old one triple, low and turfed, the modern one of white-painted corrugated iron. Behind the little settlement rose a solid red wall, Raudabergsheidi, Moor of the Red Iron Mountain, which may have contributed to the modest wealth of the church farm by yielding the inferior iron ore mined by the early Icelanders for their household needs.

Just beyond the farm is the last bluff, Lomagnupur, Peak of the Loon, with a deep indentation named Hrafnaroddar, Raven's Point. Long ago water ran through this defile, carving great rounded columns in high relief on the four-hundred-foot-high cliff walls. A little water is left: a fast stream, Hrafna, Raven's River, through the center, and waterfalls from the heights. A strong north wind drives down through the split, the fair weather wind that keeps cold spring weather lingering into June this year, to the farmers' despair. Icicles hang from the columns where the sun hits late, and some of the cascades are frozen. Others are blown by the wind so

167

that all their water flies upward like smoke. There are no ravens, but two pairs of gray lag geese circle high, evidently playing with the thermals. One pair flies away from the cliffs out into the open center, then soars upward and wheels back, wings still, nearly to brush the rock. The other pair follows, not closely, in winged counterpoint, a ballet against the sky. They honk continuously as they turn in the air, wild reedy music torn by the wind.

The gorge is about a quarter of a mile wide at the road, its mild incline strewn with old gray boulders smoothed by water. Moss campion grows between them in clumps as much as ten inches across, attesting to the centuries it must be since water flowed here. A cushion of moss campion a quarter of an inch high and one inch across may be fifty years old. The canyon narrows toward its head. The cliffs, divided only by the small torrent of Hrafna, curve in parallel lines, nearly meeting. On one side is a forty-five-degree slope of sand and gravel scraped off the wall by wind and rain. On the other the massive detritus brought down by the river closes off the defile. The north wind storms through the cut and the river cascades and eddies noisily between the giant boulders. Fulmars fly back through the corridor, circling expertly before coming to a soft landing on the nest ledges. They have found sanctuary in this wild and lonely place, a good fifteen miles from their coastal fishing grounds. Between here and the ocean lie the long flat Sands of Skeidar, habitat of the birds' chief predator, the skua. Skuas, needing open space to maneuver their heavy bodies and broad wings, will not follow their prey through this winding rock hallway, and the fulmar young are safe.

More remarkable than finding fulmars so far from the ocean is seeing sheep so far from their fields. Grass grows on the tops of the water-carved columns, and sheep graze there, sheer cliff below them, overhang above. How did they get there? How will they get down, or up? These questions remain unanswered, here and all over Iceland.

Below us, as we turn back, are the dark Sands of Skeidar laced with blue watercourses leisurely intertwining. Lomagnupur juts out, the last outpost, then there is nothing for eighteen miles. At the northern edge of the sands Skeidararjökull, Ambling Glacier (the Icelanders' name for an outlet glacier — one that has walked away from the parent glacier), is black and wrinkled where the glacial bursts from Grimsvötn, Vatnajökull's hot lake, have covered it with sand. The great mother glacier rises behind it, ice peaks shining with an almost spiritual whiteness.

Modern man has gone to extravagant lengths of engineering design, materials, labor and time to achieve what Flosi and his companions, fleeing their crime, managed with a few sure-footed ponies. The new road across the Skeidararsandur is built high. Long dikes of dirt and stones cross it at right angles, to hold and direct the periodic floods from Grimsvötn, which is contained in a hollow of one of Vatnajökull's ice mountains 5,660 feet above the plain. Today little water flows between the dikes. It will get faster and higher as the spring snows melt. The road, now high on concrete stilts, will be nearly awash within a month. It runs straight across the sands, one of Iceland's few roads that does not follow the line of convenience. Even if the engineers wanted, they could find no pony track across the Skeidararsandur on which to trace the course of their new road. Rain, wind and moving sand obliterate all paths. Much of the highway, in fact, consists of bridges. Seven of them span the shifting sands, the longest 984 yards long. Even where it is safe to build near ground level concrete buttresses raise the road above the inevitable floods. Icelanders, often thwarted by these sands, are not sanguine about the new road. Large *jökulhraups*, they know, will wash away in places, and every five years or so major repairs will be needed. But the bridges are strong and high, and as long as they remain, the highway is fundamentally still there. The conquering of the Skeidararsandur is a blessing. Now the people can at last drive all around their island, a distance of some nine hundred miles. Before the sands were bridged, in order to get by car from Reykjavik to Höfn on the south coast, a distance of two hundred miles as the crow flies, one had to go all the way around Iceland the other way, up past the west fjords, around the north country and down along the east fjords.

At the far side of the Skeidararsandur is Svinafell, Hog Mountain, Flosi's farm, a cliff at its back, the sands before it and a glacier on its doorstep. The glacier, Svinafellsjökull, a tongue of Oræfa-jökull, has advanced and retreated over the centuries. When Flosi farmed here the climate was milder than it is today, and his land encompassed wide fields and woodlands. In the cold time of the seventeenth and eighteenth centuries the glacier nearly surrounded the farm. Today the land that was glacier two hundred years ago is one of the most fertile spots in Iceland, its soil enriched by minerals left by the melting ice. Where it is not cultivated wild flowers and shrubs grow in profusion, and Flosi's brushy woodland is coming back.

We crossed a field and climbed a little hill through birches and junipers, sweet-smelling in the rain. A clear stream ran over rocks beside us. Suddenly there was the glacier that had given life to the earth below: a menacing flood of gray ice seamed with crevasses and hollowed by black-mouthed caverns, in any one of which might have dwelt the Svinafell Troll.

Between the glacier and the fresh fields was the terminal moraine, a wilderness of pebbles where, it is said, one could pick up semi-precious volcanic products such as opal, jasper, agate and Icelandic feldspar. We found none, but the rocky desert was bright-ened by pioneer flowering plants, slowly converting it into another fresh field. *Silene acaulis*, moss campion, a plant which creates its own soil, has long tough roots that can hold in gravel or sand. They intertwine to make a matted pad that holds water like a sponge. The evergreen leaves are so tightly furled as to be needle-shaped, to protect them against the evaporation of moisture. Each leaf is coated with thick wax, a further insulation against drying. The stems are so short that the clump clings to the ground like moss. It is studded all over with bright pink square-petaled blos-soms. Drifting sand cannot uproot it, rain cannot flatten it, wind cannot dry it, sun cannot burn it. Only a thin area at the top has live leaves. Below, the dead leaves, held in the spongy mat of stems and roots, break down gradually into humus which nourishes not only the plant itself but guest plants as well. The moss campion is host to many tiny plants that require sustenance richer than that afforded by gravel and rain. The growth of a moss campion colony is slow, and staunch as the cushions are against weather they are

170

frail against man. One footstep will destroy a little patch of garden that is one hundred years old or more.

In the same area of poor soil the small notched blossoms and furry leaves of *Cerastium alpinum*, mountain chickweed, like moss campion a member of the pink family, creep among the pebbles. On the lawn chickweed is obnoxious; among the gray stones of the glacial moraine its delicate white split-petaled flowers are refreshing. The attributes that make it the most persistent of pests — the spiderweb quality of the roots, the tangled, branching stems, the propensity for quick germination, producing several generations in a season — make it a rugged colonizer. The wide-spreading network of branches and roots not only insures that chickweed will not slip away in a storm, but holds the soil together, preventing erosion.

One of the loveliest of the desert flowers is *Dryas octopetala*, mountain avens, a member of the rose family. Its Latin name derives from the resemblance of its leaves to those of the oak, and dryads were said to inhabit oaks. Its evergreen leaves form a carpet from which rises the five-inch stem with its single large blossom, eight white petals around a yellow center opened widely to the sky. The leaves are waxy, the stem hairy and the sepals fuzzy, all protection against the elements. The special contribution of mountain avens to its meager environment is the making of its own nitrates, which not only help it to grow but enrich its surroundings.

Svinafell is at the eastern edge of the country of the *Njalssaga* and the end of our pilgrimage. Despite the devastation caused by eruptions and glacial bursts, the ravages of weather and the natural erosions of time, Njal's country is evocative. No influx of civilization has changed the contours of the land. The few conveniences of the twentieth century — tractors, corrugated iron houses, cement bridges — hardly trespass on the scenery. There are about the same number of people now that there were then, occupying the same farms, even looking much the same. The three boys, blond and tall, riding toward us over the lumpy field, sitting their horses with motionless grace as they maneuver among the sheep, could be Njal's sons. The little houses half buried in the ground, flowers growing in their sodded roofs, are no different from those

171

of a thousand years ago. The narrow dirt roads winding around the flanks of mountains and dipping into rivers are pony trails as old as the Settlement. It is no wonder that Icelanders feel perfectly at home with their old literature. They can look around them and see it live.

TEN

Odin's Mead

THE WRITING OF the *Njalssaga* happened at a time of an extraordinary flowering of literature. The Icelanders had been poets from the beginning, and they believed their gift came from heaven. The Æsir and the Vanir, the two races of gods that later became one, met to end the war between them. They made a treaty of peace and each party agreed to it by spitting into a jar. They breathed life into the spittle and a being was formed, Kvasir, whom they endowed with such high intelligence that he could answer any question.

Kvasir traveled over the world to teach men wisdom, but at last was murdered by the dwarfs Fjalar, Fiend, and Galar, Enchanter. They mixed his blood with honey and made a mead so potently sweet that anyone who drank it would acquire the gift of poetry. When the gods asked what had hapened to Kvasir, the dwarfs said that he had choked on his own wisdom because he could find no one who could ask him enough questions to relieve him of it.

Fjalar and Galar drowned the giant Gilling. In revenge his son, Suttung, picked them up and put them on a rock in the ocean which would be covered at high tide. The dwarfs offered him Kvasir's blood as a ransom for their release, and the giant gave it into the care of his daughter Gunnlauth, Blood of War.

Odin journeyed to the Jötunheim, Home of the Giants, to

find the precious mead. He came to a meadow where nine thralls were mowing, the slaves of Baugi, Suttung's brother. Odin offered to sharpen their scythes. They accepted, and he threw his whetstone into the air. As they tried to catch it each thrall brought his scythe down on the neck of one of the others, and they were all killed. When Baugi lamented that his laborers had killed one another Odin offered to do the work of the nine men for the payment of one draft of Suttung's mead. Baugi agreed, and Odin worked the summer long.

But at the end of the summer Suttung refused to part with a drop of the mead, which his daughter kept in a cave in three jars, Odhrörir, Mind-Exciting, Son, Sound, and Bodn, Divine Oblation. Odin persuaded Baugi to bore a hole through the rock, then turned himself into a worm and crawled through. Changing back to his natural form, he wooed the giant maiden Gunnlauth and stayed with her for three nights. After this she was easily persuaded to let him have a draft of her father's mead. He drank so deep that not one drop was left.

Then he changed himself into an eagle and flew away toward Asgard. Suttung also became an eagle and chased him. The Æsir, seeing their chief flying home, set out all the jars they had, and Odin filled them by discharging the mead through his beak. But Suttung was upon him before he could get it all out, and some of it escaped through another vent. This impure liquor fell to the share of the poetasters. To the gods remained the undefiled mead, and they shared it with those mortals whose minds were high and pure enough to make good use of it.

The gift of the gods descended pure to the Icelanders, in whom the old Norse tradition of tale-telling and celebration of heroic events in poetry found its highest expression.

This had partly to do with the nature of the country. The first settlers were dependent on sheep and cattle, and the seasonal migration to higher or lower pastures; also on fresh- and saltwater fishing, another occupation that required travel. So the Icelandic farmers were of necessity more nomadic than their Scandinavian cousins. There was much movement between districts; consequently the country never fell into culturally or economically separate divisions. The language was and still is without regional dialect, and the people feel a homogeneity of background and family unknown in any other civilized nation. From the earliest times they knew one another's family histories and shared a common love, transmitted orally by recognized poets, for the heroic events, mythical or historic, which were their birthright.

There were additional reasons why literature more than the other arts became the Icelanders' language of expression. The agricultural work of the settlers consisted almost entirely of the raising of sheep and milch cows. Little sowing or reaping was involved, as most grains would not grow during Iceland's brief summers. The haying was soon over, and with no harvest to attend to the winters were long and slow. Even though the country was culturally close-knit, the farms were isolated within the miles of land each needed for pasturage. In winter darkness and spring floods travel was hazardous, and the farmer and his dependents were thrown on their own resources not only for their livelihood but for their entertainment. Story-telling became the favorite pastime of the long winter days, and the more gifted a man was in the art of re-creating great events of the past or embellishing news of the present, the more loved he was by his weather-bound fellows.

Further, most farmers, besides having a lot of free time, had a lot of cows. Suckling calves made the finest vellum, and the preparation of the skins took a long time. Granted the spiritual impulse, the plethora of time and calfskins was a boon to the cultivation of literature.

The spiritual impulse had always been there, and as Iceland became settled and comfortable opportunity improved even more. From the tenth century to the thirteenth the country was run by an increasingly smaller group of families of ever greater wealth and power. The sons of these families had leisure, luxury and education, all conducive to the cultivation of the gentle arts. On account of the long tradition of oral story-telling, literature was their chief outlet. And there were all those suckling calves. One skin made two leaves of parchment. Most of the manuscripts extant have two hundred or more leaves.

The early poets were performers. Their dramatic recitations took the place of theater. The stories they told, tales of the gods or

175

sagas of their ancestors, handed down for generations, were as familiar to their listeners as Bible stories were to a later culture. The narrator could not change any of these "true" stories, and he provided drama and suspense by embroidering the facts, varying the details and introducing dialogue. Until the coming of Christianity little was written down. The Runic alphabet had only sixteen characters and was clumsy to inscribe. When the bishops began teaching Latin the people adopted the new alphabet enthusiastically, not only to set down the old tales but to create new ones. Poets were held in high esteem. One of the marks of an educated young Icelander was his ability, on the order of a chieftain or a king, instantly to compose complicated verse about any heroic happening. He did not do this to amuse, but to arouse. Being of good family he himself was always in the front rank of battle, so he could report the brave events in verse at first hand. Revenge, honor, death, greed for gold and power: these were the subjects of the poetry of the Vikings. They were the stuff of which the pagan myths were made, and they formed the texture of the sagas.

In its early years Christianity did not have much effect on literature. The changeover from heathen *godi* to Christian priest was only skin-deep. Iceland was so isolated that the religious fanaticism of Europe never found its way there. Some Icelandic scholars went to France and Germany to study, and came back educated but still Icelandic at heart. Where the effect took place was in the spread of education. The scholars educated abroad came home to the monasteries that were being built on the foundations of the temples to Thor. Young men flocked to them, to become historians, theologians, poets and scientists.

The Church's most important early contribution was the introduction of the Latin alphabet. It was adopted enthusiastically, and brought about a tremendous surge of interest in writing. The art of writing was first used for inscribing on parchment the laws that had been transmitted orally from one Law-Speaker to the next. The histories of the Settlement were written from the eleventh century to the thirteenth. The tales of the *Edda*, the ancient Norse religious myths, were collected and first written down in the early twelfth century. The highest flowering of the sagas was in the thirteenth century, and the composition of skaldic verse, that strange, complicated Icelandic specialty, reached its convoluted acme in the eleventh century.

The first historian to write in Icelandic was Ari Thorgilsson Frodi, the Learned, 1068 to 1148, who was educated in Iceland. Like most of the early writers he was taught by priests and was himself a priest. His most famous work is the *Islendingabok, Book of Icelanders*, which comprises a short history of the Settlement, an account of the evolution of the *Althing*, noting changes in the Constitution and listing the Law-Speakers, and a description of the coming of Christianity.

Ari Frodi also wrote part of the *Landnamabok, Book of Settlements*, a history and genealogy of the first settlers, the original version of which is lost. The version which is known today was gathered from earlier manuscripts by Sturla Thordarson, 1214 to 1284. When Ari was writing there had only been six to seven generations of Icelanders. Many of them were still living on the farms that their ancestors had built, and had knowledge, passed from father to child, of ancient boundary lines, origins of families in the mother country and complete dossiers on births and marriages since. So the history compiled by him and his successors is thought to be, in the main, accurate, though successive writers naturally tended to embroider and exaggerate, in the manner of gossips passing tasty morsels from one to another. These writers further had a tendency to explain and apologize for their histories, feeling it necessary to point out that, far from being buccaneering Vikings, the scourges of Europe, the settlers of Iceland were peaceful farmers with good family connections, who never lifted a finger in anger except in settlement of boundary disputes.

"People often say," it is written in the epilogue to one version of the *Landnamabok*, "that writing about the Settlements is irrelevant learning, but we think we can better meet the criticism of foreigners when they accuse us of being descended from slaves or scoundrels, if we know for certain the truth about our ancestry . . . Anyway, all civilized nations want to know about the origins of their own society and the beginnings of their own race."[1]

[1] *Landnamabok, Thordarbok* version

Sturla Thordarson was a thirteenth-century chieftain, politician and poet, scion of one of Iceland's most prestigious families, the Sturlungs of the west coast, whose exploits are celebrated in the lively, rambling family chronicle, *Eyrbyggja Saga*. He fought against Norwegian intervention in Icelandic affairs and was Law-Speaker of the *Althing* from 1251 to 1254. His writings include two sagas about Norwegian kings, many heroic poems, and a history of Iceland called *Islendinga Saga, Saga of Icelanders*. About 1275 he completed his *Landnamabok*, using material from earlier versions as well as details from the family sagas.

On a casual leafing through, *Landnamabok* appears monotonously addicted to names. But it is more than an arid recital of progenitors. The fierce independence of spirit of these proud immigrants shows through, along with small, telling domestic details and a spicing of humor, some of it, to modern readers, grotesque. One man, it is told, was killed in battle because his belt broke and his trousers fell down. Another took vengeance for a goat: "Herjolf was only eight years old when he killed a brown bear which had bitten a goat of his." This verse was composed about it:

> The bear with a burnt arse
> bit Herjolf's goat,
> Herjolf with the bent arse
> paid the bear back.[2]

Besides Herjolf Bent-Arse there were Thorolf Twist-Foot, Bolverk Blind-Snout, Thorir Autumn-Dusk, Ljot the Unwashed, Hergils Knob-Buttocks, Eystein Foul-Fart and Olvir the Child-Sparer (who disapproved of the spitting of children on the points of spears).

Aside from the charm of local detail and the glimpses of private lives, *Landnamabok* is historically important as the record of men and women who had the courage, because they wanted to be independent, to pick up their families, their cows and pigs, and their high-seat pillars and move to a wild country where they would have, in every sense, to begin all over again; people, further, who in the middle of the Dark Ages, had the wit to form a government of farmers where no man was set over anyone else, where the

[2] *Landnamabok*

inequalities of feudalism and the evils of despotic monarchy had no place. Their direct descendants are still there: you can read the old names in the telephone book.

At about the time Ari Frodi was writing Icelandic history another learned man was collecting the myths of the gods that had been handed down orally for generations in the cold country. Sæmund Sigfusson, 1054 to 1133, was descended directly from King Harald Hilditönn, War-Tooth, and was probably the first Scandinavian to be educated in Europe. He was born at Oddi, on the southern coast, and traveled in his youth to study in Germany, France and Italy. In 1076 he went home, to become the priest at Oddi and to establish there Iceland's first Christian center. Students came to him from all over the country to receive historical, scientific and clerical instruction, and he became revered as one of the wisest of men. Among his students were old-time poets, singers who had been baptized but were old enough to have learned their skills from pagans before the coming of Christianity. From them Sæmund in turn learned. They sang him the ancient lays: the *Völupsa*, the *Seeress's Prophecy*, in which is told of the creation and destruction of the world; *Odin's Rune Song*, of his sacrifice to gain wisdom; tales of the wiles of the devil-god, Loki; stories of dwarfs' and giants' plots against the gods; the songs of the Volsungs, Odin's children on earth, which included the *Lay of Sigurd*, the *Lay of Fafnir*, the *Lay of Gudrun*, *Brynhild's Lament*, the *Killing of the Niblungs*; the *Ragnarök*, song of the world's doom, when Asgard and the earth were destroyed by the geniuses of frost and fire. Sæmund wrote them all down in a series of beautiful, passionate long poems now called the *Elder*, or *Poetic*, *Edda*. His fascination with the pagan songs was so great that his countrymen regarded him as a sorcerer, but a "white" one, doing only good.

After Sæmund's death the farm estates at Oddi continued to prosper, and the parsonage remained a shrine of learning under his two sons and his grandson, Jon Loptsson. The latter took as foster son three-year-old Snorri Sturleson, 1179 to 1241, another of the renowned Sturlungs of western Iceland, who remained at Oddi until he was twenty. Snorri (the name means "sharp-witted one," and it was inherited from a canny progenitor, one of the protagonists of *Eyrbyggja Saga*) became a historian of great learning

179

and a brilliant poet, probably the most skillful of his time. He wrote *Heimskringla, Disk of the Earth* (named for the first words of the manuscript), the history of Norway to the time of King Sverrir in 1177, and is thought to be the author of several of the sagas, *Egilssaga* being specifically assigned to him. The work for which he is now best known is an extraordinary textbook on poetry which contains the *Younger*, or *Prose, Edda*.

Despite his original mind and his fine sense of the beauty of poetry, Snorri was a most unpleasant man. He quarreled with his own children, divorced his wife so he could marry a wealthier woman, took a traitorous position as cup-bearer and official historian at the court of King Haakon of Norway although his country was at the time trying to fend off the unwelcome interference of that king. He was avaricious, extravagant and unscrupulous, and no one liked him. But, being extremely rich and powerful, the head of Iceland's strongest clan, he succeeded in being twice elected Law-Speaker. However, he was unwisely perfidious: he deceived his benefactor, the king of Norway. Promising to aid the Norwegian cause in Iceland, he returned home to build a magnificent residence at Reykholt, his ancestral home, from ideas of grandeur he had absorbed at King Haakon's gaudy court. There he sat in state, contriving plots against the king who had favored him. Haakon directed his representative, Gizur Thorvaldsson, to have him accused of high treason and exiled or executed. Gizur entrusted the arrest to the husbands of Snorri's three daughters, with whom Snorri had fatally quarreled. Interpreting their mission more stringently than was intended, they chased their father-in-law down into the cellar of his grand new house and murdered him.

Unattractive as he was in life, in death he was redeemed by his work. Today Snorri is regarded as a national hero in a country which reveres its poets above its warriors.

Snorri's textbook teaches the verse forms, poetic diction and metric variations of the elaborate Icelandic genre, skaldic poetry. He illustrates the use of the rules in an entertaining and original manner by telling stories. Though the technical aspect of his exposition is no longer interesting except to students of that highly artificial verse form, the stories, particularly *Gylfaginning, The Beguiling of Gylfi*, are as glowing today as when they were written. Where Sæmund's *Edda* is a collection of songs only loosely connected, Snorri, using Sæmund's lays, tells a straight tale in the form of a dialogue between Gylfi, King of Sweden, and three wise ones of Asgard, of the whole of Norse mythology. It is spread before us in eloquent language, a glorious, many-colored tapestry of gods and goddesses, dwarfs and giants, from the first frost giant, Ymir, from whom the earth was made, to the final coming of Surtur and his forces of destruction to annihilate the world.

The name *Edda* was, at the time, given only to Snorri's work. Scholars differ as to the meaning. Some argue that it means "great-grandmother," the thesis being that the earth mother of mankind sat in the circle of her children telling them the lore of her past. Others say that it means "reason" or "soul," hence "soulful utterance," or "poem." Both these meanings, however, were assigned to the word in manuscripts written after Snorri's death. And neither of them accords with the prosy attitude of the Icelanders in assigning names. A more reasonable, but unproven, hypothesis is that Snorri himself named his manuscript *The Book of Oddi*, later corrupted to *Edda*, in recognition of the parsonage where he spent his childhood, which breathed the tradition of its founder Sæmund. Not only was the sensitive mind of the young poet inspired by the atmosphere of the sanctuary, but there were all the works of the old scholar for the new one to peruse and digest. This seems the simplest theory. It was not until the seventeenth century that the name was applied, by mistake, to Sæmund's pagan songs.

Whatever the origin of the name, Sæmund and Snorri have given the world, in some of the most beautiful words ever written, a panorama of the heroic paganism which was their people's birthright. The fact that this mythology and its ethos have been subverted in this century to serve a modern savage should not be allowed to mar the perspective. The Norse people, with all their panoply of extraterrestial beings and their philosophy of stoic heroism, belonged in their time. This was the way they lived and thought; the early destructive missionary zeal and later scornful humanism of Christianity cannot take them and their beliefs from their place in history.

At first sight the sagas appear to be closely related to *Landnamabok* and its predecessors. They are family chronicles, most of them dealing with events that happened in the first century of Iceland's settlement. Their subjects are the early immigrants and their direct descendants to the third or fourth generations, and many of the happenings appear also in the straight histories. The narrative style, to a modern reader, is dry, sparse and excessively matter-of-fact. It is almost textbooklike in the disregard of physical characteristics, whether of people or of places, the meticulous attention to genealogy, the unemotional recitals of local politics and feuds. The characters are many, their doings seemingly trivial. As you plod through one of the long ones, *Njalssaga* or *Eyrbyggja Saga*, you wonder at first why you bother; then insidiously the thing begins to take you over. You find, as you get used to the bald style, that the characters, even the least important, are sharply delineated, a few words sketching a masterly line drawing. The dialogue is terse and feather-edged. The events are harsh, related coldly, then dropped, their results to appear later in a complex web of plot that leads to a shattering climax. Emotions are more poignant for being implied, events more dramatic for the frugality of their telling. These long, busy tales are not dusty curiosities, they are live creations. They have a spiritual relationship to the Greek tragedies, their protagonists, ruled by fate, facing inescapable doom with high courage. Their form goes back to an earlier Greek, Homer, who also gathered into a coherent and glowing whole a mass of scattered folk tales known for generations only through the spoken word.

No one knows who composed the sagas. In some form they were related orally for many years before they were written down. (The word *saga* is derived from *segja*, to say.) It seems impossible that any narrator could have remembered the complicated events and numerous characters. But before the art of writing was generally used people had to store facts and figures in their heads, since they could not go to books to look things up, and their minds developed extraordinary strength in the direction of memory. The Law-Speaker, who had to recite the entire body of law at the *Althing*, was a prime example of a man with a well-muscled memory. With the adoption of the Latin alphabet the remembered stories were inscribed by the new scholars — but not in Latin. Icelandic independence extended to every area of life, including language. Though well versed in Latin and knowledgeable in all fields of European learning of their day, the scholars adapted mathematics, astronomy, geography and theology to their own tongue. The sagas, written down in the language in which they were spoken, have the directness of natural speech.

Yet they are too artful to be solely spoken hand-me-downs. Oral transmission is usually primitive; the sagas are complex literary epics composed with a high degree of intelligent imagination. The stories are intricately woven, the characters revealed with penetrating subtlety. Furthermore, they were all written in the twelfth and thirteenth centuries, though they took place in the tenth, and the authors, while anonymous, were obviously men finely trained in literary execution. The manuscripts extant are copies, and there exist variations of the same sagas as each inscriber added his own bit of creativity. Sometimes the same event is described in two sagas, with different emphasis, as one character is given precedence over another according to the demands of the plot. The historical facts are not firmly accurate; the authors bent the truth to fit the story line. In at least one case, *Hrafnkatla*, a consistent, sober, unexaggerated saga which used to be regarded as the acme of historical reliability, two important characters well documented as to antecedents and domicile have been found to be entirely fictitious. They are essential to the development of the story and an imaginative author simply invented them, along with a set of convincing ancestors, to fill his need.

The scholars who inscribed the sagas, as well as being heirs of wealthy farming families, were highly educated priests, conversant with ecclesiastical Latin. They were necessarily influenced by the elaborate and esoteric literature that flowed continuously from medieval Europe's cloistered monasteries, the antithesis of the simple and savage folk history that had been related by their grandfathers. In a literary miracle which has never been explained, they mingled rich ecclesiastical verbiage and primitive spoken word, to produce dramatic works of art remarkable far beyond the bounds of a mere blend of two styles.

Skaldic poetry, also called court poetry, originated in Norway as libelous love verse. ("Skald" and the English "scold" are akin, originally signifying one who scratched libels and imprecations on poles.) It is a highly artificial verse form with no known prototype. Apparently it sprang full-grown into existence with Bragi, a ninth century Norwegian, who is the first one known. He could not actually have been the first, however, because his poetry is already bristling with the artful conceits of the genre, and is too complicated to be a mere forerunner; it is also too complicated to have been invented by one man. Bragi must have learned his art. But no other poetic practice in Europe has ever been anything like it, and scholars cannot even guess at its antecedents. Though it arose in Norway it was abandoned there after a century. The Icelandic colonists, like most emigrés fonder of tradition than those they left behind, took over the form and it became a literary phenomenon peculiar to Iceland, a specialty of educated young aristocrats. It came to be an accepted tenet that every young gentleman of good birth could compose *ad lib* in skaldic meters.

The new nation soon found that trade was essential to her existence: the exchange of native wool and homespun for vital timber and grain. Her representatives, sons of chieftains, who had time and money to travel and skill to entertain, were sent as liaison men to all the courts of Europe and the Middle East. In the manner of troubadours and minnesingers, but with a far more difficult verse form, the young travelers ingratiated themselves by reciting poetry they had composed in honor of the chiefs to whose courts they went. They could improvise in fluent verse on any subject, and they came to be much sought after as additions to royal entourages. Many stayed abroad, becoming not only entertainers but advisers and confidants to kings. As court minstrel the young poet was expected to sing of his master's adventures, praising his courage, lauding his successes and lamenting his losses. However, he did not fawn. Keeping his independent spirit, he criticized, warned and scolded his master when it was warranted. Sometimes he aroused the king's anger, oftener his gratitude. It was a proud relationship, highly valued on both sides.

Useful and graceful as were these courtiers, the language in which they spoke so eloquently, to the complete comprehension of their listeners, is to us arcane and impossibly complex. Its rules are formal, including strict alliteration, a prescribed number of syllables to each line, internal rhymes and assonances precisely regulated, stressed and unstressed syllables in predetermined places. Nothing is expressed directly; phrases, even whole sentences, are

184

interpolated in the middles of other sentences. Nothing is mentioned by its own name; all is in kennings, or metaphors. The kennings, set by tradition, had immediate significance in their time. But they grow out of one another in an ornate branching that even then must have seemed artificial. To a modern reader the meaning is totally obscured in a dense undergrowth of outré verbiage. Here is an example:

"The appeaser of the hunger of the gull of the tumult of the glamor of the animal of Haki."[3] The whole phrase signifies one word: warrior. Haki is a sea-king. The animal of Haki stands for a ship. The glamor of the animal of Haki is a shield — shields were fastened for decoration on the railings of Viking ships. The tumult of the glamor of the animal of Haki is battle. The hungry gull in this rococo conceit is a raven, a symbol of battle. His appeaser is the fighter who gives him the bodies of men slain in war — hence warrior.

It isn't all this silly. Sometimes wit and emotion shine briefly through the cloud of words, and one can glimpse the skilled charm of these medieval poets within their exacting medium. Here are two light little love poems:

> All the girls fain would
> with Ingolf have lalliane —
> those who were grown up
> or grieved they were too little.
> The old hag said: "I too
> with Ingolf shall dally
> while two teeth still
> are 'twixt my gums."[4]
>
> Brightly beamed the lights-of-
> both-her-cheeks upon me —
> e'er will I recall it —
> o'er the heaped-up wood-pile;
> and the instep saw I

[3] *Olafsdrapa, Heroic Song of Olaf*, Hallfred Ottarsson, born *circa* 970.
[4] Gunnlaug Illugason, born *circa* 984.

185

of the shapely woman —
no laughing matter, lo! my
longing — by the threshold."[5]

And two passionate stanzas from a battle poem:

Grim in mind, the martial
maiden urged her father
on to stem the steely
storm-of-arrows — fiendlike,
when she bore, with baleful
brow, the necklace wrought by
dwarfs, she double-hearted,
down to the trees-of-combat.

. . .

Not for knavish yielding
neckrings she him offered —
she who brought brave warriors
back to life from deathwounds;
feigned aye — though to Fenrir's —
frightful-sister she did   [Hela, goddess
egg the earls to journey —   of the underworld]
eagerness to bate strife.[6]

The remarkable blooming, of which the subtle and intricate
skaldic poetry is the most sophisticated if not the most winning
example, was at its most productive from the middle of the twelfth
century to the middle of the thirteenth. Most of the sagas and the
best of the poetry were written in this time, which is called the
age of the Sturlungs. This family, which produced warriors, states-
men, scholars and poets, dominated Iceland's literary and political
life until the fall of the Commonwealth in 1262. Hvamm-Sturla,
Sturla of the Green Valley (the name of his farm), 1115 to 1183,
was a direct descendant of Thorolf Mostrar-skegg, Mostrar-Beard

[5] Kormak Ogmandarson, born *circa* 945.

[6] *Ragnarsdrapa Lodbrokar, Poem of Ragnar Shaggy-Breek* (mythical
Danish king), Bragi Boddason the Old, first half of the ninth century

(Mostrar was the Norwegian island from which he emigrated), the first settler of Breidafjord, Broad Firth, in the west. Hvamm-Sturla was a cunning and ruthless man who manipulated himself into the overlordship of most of the western farms. The clan produced a number of strong leaders over the hundred years of its dominance, the most powerful being Hvamm-Sturla's son, Snorri Sturleson, and his grand-nephew, Sturla Sighvatsson, both of whom amassed even more wealth and lands through political maneuvering and judicious marriages. Both were murdered, a not unusual end those days to an ambitious career.

There were half a dozen other families of great power in this time but the Sturlungs have given their name to the era because of the *Sturlunga Saga,* a collection of loosely related sagas, much of it written by Sturla Thordarson, the compiler of *Landnamabok,* describing events of the twelfth and thirteenth centuries with particular reference to that family. The author did not stay his pen; it is a sharply realistic picture of political corrosion and ferocious immorality. Iceland's decadent savagery was not out of line with the spirit of the time in most other European communities, but the light of the *Sturlunga Saga* shines harshly on it.

The story of the Sturlungs is typical of what was happening to Iceland's political and moral structure. Much of the creeping deterioration can be attributed to the changes made by the coming of Christianity. Each chieftain had also been the priest of the pagan temple of his region. Some of them, after being baptized, chose to become ordained as Christian ministers. In order to remove themselves from the feuds of their peers, which did not accord with the tenets of the new faith, they resigned their *godord* authority. Where there had been a good balance of many small-holding *godar* with equal power, political influence came to be vested in the heads of a few influential families. These chieftains, becoming ever more ambitious and arrogant, ignored the law and administered their own form of justice. The resultant feuds, which had been between individuals and relatively easy to settle, became vast, bloody and violent, as the families enlisted whole armies to settle disputes, exact penalties or carry out vengeance.

As the *godar* turned to Christianity, their lands went to the Church, which began to amass huge tracts, and became a landlord on a large scale. A new class of tenant farmers arose and the small freeholding farmer began to disappear. With him went the old vital interest in the running of the country, in which every landed farmer had had a say. This gave the ruling families further power. In the early days their strength had depended on the goodwill of the free farmers of their neighborhoods; now they could range far afield and buy as many supporters as they wanted.

Among the available mercenaries were numbers of freed slaves. The Christian religion did not officially countenance slavery (though it was tolerant — the institution continued in the rest of Scandinavia for another two hundred years). Though slavery had never been very important in Iceland, its decline brought a further increase in the number of men who worked for a living. As the slaves were freed or bought their freedom, they found that there was no empty land left, and none could be bought cheaply. All the arable land had been taken in the sixty years of the Settlement, and now, with the gobbling up of small freehold farms by the Church and a handful of wealthy chieftains, there were no plots left for the new freedmen. They had to hire themselves out in order to eat, and they owed allegiance to no one.

Iceland's new landlord, the Church, became just as demanding and greedy for power as her old families. In addition to the power struggles, the outside world began to touch Iceland as some of the more jealous and thrusting of the bishops called on the authority of the Archbishopric of Norway to help them in their disputes with the headstrong *godar*. The chieftains, in retaliation, invoked the aid of the Norwegian throne. Allying themselves with it against the Church and one another, they became at last so indebted, practically and morally, that their country was ready to drop like an overripe plum into the waiting hand of the Norwegian king.

King Haakon IV, one of Norway's stronger kings in that country's continuing strife between aristocratic landowners and the central power of the throne, had been working toward this end for a long time. He bribed Iceland's best men with honors and promises, among them the talented but ruthless Sturlungs, Snorri Sturleson and Sturla Sighvatsson, who were murdered for their pains. He encouraged the discontented *godar* to come to

188

him for help and received their allegiance in return. By the middle of the thirteenth century Iceland was so torn with feuds that the chieftains voluntarily gave up their *godord* authorities and appealed to Haakon to take them over. In 1262 the *Althing*, helpless against the pressure of the apostate *godar*, agreed to pay tax and allegiance to the crown of Norway. Iceland became a tributary state. Her people had fled Norway to keep their freedom. For a while that freedom had been a bright flame in a dark world. But it had proved too much for the young republic. It would be nearly seven hundred years before Iceland would again hold up her head as a sovereign state.

Where the Church had been a benign influence on literature in the beginning, with the spread of education and the introduction of the Latin alphabet, its ideals of meekness and forgiveness gradually began to undermine the heroic concepts on which the poems and sagas were based. Honor, pride and revenge had no place in the new religion, nor did stoical self-reliance, personal loyalty to a hero leader, the code of battle as a strong man's chief aim. As men began to give up the old standards of value, not yet having assimilated the new, they became disoriented. Family solidarity was crumbling, the ancient Viking moral code was frowned on, and men had nothing left to which to fasten their ideals. Trying to hold on to their individuality at all costs against the encroaching dogma of man's insignificance, they began to indulge in violence for its own sake, in their literature as well as in their lives.

The description of the killing of Sturla Sighvatsson in the *Sturlunga Saga* shows to what depths of irrational fury the once proud hero warriors had sunk. Sturla, mortally wounded in the throat, lay on the ground faint with loss of blood. One of his companions covered him with a shield, but Gizurr Thorvaldsson, shouting, "This is my business," tore it away and struck the dying man on the head with a broad-bladed axe, hewing so hard that his feet left the ground. Another man then stuck the already dead Sturla through the throat and up into the mouth, into the same wound that had felled him, so that one could put three fingers through it. Another slashed his stomach and still another struck him again in the throat with an axe. They then plundered his body and left it naked. This senseless and cowardly ferocity, this savaging of a man already dead, contrasts sadly with the old heroism of men like Gunnar, trapped inside his house and fighting off his enemies to the last breath with his bare hands, or Grettir the Strong, felling twelve berserkers single-handed to protect the house in which he was a guest.

As the style and content of the sagas changed with the general deterioration of morals, other influences were coming to bear on the poetry. Iceland was no longer removed from the literary world of Europe. People were reading Christian tales such as the legends of Arthur and the romance of Tristan and Isolde. Love replaced battle as some poets turned from heroism to chivalry. Other poets took to religious writing, chronicling the lives of saints. The clear, radiant voices became prosy as they sang in a style not native to them.

It was not only imitation of an alien genre that spelled the death of Iceland's bright literary soul. The loss of independence in 1262 led to an ebbing of spirit. The Norwegian takeover signaled the beginning of poverty, as all native industry, trade and commerce came under foreign control. The low state of morale was exacerbated in the following hundred years by repeated volcanic eruptions, livestock epidemics and disastrous famines. The climate was entering one of its cold phases; chill rainy weather and ice-bound fjords added to the miseries of daily life. It was not a time when anyone felt like writing heroic sagas.

By the middle of the fourteenth century the strange and unique flower that had grown on this island out of the world had withered and fallen, and the common field flowers came up where it had been.

That incomparable literature is little read today outside of Iceland, but its effect lingers, part of our unconscious birthright. If it were not for the northern poets who listened to the old songs and stories and wrote down what they heard, our knowledge of Norse mythology and the pre-Christian, pre-Roman civilization that gave rise to it would have vanished from the world. Along with the lore of the Greeks, the Romans and the Jews, these tales are the legacy of our ancestors. We are in great debt to Iceland.

ELEVEN

Dwellers on the Sand Spit

ODDI, WHERE IT all started, is in the southern part of the Rangarvellir, here a bare plain where the thin grass, just beginning to sprout, is very green on the dark sand. The word *oddi* means a triangle, or a point of land, and the hamlet lies near the point where the Rang River makes the abrupt right-angle turn that gave it its name, Crooked. One can see the church from afar, in an oasis of lumpy little hills whose short thick grass makes them look like part of a golf course. Oddi can hardly even be called a hamlet. It consists only of two farm buildings and the small church, Iceland's typical country church that always makes one think of the childhood rhyme: "Here is the church and here is the steeple . . ." One of the farm buildings is a white barn of concrete blocks with a tawny-colored roof, the other is a new iron dwelling with a bright yellow roof. The cemetery in the churchyard has no graves over a hundred years old. Nothing in this simple modern farmstead hints that here was the wealthy, thriving monastery where Sæmund gathered around him the singers of the ancient lays, that here were drawn the best of Iceland's young aristocrats, to become foster-children to the priests and to soak up the learning they would later convert into some of the most beautiful writing the world has ever known.

The wide, quiet Rang River flows below the church. Far across the sands is the fine blue line of the ocean. To the north, above the inland rock ranges, the peak of Hekla shines alone, and in the east Eyjafjall Glacier is a dazzling white dome over the black barrens. The only sound is the bubbling call of the whimbrel as it rises from the river shore and wheels, long-winged, in slow rising circles. The present day is far away as Sæmund and his lay-singers.

The land of the Sturlungs is north and west of Oddi, on the peninsula of Snæfellsnes, Cape of the Snow Mountain. When Snorri Sturleson left his foster father, Sæmund's grandson, to go home he traveled to Reykjavik over the roads along which we have traced Njal's journey south. North of the capital Snorri's road follows the shore, as it must do, for just back of the coast rise flat-topped mountains, their summits sliced off evenly by glacier during the Ice Age. Every few yards a rapid stream or waterfall pours down the rock, bringing sand and pebbles to wear out the road. Trucks pass us, some carrying gravel, others loaded with the little green huts for the road-mending crews. In an open space there is a temporary settlement of them; here the road has slipped into the sea in a muddy landslide under the constant assault from the hills. Iceland's roads require — and get — constant maintenance.

The road turns inland along the edge of a long, narrow cleft, Hvalfjord, Whale Fjord, where whales used to sport but do so no longer. The fjord cuts twenty-two miles into the countryside, curving as it goes, so that at its head it appears to be an inland lake surrounded by mountains. Around its northern side the mountains give way to alluvial plains, green and flat, with pale bare rocks coming through the grass like the bones of animals. Little streams wind quietly through the fields, halting to form marshy pools. Redshanks walk elegantly in the mud at the edges of the ponds, lifting their long red legs with delicacy, plucking out crustaceans with their slender beaks or darting suddenly after small fish. This large, handsome sandpiper, the commonest bird of the watery plains, is also the most raucously suspicious. Perhaps some of them have scratched nest hollows in the long grass of the hummocks, but their shocked yelps and hysterical circling seem an overreaction to our still presence on the road fifty yards away.

We have left the car not to view the redshanks but to watch a pair of northern phalaropes which are as unconcerned about us as the other birds are emotional. These small sandpiperlike shore birds have but recently arrived from wintering grounds no one has ever seen, some four or five thousand miles south in the Atlantic, to spend their short nesting time on the muddy shores of Iceland's lakes. They are brown and gray with red neck patches, brighter in the female than in the male. She is also bigger than he, and in everything but egg-laying she assumes the role of male. At the moment the female of this pair is courting the male. He circles rapidly, roiling up the shallow water to bring insect larvae to the surface. She follows him in his gyrations, almost pushing him as he tries to feed. He evades her, turning his head sideways and spinning away from her. She persists and at last — one thinks more to be rid of her than from any inner conviction — he mounts her in a fast flurry of wings. The next step will be a grass-lined nest in a hollow at the edge of the pond, excavated and lined by him, followed by the brooding of the eggs, also a function of the male, while she will keep watch and warn of danger with sudden flight accompanied by low calls. When the two join their kin late in August for the flight south, having shed their bright neck feathers and turned light gray and white, the flocks will swell to 250,000 or so. Swirling down over the bays and oceans toward their mysterious southern home, they will alight occasionally, spinning in the water, rising and circling briefly, touching down again like feathers. They are so light that they cannot dive, and they hold their heads high, except when eating, over the thick, buoyant breast feathers. They look like animated little decoys bobbing in the swell. Fishermen watch where they land, because there will be schools of mackerel. Both the birds and the fish feed on brit, the young of the herring. The mackerel dart deep when the birds come, frustrating the fishermen, who don't know whether to bless or curse the phalaropes.

Unexpectedly two black-tailed godwits leap into the air beyond the phalaropes' pond, screeching nasally the two-syllable sound that gives them their name. Perhaps a grazing sheep came too close to their grass-covered nest hollow. They are tall, striking

193

shore birds with bright rusty-colored heads and necks, sharply black and white tails, and long upturned bills. Closely related to our rare and dwindling Hudsonian godwit, they are plentiful in Iceland.

Mountains rise at the edge of the alluvial plain, layers on layers through mist. Behind them, invisible today, is Snæfellsjö-kull, Snow Mountain Glacier, an extinct volcano that towers 4,746 feet at the end of Snæfellsnes. This is the mountain into which the reluctant geologist Henry Lawson, his fanatical uncle Professor Hardwigg and their stolidly cheerful Icelandic guide Hans descended in 1864, carrying "two pickaxes, two crowbars, a silken ladder, three iron-shod Alpine poles, a hatchet, a hammer, a dozen wedges, some pointed pieces of iron and a quantity of strong rope,"[1] together with a few days' supplies of concentrated essence of meat and biscuit. The volcano, which has exploded and fallen in on itself, leaving an immense *caldera* surrounded by peaks, was a favorite climbing feat for nineteenth-century Englishmen, from one of whom Jules Verne may have gotten his painstakingly accurate picture of the mountain's exterior. It has three main peaks, two of which are black rock in summer, glassy ice in winter and spring. The third is covered all year round by glacier. Snæfells-jökull has not erupted in historic times — but neither had Heimaey's Helgafell. In Iceland there is no such thing as a harmless volcano. The mountain is visible from Reykjavik. On a clear day it seems to rise directly out of the ocean in the northwest, its gleaming ice pale gold in the morning light, lavender in the evening.

Snæfellsnes is the home of the *Eyrbyggja*, Dwellers on the Sand Spit. It projects some seventy miles into the ocean, the Bay of Faxafloi, Reykjavik's water, to its south and the immense Breidafjord, Broad Firth, on the north. *Eyrbyggja Saga*, the story of its early settlers, is an episodic family tale written about 1200 but concerning events of some two hundred years earlier. It encompasses four generations of the Settlement years, from the first settler of the West, Thorolf Mostrar-skegg, to his great-grandson, Snorri Thorgrimsson, a famous wise man and *godi*, direct ancestor

----

[1] *A Trip to the Center of the Earth*, Jules Verne

of Snorri Sturleson, Iceland's controversial thirteenth-century poet-historian. Early in his youth Snorri Thorgrimsson showed some of the characteristics transmitted through the generations to his descendant namesake, being more wily than foolhardy, and substituting cunning for courage whenever possible. Though this was not in accord with the spirit of forthright battle that was the style in his time, the first Snorri was greatly admired for his calm wisdom. People came from all over the country to request his advice and hear his Solomon-like judgments.

It is impossible to tell the story of *Eyrbyggja*. It is elegant and incisive in style, often humorous, sometimes even malicious, with characters as sharply etched as those in any of the sagas. Winding through the years, it deals as it meanders with a huge cast, relatives by marriage, friends and enemies. It even includes the story of the murders that sent Erik the Red on his first expedition to Greenland, though he is no relation to anyone else in the tale. It is rich in detail of medieval life and mores; its aristocratic author properly sneers at slaves and reveres the Viking twin obsessions of honor and personal courage. Christianity has little place in it, although the author has obviously been clerically trained. He rather scoffs at the new religion, saying that too many churches were built by the chieftains when priests promised that as many could be tenanted in the Kingdom of Heaven as could find standing room there; but that the churches stood empty because no priests showed up to introduce the supplicators to the Promised Land.

The locale of the events of *Eyrbyggja Saga* is a green country of hills that come right down to the sea. It has little flat land and, except for Snæfellsjökull, no high mountains. Some of the interior hills are bare rocks, and here and there are patches of the inhospitable *apalgryti*, or *aa* lava on which nothing grows but moss. But most of it is fresh and verdant, rather English. The air, though cool, is soft and damp. It rains a great deal, and minutes after rain the sun shines. It is a country of rainbows.

Budir, where we stay, announces itself to us with a post-box on the road and a hand-lettered sign, "Hotel Budir." Down by the sea on a quiet inlet is a tiny church and a blue-roofed white building, the hotel. Three other buildings are tumbledown and

195

uninhabited. It is even less of a village than the usual Icelandic hamlet. There used to be activity here. The little harbor is calm and deep enough for small trading vessels. A visitor in 1810 found that the town consisted of "a merchant's house, a large wooden store house, a church, and a considerable number of cottages . . . The war between England and Denmark has been severely felt . . . No vessel has come to Budir for three years past . . ."[1] All Iceland suffered in that war, as the mother country, Denmark, was unable to send the grain, timber and iron which the people needed, and their storehouses were filled with their own produce, which they were unable to sell. Budir must have died then; there is no longer a sign of trading or indeed of any activity at all. The merchant's house, renovated and covered with corrugated iron, is the hotel. It is small, clean and comfortable and it serves simple and beautiful food. Its present owner is trying to revive the village by attracting customers to his hotel and rebuilding the store. While we were there a conference of representatives of meat producers from all the Scandinavian countries, fifteen bright young men, met there. In our country similar progressive young businessmen would have gone to Miami or at the very least to Atlantic City. Here the only diversions were families of eider ducks playing in the harbor and seals sporting in the surf beyond it. The conferees seemed to like it that way.

Budir's beach is orange, with jade-green streaks. It is lonely and wild. The only footsteps besides ours are those of a horse. The ocean rolls up in long breakers, not as frightening as the monster waves at Dyrholaey because the sand slopes gradually and the water is shallow. But it is a heavy sea, full of life and noise. Spray flies over the beach in sun-touched clouds. Rain is behind us, and a rainbow touches the dark ocean, far out. A seal almost stands on its tail to watch us, just beyond the breaking waves. Fulmars fly low through the rainbow and terns wheel around our heads with harsh clamor. A flock of ringed plovers feeds at the edge of the water, picking out marine worms and crustaceans as the waves fall back, fleeing up the beach before them as they break,

[1] *Travels in the Island of Iceland*, George Steuart MacKenzie, 1812

196

relying more on their fast legs than their long wings. Above high tide line one of them, apart from its flock, runs away from us dragging a wing and crying distressfully. Its nest is a meager hollow in the sand, lined with bits of shell and seaweed, in which are four eggs so much like their background, mottled brown-black on stone color, that if not for the agonized actions of the parent we would not have thought to look for it. It is probable that the bird's mental powers cannot encompass anything as tricky as a reasoned ruse, and the display is the bird's traumatic response to two conflicting emotions: should it fly in fear or stay to defend the nest. As we walk away it gradually calms down, though it still does not fly, and the woeful cries give way to a simple call of two cool, pure notes repeated over and over.

The seaweed lying on the sand is built to withstand handling by that rough ocean. The ribbon-like fronds of bladder wrack, some as long as five feet, are tough and leathery. Tangle, one of the deep-water laminaria, is large and yellow-brown, with a fan of strap-shaped fronds through which the waves can stream without breaking them. When you pick it up it all falls together like heavy hair. Its thin, elastic stipe ends in a sinewy holdfast that looks too small for the ponderous head.

Ten miles up the road from Budir is Arnarstapi, Eagle Rock. The town is named for the steeple-peaked mountain behind it where, presumably, Iceland's disappearing white-tailed eagle once nested. Here lived Gudrid, granddaughter of Vifil, a freed slave who had been well-born in the British Isles. Her first suitor was Einar, the son of another wealthy freed slave, a successful sea-going trader and "a handsome and courteous man with a taste for the ornate." He was contemptuously rejected by her father: ". . . that I should marry my daughter to the son of a slave! . . . She is rather particular about husbands."[2] Gudrid then married Leif Eriksson's brother, and after his death Thorfinn Karlsefni, the most enterprising of the Vinland settlers. Their son was the first white child born on the American continent. Gudrid's later descendants included three important bishops. The saga does not

[2] *Eirik's Saga*

197

relate what became of Einar, the slave's son. This story has no moral.

Today the town has more life than Budir, being a small fishing port for capelin and lobster. The harbor is tightly enclosed with grass-grown cliffs and looks like a green-sided box. Boats rock at anchor and seining nets are spread on the fields above. On the cliffs fulmars nest, spreading ample breasts over the single eggs. Houses perch on the hillside over the harbor and a fisherman's wife tends her potato patch. Life is all around, pervasively peaceful. Arnarstapi is a lovely town.

Crossing the peninsula, the road winds steeply up to the foothills of Snæfellsjökull through the gorge of Frodarheidi, Heath of Frodi's River. It is a rocky landscape. It looks as if someone had stood on top of the mountain and thrown stones all over the countryside. Here and there a hill rises in a jumble of cracked spires so sharp that stones have found no resting place. These polished, mud-brown hills are of the young rock palagonite, basaltic glass. During the Pleistocene Ice Age, when Iceland was rising through volcanic eruptions under the glacier, the rock thus formed, lava hardened under ice, came to have a glassy consistency. The shattered hills look like demented visions of Italian hill towns. Nothing grows there. One raven flies between the broken towers. This bird of inaccessible mountain peaks and gorges, a superb flyer and a creature of confident courage who will attack a gyrfalcon or seize food from a dog, is so unspecialized that it can adapt to whatever life offers. Sophisticated, flexible, even humorous, it is, like man, one of the highest forms of its class. The Icelanders regard it with awe and affection as a symbol of sagacity. Two ravens, Huginn and Muninn, usually were said to accompany Odin as his familiars and messengers. Ravens which attach themselves to farms in Iceland are safe (even if they steal the chickens). If one of a pair is harmed, misfortune, believe the farmers, is sure to befall. The raven in Frodarheidi circles upward on still wings like an eagle, rides the wind, then sideslips and tumbles toward the earth in a series of somersaults, to climb again and repeat the agile maneuver. It is evidently playing.

The farm of Froda, Frodi's River, is beyond the pass near the

ocean, where the foothills are green-covered and soft. The palagonite hills back up its fields and the white ice and black rock of
Snæfellsjökull rise far above. A long bleak curve of uninhabited
coast lies below. It is not a cozy place to live. It is easy to imagine
Froda haunted, as it was. It was grotesquely ghost-ridden, due to
the greediness of a farmer's wife. Thurid coveted the "fine English
sheet and silk counterpane" as well as a scarlet cloak and other
beautiful clothing brought by a visitor from the Hebrides. The
visitor died after a shower of blood from the sky had presaged
her death, having on her deathbed specified that her bedclothes
were to be burned or evil would befall the entire household.
Thurid refused to burn them, and the visitor came back, at first
naked, to cook supper over the fire, later in the form of a seal
which got into the dried fish stores and ate all the fish out of their
skins. Successively a shepherd died of a strange illness, the farmer,
Thurid's husband, drowned at sea with six others, eighteen of the
thirty servants perished mysteriously. All these people kept coming
back, the shepherd to stand in the doorway and throw against the
door anyone who tried to enter, the drowned men to sit dripping
wet at the cooking fire and wring out their clothing, the buried
corpses, all covered with earth, to shake out their garments and
scatter earth over the floor. The family, much reduced, set the fire
in another room, but the huge train of ghosts followed them all
over the house. At last Snorri the Wise was called and he advised
the Christian procedure of ghost-banishing. After the customary
sprinkling of consecrated water and hearing of confessions the
ceremony reverted to the pagan. First the bedclothes, the original
evil omens, were burned. Then a court was set up before which
the farmer's fourteen-year-old son summoned the ghosts one by
one and cited them for "haunting the house without permission
and depriving people of health and life."[3] Each spirit accepted the
verdict, and each departed with a short brisk farewell. "Sat I have
sat while the sitting was good," said one. "Go I shall now, though
I think I should have gone before," said another. The last, the
farmer himself, summed up: "There is no welcome here; let us

[3] *Eyrbyggja Saga*

199

away all."[4] The entire preposterous episode is recited with an air of ingenuous veracity. It is clear that the sophisticated author was having a joke at the expense of superstition and Christianity alike.

Beyond Froda the coastal land rises and falls. Sometimes the road skirts the tops of cliffs, sometimes it follows small fjords and harbors with sheep grazing in hummocky fields right down to the water. Across one narrow fjord there is a bridge because the road cannot traverse a flow of rough *apalgryti* lava that tumbles down to the edge of the sea. This is called Berserkjahraun, Burnt Field of the Berserkers. The gray-black cindery field is angry-looking, as if the wild men had torn it up in uncontrollable rage. To one side of it rises the small volcano from which it issued, a round mountain deep red on its sides, black at its foot. An explosion crater lower down is filled with water. A few small craters appear to be bottomless. One of these is the grave of the berserkers.

They were two brothers, Halli and Leiknir, from Sweden (berserkers, in the sagas, were never Icelandic; in Norwegian literature they were never Norwegian; no one wanted to claim them), who sometimes "went about like mad dogs and feared neither fire nor iron."[5] When not in their mad state they were good servants, willing and extremely strong, but if they were crossed they went into frenzies of anger. A man named Vermund brought them from Norway as bodyguards for protection against his brother Styr, who was encroaching on his property. As soon as they came to him they started requesting favors, which Vermund had to grant. When he hesitated they grew vicious, and he decided to give them to his fractious brother, whose unruly personality was more akin to theirs. One of the berserkers, Halli, fell in love with Styr's daughter and demanded her hand in marriage. When he refused the Swedes broke open his bed closet by forcing the joints apart with their fingers. At a loss, Styr went to Snorri the Wise for advice. Cunning Snorri told him what to do to rid himself of the brothers — everyone was now sorry they had been invited into the country. Halli could have his daughter, said Styr, even though he had no possessions, if he would earn the marriage

[4] Ibid.
[5] Ibid.

by work. The Swedes were to clear a pathway over the lava field, build a boundary wall between Styr's and his brother's farms, and construct a sheep enclosure on the lava. The two men, summoning their berserk strength, did all the work in one day, throwing great hunks of lava around as they strove. The young woman, "vain and showy and rather haughty,"[6] paraded past them all day, exciting love songs from the two hefty laborers.

In the meantime Styr had a bath dug down into the ground with a trapdoor through which water could be poured. When the berserkers went home, tired and weak after the ebbing of their mad strength, Styr thanked them for their work and invited them to use the bath. When they had entered Styr closed it and piled rocks on the trapdoor. Before the entrance he laid a fresh oxhide. Then he poured hot water through the opening. The Swedes, scalded, ran for the door and broke it open. Halli slipped on the raw oxhide and Styr gave him his death blow. When Leiknir tried to escape by the trapdoor Styr thrust his spear through him and he fell back dead into the bath.

Styr gave them a good pagan burial, putting their bodies in a hollow in the lava "so deep that one can see nothing from it except the sky above."[7] He threw rocks over their bodies so that they could not rise to haunt the neighborhood. (It was believed that actual corpses, along with their attendant spirits, would come out of their graves if not correctly and thoroughly buried.) Over their burial place he spoke this verse:

> "Dangerous and difficult
> my daughter's suitor ever,
> the swaggering sword-wielder,
> seemed to me to deal with.
> In dread I dwell no more of
> dour warrior's overbearing:
> promptly the pair by me
> places of rest were given."[8]

[6] Ibid.
[7] Ibid.
[8] Ibid.

He then had another conference with Snorri, the upshot of which was that Snorri himself married the girl for whom the berserkers had died, and both he and Styr "became more powerful through this alliance."[9] It can be seen that Christian ethics played small part in the Iceland of the early Sturlungs.

Thorolf, the first settler of Snæfellsnes, in the year 884 followed his high-seat pillars into a calm inlet of a water-indented peninsula he named Thorsness. The bay he named Hofsvag, Temple Bight. There he built a farm and called it Hofstad, Temple Farm. Near it he raised a temple to Thor with the wood he had brought from Mostrar Island in Norway after razing his temple there. Under the image of Thor he put earth he had taken from beneath the old image. There was a little mountain on Thorsness for which Thorolf "had such great reverence that no man might look at it without first having washed. Nothing was killed on this mountain, neither cattle nor human beings . . . That mountain he called Helgafell [Holy Mountain] and he believed that he would enter it when he died, and also all his kinsmen on the ness."[10] His *thingmen* assembled, in Iceland's first *thing*, fifty years before the establishment of the *Althing*, near where he had come ashore, and "this too was such a holy place for him that he would not allow it to be defiled in any way whatsoever, either through bloodshed or human excrement. For this purpose a skerry was set aside which was called Dirtskerry."[11]

Thorolf's land included a number of small islands which he called the Helgafell Islands, where eiders and seabirds nested in multitudes and seals were wont to congregate. He found a good living there, as birds, seals and fish between them supplied nearly every need for his family and followers. The fields provided good pasture for his cattle and sheep and horses.

The farm of Hofstad sits in the middle of level fields lush with grass and wild flowers. The inlet is shallow and full of rocks, any one of which could have been Dirtskerry. Beyond the farm are the coastal hills and cliffs and behind them rise the palagonite

[9] Ibid.
[10] Ibid.
[11] Ibid.

ridges of the interior, dark lines leading to the black and white of Snæfellsjökull. This serene place was the arena of a bitter fight when some of the later settlers, finding the Thorsness people arrogant, refused to observe the sacrosanctity of Thorolf's meeting place. They said that "they would ease themselves on the grass as anywhere else . . . They stated that they would not wear out their shoes going to the skerry for their needs."[12] Thorolf's men fought the newcomers on the beach in a long and bloody battle in which some were killed and many wounded on both sides. At last one of the older men intervened. A compromise was arrived at. The field had been defiled by bloodshed and could no longer be considered sacred, so meetings could not be held there anymore. The opposing sides would choose a new place and help one another maintain its holiness and cleanliness. There was to be no indemnity for the killed and wounded, as their number and status canceled out, and a daughter of one side married the principal offender on the other.

The Helgafell Islands are scattered in the sea beyond what is now the town of Stykkisholmur, Rocky Islets, an attractive fishing village on a steep slope, with modern concrete houses of many colors perched felicitously overlooking the harbor. The islands are small and rocky, some green-topped, and today as then they are haunts of birds and seals. To the east of them are several larger islands including Brokey, Island of Black Grass, and Oxney, Oxen Island. To this group Erik the Red moved when he was outlawed on the mainland, and from here, beset by enemies, he set sail on his first voyage to the unknown land to the west.

Thorolf's son, Thorstein, when he was twenty-five years old, rowed one day out to one of the larger of the Helgafell Islands, Höskuldsey, Gray Stack Island, a sharp-peaked rock, to fish. He did not come back. The next evening, when his shepherd went north of Helgafell Mountain to bring in the sheep "he saw the northern slope of the mountain open, and inside he could see great fires, and he could hear noisy merriment and the blaring of horns coming from there. And when he listened . . . he heard Thorstein

[12] Ibid.

203

and his shipmates being welcomed and Thorstein being invited to sit in the high seat opposite his father."[13]

Helgafell is a flat-topped knob of dark gray columnar basalt. The columns are oddly regular and resemble massive gates. On a misty evening an impressionable shepherd of those pre-Christian times could easily have imagined them slowly swinging open to reveal the happy spirits inside. There is a church at the bottom of the hill, replacing the one that Snorri the Wise had built when Christianity came, to refute the tales of banqueting corpses — even though there was no priest to hold services. From the top of Helgafell, a short steep climb up between the columns, where cinquefoil grows, yellow-gleaming, in the smallest earth crevices, the watery peninsula and the island-studded fjord are spread before us, the snowy mountain behind.

On the other side of Thorsness are two long fingers of the sea. Alftafjord, Swan Fjord, is a narrow inlet cutting far inland and its subsidiary, Vigrafjord, Spear's Head Fjord, so named for its shape, approaches Hofvag, nearly severing the cape from the mainland. The east shore of Alftafjord is a landslide area, stony and steep. At the head of Vigrafjord land merges so imperceptibly with the shallow water that at ebb tide the fields run right into mud and in winter the whole fjord is frozen over. On these two grounds, the stony one affording vantage points for attack, the flat one a hard ground for frontal maneuvers, were fought *Eyrbyggja Saga's* two main battles, fiercely bitter conflicts between the men of Thorsness and their cousins who had settled on adjacent capes. The origins of these battles, deeply embedded in continued small lacerations of honor, are impossible to disentangle. The ill feeling came to a head when Egil, a strong slave who wished to gain his freedom, was sent to earn it by killing one of two belligerent brothers. He fumbled the killing because one of his long tasseled shoelaces came loose. When he stepped over the threshold, having craftily crept toward the house hidden in smoke from the fire, one foot came down on the dragging lace, trapping the other foot. He tripped over his foot and fell into the hall, landing "with such a thud that it sounded as though a flayed beef carcass had

[13] Ibid.

been flung down on the floor."[14] (In the finer areas of the aristo-cratic province of battle craft, such as stalking an enemy, a slave was considered to have no finesse. He invariably fluffed his entrances and turned out a clown.) Egil was arrested and thrown into a shed, his feet tied together, until the next morning, when he was killed. The men waited overnight because it was the custom not to kill a man, even a slave, until a day had passed, to give passions a chance to cool in case there might turn out to be extenuating circum-stances. It was said that "night slayings are the same as murder." The law further declared that when a slave was killed the owner was to be reimbursed by the slayer within three days with twelve ounces of silver. Egil's killers gathered in a band of eighty, all armed, to deliver the worth of Egil to his master. One word led to another and there ensued two enormous battles among the rocks and the frozen mud. At the end of the fighting, where much heroism was shown and bloody wounds endured stoically, such fair settlements were arrived at under the judgment of Snorri that no more during the sage *godi's* lifetime was there trouble on Snæfellsnes.

Alftafjord was, however, the scene of another of those matter-of-factly macabre hauntings. A strong and violent Viking named Thorolf Lamefoot, after a fight with his son Arnkel, feeling that he was thwarted by the world, went into a depression and died sitting in his high seat. Arnkel took the proper precautions after this unnatural death to prevent his father putting the evil eye on anyone or coming back to the house. But Thorolf Lamefoot rose anyway and bothered the neighborhood. "The oxen which had drawn his body away from the house became troll-ridden, and all the cattle which came near the grave . . . went mad and bellowed until they died." A shepherd was found near the grave dead, black and blue all over, and all his sheep were also dead. "If birds settled on the grave of Thorolf they fell down dead." Others died horribly and the survivors began to desert their farms. Thor-olf's son had to do something about it. He dug up the body and found it "undecomposed and most hideous to look at." Arnkel buried him again, on a headland in the fjord, and had a wall built

[14] Ibid.

205

across "so high that nothing could get over it except a bird in flight." As long as Arnkel lived his father was quiet. But after his death by violence the old man rose again to terrorize the countryside. They went to his grave and "his body was still undecayed, and most troll-like in appearance. He was black as Hela [goddess of the underworld] and as big around as an ox." This time they took him down to the beach and burned him. They watched until the fire and Thorolf were all cold ashes and the wind blew him out to sea. That was the end of Thorolf's ghost.

Alftafjord is a properly forbidding scene. The few farms of the haunting lie on narrow fields enclosed by cliffs and always threatened by landslides. They look across the water to the disorderly litter of rocks falling into the sea, where the battle took place. There is not a house on Vigrafjord, site of the other battle. Low banks of rock frame a long flat field with puddles in it, gray reflections of the cloudy sky. Away from the banks the puddles grow larger and the land shrinks; there is no definite place where earth ceases and sea begins. One cannot walk there at all in summer. In winter, frozen hard, it would be a fitting bleak and desolate place for a battle.

Despite its ragged cliffs, its strange palagonite hills and its stretches of appalling *aa* lava, Snæfellsnes is a gracious place to live. It is up and down country where the eye never tires. The fields are greener in contrast to the rocks that rim them. The waters of Breidafjord, full of islands and teeming with birds, fish and seals, are calmer than more of Iceland's coastal areas. Its settlers found here the best living in Iceland, and they prospered. By the time the Sturlung generations reached Hvamm-Sturla in the twelfth century this fertile land had given the clan all the wealth it needed to become one of Iceland's most powerful family blocs.

Snorri Sturleson reached the family's pinnacle of wealth in the early thirteenth century, just a few decades before Iceland's golden age fizzled out in war, poverty and occupation. He built himself a large ornate villa at the head of Snæfellsnes in Reykholtsdalur, Valley of the Smoky Copse, named for the hot springs that sent their steam up through the woodlands of birch and mountain ash. The outstanding feature of his estate was the bath, "a circular basin, constructed of stones, without any cement, but nicely fitted together . . . about fourteen feet in diameter and about six feet deep . . . The hot water was brought from a spring about one hundred yards distant, by means of a covered conduit, which has been somewhat injured by an earthquake . . . The cold water had been brought into it, so that by mixing the hot and cold together, any desired temperature might be obtained. All around the inside, a little way under the surface of the water, is a row of projecting stones, placed to serve the purpose of steps."[15] Besides this unusual luxury Snorri's household used the hot springs for cooking. The valley has a number of craters a few feet across, where hot water bubbles nearly to the brim. Pots were suspended between bars and sunk into the springs, where the meat stewed cheaply and conveniently. It is said that today fishermen catch trout in the Hvita, White River, nearby, a stream famous for a particularly delicate species of brook trout, and flip them right out of the cold water into the hot spring, where they cook while still on the hook.

Snorri was far in advance of his time. The same nineteenth-century British traveler observed that Iceland's hot springs were mostly ignored, that few had the initiative to use this abundant commodity for heating or cooking. "Their not having taken advantage of this natural source of comfort must proceed from that want of enterprise which is so conspicuous in the character of the Icelanders,"[16] he wrote, in a period when Iceland was more than usually downtrodden and impoverished and her people were not feeling very brisk. This is not true today. Iceland entered modern civilization at a smart pace, all in the twentieth century. It was only about fifty years ago that the wealth of hot water was finally put to use to heat the houses of Reykjavik and other *solfatara* areas.

Reykholtsdalur is a rich green valley edged on both sides by rows of hills with no tops, like one long hill. The hills are green too, covered with dwarf birch. Cattle graze in the long grass, moving placidly between plumes of steam. Beside the road runs a

[15] *Travels in the Island of Iceland*, George Steuart MacKenzie, 1812
[16] Ibid.

207

smoking brook which widens into a sulphurous pond with a temperature of about 110° F. Pipes lead from the pond to the farmhouses nearby. In and around the town of Reykholt, where Snorri's house was, are large greenhouses with tomato plants pressing against their glass all the way to the roofs.

Neither the villa nor the famous bath exists today, probably destroyed by earthquakes, to which the valley is prone. The whole town is new-built. But Snorri himself, in stone, stands on a grassy plaza before the modern school building, looking over his green and steamy valley. He is surrounded by a grove of birch and mountain ash which have been coaxed in this warm bottomland to grow up to ten feet tall. His dress is the simple garb of a medieval priest-scholar, a straight, belted tunic down to mid-calf, laced boots and a plain round-crowned hat with a narrow brim. He stands in the rain, looking patient and modest, qualities notably absent in life. He is briefly rewarded in his vigil by the sight of a double rainbow, one flat in the grass, the other arching above it through a tuft of hot cloud. His estate is peaceful and bucolic, which it was not when this brilliant, turbulent, greedy man occupied it. It is hard to imagine here the jealous ambition, the infighting, the treacherous intrigue which led to the murder of the greatest of the Sturlungs, and at last to the collapse of Europe's first republic.

TWELVE

Wild Wheat and Grapevines

ICELAND LED EUROPE in the creation of her farmers' republic. Her literary flowering came long before Europe's Renaissance. In a third field the little country was five hundred years ahead of her world: seagoing exploration and settlement to the west.

In every Icelandic farmer there lived a sailor. The blood of the Vikings was undiluted. The Settlement had been a logical progression from the early Viking raids, a part of the massive Scandinavian migrations outward in all directions. Though the Norsemen who founded Iceland were colonizers, not raiders, they remained sea-minded. They could not settle inland, where the soil was thin, and rock and ice discouraged cultivation. Most of their farms were poised at the edge of the sea, near the shallow coasts of bays, where boats could be safely beached, at the heads of fjords whose cliff-protected waters invited anchorage. The new settlers were always ready to take to the water, to fish, to escape enemies, to explore or simply to visit one another.

Nowhere is this oceangoing disposition more evident than on the great Northwest Peninsula, a many-fingered hand reaching into the Denmark Strait toward Greenland only 180 miles due west. Its multitudes of capes and fjords stretch outward from two inhospitable highlands, one of rock, appropriately named Glama, Moon, the other of ice, Drangajökull, Lonely Rock Glacier, making the peninsula so exclusively water-directed that even today

209

many of its settlements are connected with the rest of Iceland only twice a week, by mailboat.

The Northwest Peninsula was inviting to sailors from the beginning. Here came Floki, Iceland's first intended settler, to find after circling south Iceland his most attractive landfall at Vatnsfjord on the Northwest Peninsula's south coast. Here later settled Thorvald, son of Asvald, who had to leave Norway along with his son, Erik the Red, because of killings they were involved in. Here also lived Thorfinn Karlsefni, the most prominent of the Vinland settlers, father of North America's first white child and chief source of information for the *Grænlendinga Saga*, one of the two important tales of the explorations and settlements of Greenland and North America.

It was not only tradition and local conditions that oriented Icelanders toward the sea. Five days of rough ocean between Iceland and her nearest European neighbor, Ireland, were an obstacle to European visitors. But to Icelanders the sea was a necessary passageway, not a barrier. The essentials of life lay across that wild ocean: timber, metals, flour, malt, honey, wine, beer, linen. Wool, sheepskins, hides, cheese, tallow, sulphur and falcons — and native poets and courtiers — were their materials of exchange. The boats were not the slim, swift longboats of the earlier Viking era, made only for the buccaneering grab-and-run of coastal raids, but broad-beamed cargo boats propelled by a big square sail and directed by a long steerboard on the right side (the origin of the word "starboard"). They were seaworthy in open ocean and could make about ten knots in fair weather, the fastest craft of their time. But they could not be held on course in a crosswind. Their sailors, who navigated by sun and stars, had no way of reckoning longitude, and they were always being blown off course. That was what had found them Iceland and it was to lead them to Greenland and North America.

Their knowledge of European geography was equal to that of the mother country and in one direction, north, surpassed hers. Icelandic sailors discovered and mapped Spitzbergen before 1170 and Jan Mayen in 1194. In a *Geographical Treatise*, written in 1300 but based on a twelfth-century manuscript, the northern coastlines are described in detailed sequence, from the Arctic

210

regions of Russia around Finnmark to Greenland; south and west around Cape Farewell to the near land on the other side, described thus: "To the south of Greenland lies Helluland [Baffin Island?] and then Markland [Labrador?]; and from there it is not far to Vinland, which some people think extends from Africa." This is the earliest known reference to North America.

By the second half of the tenth century Iceland's arable regions had been fully settled. There was room for more; Iceland has never had an overpopulation problem. But the early Norseman would not stand for subdivisions. The old urge to move on arose again. As in the original step from Norway, the people who organized the latest migrations were not the poor and down-trodden — there were none of these in Iceland — but wealthy and powerful dissidents.

In 900, twenty-six years after Ingolf landed, an Icelander named Gunnbjorn, son of Ulf Crow, was carried by storms far to the west. He came upon some rock islets and saw land beyond them. From his descriptions, and from later voyages, it has been ascertained that this first sighting, then called the Gunnbjarner Skerries, is the present-day Angmagssalik on Greenland's eastern coast.

In 978 Snæbjorn Galti, son of a rich farmer of the west, was involved in a revenge killing on behalf of his cousin. He had over-done it a little and decided that, rather than face the courts, he would outfit a ship and go to find Gunnbjorn's land to the west. One of his companions had a dream before they sailed and warned the others:

> "I can see death
> in a dread place,
> yours and mine,
> north-west in the waves,
> with frost and cold,
> and countless wonders;
> that's why Snæbjorn, I see,
> will lose his life."[1]

[1] *Landnamabok*

211

Undeterred, they set sail, sighted the Gunnbjarner Skerries and landed safely at an icy fjord they called Blaserk, Blue Shirt, under a six-hundred-foot glacier. There they built a house which was quickly snowed in. Violent to begin with, the men soon could not stand one another's company in the cramped quarters. Before the winter was out, which they knew only by "a drop of water on a fork sticking out through the skylight,"[2] several killings occurred, including that of Snæbjorn by the man who had foretold it. The few survivors returned home to a horrible vengeance.

Erik the Red was an intelligent and adventurous man with a forceful temper. Expelled from Norway with his father in 960 following their too spirited participation in a revenge killing, the two, being latecomers, settled perforce on a poor piece of land on the east coast of the Northwest Peninsula called Drangar, Lonely Rock (a common place-name in Iceland, where basalt stacks isolated by water erosion are a frequent sight along the coasts). Erik lost no time looking for and finding an advantageous match. His wife came from the West Fjords, and Erik settled there in Haukadale, Hawk Valley, a fertile region at the head of Snæfellsnes. He did not remain long at peace. His slaves launched a landslide in a nearby farm, the neighbor killed the slaves, and Erik killed the neighbor. He was banished from his new farm as a consequence. He took possession of the islands Brokey and Oxney north of Alftafjord. There he kept a force of fighting men and engaged in a series of energetic set-tos with his enemies which resulted in his being outlawed. He hid in his islands, dodging enemies, until he was able with the help of friends to outfit a ship. In 981 or 982 he set sail. Two hundred miles due west on the 65th parallel he came in sight of the landmark glacier Blaserk where his predecessors had built the house that became their prison. Warned by their ill luck he turned south and sailed around Cape Farewell. The first winter he spent on an island he named Erik's Island in the mouth of a great complex of fjords on the west coast near what is today Julianehaab. When spring came he moved inland up the largest fjord, today's Tunugdliarfik to Brattahlid, Hillside, where he found mild temperatures and good fields for grazing.

[2] Ibid.

He explored inland and northward for another year, then returned to Iceland to recruit colonists for the new land. He gave it the name Greenland to offset the story of Snæbjorn Galti's ugly winter, and painted an attractive picture of ice-free fjords and gentle pastures going down to the sea.

Erik was an imperious man who was happiest leading others, and there is no doubt that he was ambitious for settlers in a new land where he would be chief and patriarch. But he was not inventing the green pastures of his virgin land. Julianehaab is on the same parallel as southern Iceland. Though no warm ocean currents melt its snow in winter, the coastal strip between the ocean and the forbidding icecap of the interior is entirely habitable in summer and not unlike Erik's two original homes, Drangar under the glacier in the north and the snow-backed valleys of Snæfellsnes. Erik considered that he had found another Iceland.

In 985 or 986 twenty-five ships sailed from Iceland, but only fourteen reached Greenland. Some were driven back by storms and some were lost in what is now thought to have been a submarine earthquake, fairly common in the Denmark Strait. The catastrophes of this voyage did not discourage settlers, for more followed and within a few years there were 190 farms in the area called the Eastern Settlement around Erik's home in Brattahlid. Other colonists sailed two hundred miles northwest, to found the Western Settlement of ninety farms at another pleasant confluence of fjords where today is Godthaab.

For about two centuries Greenland was an exciting, somewhat exotic lure. Young men went there adventuring, liked what they saw, and came back again later, bringing wives and possessions, to homestead in the new land. They did not consider themselves cut off way out there across the Atlantic. The ocean's dangers never daunted an Icelander. It was no worse crossing the Denmark Strait than braving North Atlantic storms to reach the British Isles or sailing over the fierce waters of the Norwegian Sea to Norway. From Western Iceland to Cape Farewell in Greenland was four days' sail; it was five days from Reykjavik to Ireland and seven days from the East Fjords of Iceland to Norway. Visiting back and forth was easy, as was the transport of the necessary imports and exports to keep life comfortable in the colony. At the height

213

of its Norse colonization Greenland had a population of about three thousand. It was an independent republic with a constitution modeled on that of its mother country.

The years of the Greenland settlement were warmer than the present, and the newcomers flourished. The grasslands indeed came down to the water's edge, and the colonists could raise sheep, cattle, ponies, pigs and goats. The fjords abounded in fish and there was some larger game: reindeer, seals, walrus and polar bears. Their exports were items rare and greatly valued in Europe: seal and walrus skins, walrus ivory and furs. Though all necessities but food had to be imported, they prospered. Their farms were large, the dwellings spacious. Erik's home farm had four barns and room for forty head of cattle, as well as its own small turf-and-timber church that his wife had built. She was one of Greenland's first Christian converts, much to Erik's annoyance, as she refused to sleep with her still heathen husband.

Greenland lost her independence to Norway in 1261, a year before Iceland succumbed. A killing trade monopoly ensued as the Norwegian government forbade the Greenlanders to trade with any other country, contracting to send two ships a year. After a few years the two ships came only irregularly and finally stopped altogether. The climate began to get colder in the thirteenth century; glaciers all over the world started to expand and drift ice increased in the northern seas. No boats were made that could negotiate the floes, and the route was moved farther south. After a hundred years that too became impassable as the East Greenland Current brought down ever more ice from the polar regions. By the early fifteenth century all traffic between Greenland and Europe had ceased. In the sixteenth century, when boats began to reach Greenland again, there were no Norsemen left in the neglected settlements, only cattle running wild.

With the end of their European ties the colonists had been thrown on their own resources. They had no grains or fruits, no iron for weapons or farm implements, no wood to build ships. They had to live on a diet of meat and fish, whatever they could meagerly catch. That diet is known to cause physical and mental deterioration in people not accustomed to it. They survived, but in a diseased condition.

The colder climate brought another new terror. There had been no early records of meetings with natives in Greenland though they were to become distressingly familiar to the explorers and settlers of the North American continent. Greenland Eskimos, in the warmer centuries, had gone north following the bear and the walrus. By the late thirteenth century heavier ice in Baffin Bay and Davis Strait began driving their livelihood south. The hunters followed. Drifting down the coast they began to run into the white settlements. Cold weather was no problem to the Eskimos, who thrived on the regime that was crippling the Europeans. Their clashes with the already weakened Norse farmers always ended in disaster to the white men in spite of their superior weapons. One report states: "Skrælings attacked the Greenlanders, killing eighteen of them and carrying off two boys into captivity."[3] *Skræling* was a derogatory name given to natives of the New World, first Eskimos, later Indians. It means literally, "one withered by the sun," and probably originally referred to their appearance: a small people with skin wrinkled by sun, wind and frost. "These people," wrote a sixteenth-century Icelandic geographer who mapped the coast of North America, ". . . get their name from their aridity; they are dried up just as much by the heat as the cold."[4]

The same excavations that disclosed the roomy dwelling places of happier years uncovered a sad history of the devolution of a race. The later skeletons were undersized and malformed, evidence that the robust farmers had degenerated into a stunted and sickly people deformed by malnutrition. By the end of the fifteenth century, when Columbus started the new wave of exploration from Europe the old one, ignored and then forgotten, had entirely crumbled away. Only the skeletons tell of its horrible and lonely death.

For the details of the Norse explorations and settlements in North America we have the word of the sagas, specifically two, *Grænlendinga Saga* and *Eirik's Saga*. There is no guarantee of

[3] *Icelandic Annals*, 1379

[4] Sigurdur Stefansson, *circa* 1590, explanatory note to his map of North America

their accuracy; the saga authors, as we have seen, writing long after the fact, had less solicitude for exact truth than for the making of drama. If these two sagas are not scrupulously factual, however, they have a general ring of authenticity. There is a genuine sound to the travelers' wonder at the beauty and fertility of the new shores, mingled with their disgust and fear of the indigenous peoples; the minuteness of detail concerning their landings and abortive settlements. Though these two sagas were written long after the events they describe, there is earlier documentation of the Vinland events: one account, by a German priest named Adam of Bremen, written only sixty years after the attempted settlements,[5] another by Ari Frodi, author of *Islendingabok* and an early version of *Landnamabok*, who knew some of the immediate descendants of the explorers. Though these various accounts are probably not the undiluted truth, only a historian of unswerving prejudice would presume to deny the basic premise: Norsemen were here five centuries before Columbus.

The North American coast, like Greenland, was found by mistake. Bjarni Herjolfsson, sailing from Iceland to find his father, who was farming in Greenland, ran into fog and northerly winds which pushed him south so that he missed Cape Farewell. After many days he sighted a wooded land of low hills. As it was obviously not Greenland it did not interest him. He set out to sea again and made landfall two days later on a flat, forested coast. Since this also was clearly not his goal, Bjarni refused to let his men go ashore even though they needed water and wanted to collect wood. Once more they hoisted sail and ran before a southwest wind until they came to a stony, mountainous land with glacier behind the mountains. Again the men asked Bjarni to let them land but he answered, "No, for this country seems to me to be worthless."[6] They sailed east for four more days and at last came to Greenland, with luck to the very promontory where Bjarni's

[5] "He [the King of Denmark] spoke of an island in that northern ocean, discovered by many, which is called Vinland, for the reason that vines yielding the best of wine grow there wild. Moreover, that grain unsown grows there abundantly is not a fabulous opinion but, from a relation of the Danes we know it to be true." *Hamburg Church History*, Adam of Bremen, 1074

[6] *Grænlendinga Saga*

father had his farm. Bjarni settled there and never went to sea again. His lack of interest precluded any exact record of the lands he had sighted.

He was criticized for his want of curiosity about the new shoreline of forests, a rare resource to a Greenlander. The first to organize an expedition to remedy this ignorance was Leif, one of Erik's three sons. In 1001 he sailed west and found the last land Bjarni had sighted. Agreeing with his predecessor's comment on its worthlessness, he named it Helluland, Land of Rock Slabs (probably Baffin Island), and continued southwest, aided by a northeast wind. The next land was "flat and wooded, with white sandy beaches . . . and the land sloped gently down to the sea."[7] Leif named it Markland, Forest Land (probably Labrador). The northeast wind continued and they sailed before it for two days, when they reached land again, an island north of a mainland. "They went ashore and looked about them. The weather was fine. There was dew on the grass, and the first thing they did was to get some of it on their hands and put it to their lips, and . . . it seemed the sweetest thing they had ever tasted."[8] (This was thought to be Belle Isle, off the coast of Newfoundland.)

They went back to their ship and sailed into the sound between the island and a promontory of the mainland. They entered a river which flowed out of a lake, and there they found the land so fair that they decided to stay the winter. It was a new experience for men accustomed to the chill winter darkness of Greenland and Iceland. On the shortest day of the year the sun was up before nine o'clock and did not set until after three. "There was never any frost all winter and the grass hardly withered at all."[9] There were salmon in the river and the lake. One day Leif's foster-father, a German, came back from an expedition babbling in German, "rolling his eyes in all directions and pulling faces."[10] When they had calmed him down he managed to tell them in Icelandic that he had found grapevines and grapes, which he knew well from his native land.

[7] Ibid.
[8] Ibid.
[9] Ibid.
[10] Ibid.

They also found there wild wheat, the lyme grass of the Icelanders, their only native grain, from which came not only food but many household necessities. The trees, especially the maples, were excellent for building. The explorers were most ecstatic about the grapes, but the abundance of all this natural wealth was a windfall for people who up to then had had to import everything but food. When spring came Leif went back to Greenland with a cargo of timber and the towboat full of grapes. He called the country Vinland.[11]

Leif did not have to work any harder to entice footloose compatriots to the Land of Wine than had his father to lure them to Greenland. His brothers and a half-sister, Freydis, followed his initial expedition with several of their own. On the first one came the first encounter with natives and the first death. While exploring to the south along the coast, a party led by Leif's brother Thorvald was set on by a horde of Skrælings in skin boats. Thorvald was wounded by an arrow in the armpit. He asked his men to take him to the lovely headland where he had wanted to build his house. "I told the truth when I said that I would settle there . . . Bury me there and put crosses at my head and feet, and let the place be called Krossaness for ever afterwards."[12]

This is the account in one saga of how Thorvald Eiriksson died. In the other his exploring party saw a Uniped come "bounding down to where the ship lay." It shot an arrow into Thorvald's groin, whereupon the Norseman pulled the arrow out and remarked, "This is a rich country we have found; there is plenty of fat around my entrails,"[13] and died. A Uniped is a creature of medieval legend, said to be an inhabitant of Africa. Its inclusion in the story by a Europe-educated scribe who worked on polishing this saga reflects the widespread impression that the land to the west was attached to Africa.

[11] The settlements of Leif and succeeding explorers were thought to have been on and near Cape Bauld, Newfoundland, where the sites of two large Norse dwellings and several smaller buildings have been excavated at l'Anse aux Meadows. The buildings, the largest of which is seventy feet long by fifty-five wide, are in the style of the Greenland and Iceland farm dwellings of the period. There is no evidence extant that the Norse explorers got as far south as New England, grapevines notwithstanding.

[12] Ibid.

[13] *Eirik's Saga*

Leif's second brother, Thorstein, also died, of an illness caught from some shipwrecked men whom he rescued. Their half-sister, Freydis, "an arrogant, overbearing woman,"[14] despised her husband Thorvard, whom she had married for his money. She was not interested in Vinland as a place to settle but only for its money-making possibilities. She persuaded two Greenland brothers, Helgi and Finnbogi, to join her with their ship on a Vinland expedition to cut timber and gather grapes. Once there she cheated the brothers and at last bullied and shamed her husband with lies about them, until he reluctantly took his men to set on them with their whole crew while they were asleep in bed. When his men dragged them out of the house one by one Freydis ordered each one put to death. No one wanted to kill their women, so Freydis, saying, "Give me an axe,"[15] killed all five of them herself. She then alternately bribed with money and threatened with death anyone who said a word of this, loaded all the produce of Helgi and Finnbogi off their ship and onto hers and sailed back to Greenland much richer than when she had left.

On this same expedition some of the men were attacked by Skrælings with catapults and retreated in terror before the unknown weapon. This formidable woman, pregnant at the time, berated her companions for their cowardice. Unable to move fast, she snatched up a sword of a man who had been killed by a flint-stone flung at his head, stood waiting for the Skrælings to approach, then pulled one of her breasts out of her bodice and slapped it with the sword. The Skrælings were so taken aback that they fled to their skin boats and took off at once.

Freydis's crimes were found out. Neither money nor threats could keep the gossip down. Leif tortured three of his sister's men until they told the whole hideous story, but he had not the heart to punish his own flesh and blood. However, he prophesied that her descendants would never prosper, "and after that no one thought anything but ill of her and her family."[16]

Next to Leif, who started it all, Thorfinn Karlsefni was the most courageously adventurous of the Norse explorers and the

[14] *Grænlendinga Saga*
[15] Ibid.
[16] Ibid.

one who first envisaged the possibility of establishing a colony in Vinland. He was a seagoing merchant from northern Iceland who went to Greenland to trade. There he stayed with Erik at his large hospitable farm in Brattahlid, where he met and fell in love with Erik's widowed daughter-in-law Gudrid, she whose slave-born father had been so scornful of a freed slave. Marrying her brought Karlsefni into the undertakings of this adventure-minded family. Soon he outfited his own ship for a long journey, stocked it with cattle and sheep, and gathered a party of sixty men and five women. Another ship with about seventy-five people joined the expedition. In 1010 they set sail for the west intending to make a permanent settlement in the new land. Following Leif's voyages they sailed directly across the 65th parallel to Helluland, turned south to Markland, then spent several days passing long sand beaches with no harbors, which they called Furdurstrands, Marvel Shores (probably Labrador). They stopped for the first winter at a fjord they named Straumfjord, Fjord of the Tide-Race, north of Vinland. "There were mountains there and the country was beautiful to look at, and . . . there was tall grass everywhere . . . The male beasts became very frisky and difficult to manage."[17] (This was probably the Strait of Belle Isle.) The party gathered timber for building, caught game, and lived for part of the winter on a beached rorqual (finback whale). But the weather was severe, the hunting failed and they ran short of food. In spring they moved south to Vinland and found an estuary they named Hop, Tidal Lake (probably between Quirpon Island and White Bay, Newfoundland), flooded with seawater only at high tide. "They found wild wheat . . . and grapevines . . . and streams teeming with fish. They dug trenches at the high-tide mark, and when the tide went out there were halibut trapped in the trenches. In the woods there was a great number of animals of all kinds."[18] They decided to settle there. The winter was kind; there was no snow at all and their livestock grew fat on the fine grass.

In the first autumn after they left Greenland Karlsefni's and Gudrid's son Snorri had been born. He lived in the new land until

[17] *Eirik's Saga*
[18] Ibid.

he was three, when all the settlers sailed back to Greenland forever. It was not the land or the weather that drove them off. Everything about Vinland favored a permanent settlement. It was the Norsemen's queasy abhorrence of the natives that they could not overcome. It is surprising that people as tough and resourceful as the Norse discoverers of America should be turned away by Stone Age men with primitive weapons and unsophisticated mentality. Cortés, with a handful of adventurers, was to conquer a far more capable, numerous and menacing enemy. The Conquistadores, however, were motivated strongly by the desire for gold and territory for the Crown. The Norsemen, coming by mistake on a fair new shore, had in the beginning only the incentive of cutting timber and picking grapes. They had no immediate inclination toward colonization. They no longer needed, as they had when the republic of Iceland was founded, to escape tyranny or to spread into fresh lands. The centuries of Norse aggressive peregrination were coming to an end; the migratory impulse was at last petering out. Their efforts in America were halfhearted, and it was easy for the natives, with their superior numbers and repugnant appearance, to frighten them off.

It is impossible to say where the fault lay. There never was a friendly meeting between the new population and the indigenous. The natives regarded the Norsemen as aggressive invaders, as indeed they were, and the settlers considered the Stone Age people ugly, stupid and altogether wretched. "They were small and evil-looking, and their hair was coarse; they had large eyes and broad cheekbones."[19] They also, to the Norse, had the faults of a poor-spirited people, slyness and cowardice. The attitude on both sides was defensive and belligerent at the same time. But from the beginning the Skrælings had the upper hand. They were invincible in a crowd.

There was a feeble effort at trade. One day a group of Skrælings appeared out of the woods bearing packs. The cattle were grazing in the fields and when the bull began to bellow the Skrælings fled terrified back into the woods. After a while they filtered back and tried to get into Karlsefni's house but he barred

[19] Ibid.

the doors. Then they opened their packs and disclosed furs and pelts of all kinds. They indicated that they wanted swords and spears in exchange, but Karlsefni forbade anyone to sell them weapons. Instead he told the women to carry milk to them, "and so the outcome of their trading expedition was that the Skrælings carried their purchases away in their bellies, and left their packs and furs with Karlsefni and his men."[20]

After this Karlsefni built a palisade of tree trunks all around the houses. When the Skrælings returned the women brought them milk again and they threw their wares over the palisade. A third time one of them got in and was killed trying to steal some weapons. His companions ran in fright, leaving their clothing and wares behind. That time they did not even get milk.

Another item the Skrælings liked was red cloth. They took "a span [about nine inches] of red cloth for each pelt, and tied the cloth round their heads . . . After a while the cloth began to run short; then Karlsefni and his men cut it up into pieces which were no more than a finger's breadth wide; but the Skrælings paid just as much or even more for it."[21]

However easily cowed the Skrælings were, the Norsemen were equally terrorized. The sheer numbers of the natives, swarming over the shore from their skin boats, slinging their catapults, thongs of animal hide and sharpened flintstones, with lethal accuracy, had a numbing effect on warriors accustomed to hand-to-hand combat with the familiar sword and axe. A man could parry these and strike back. The newcomers had no defense against hordes of sling-shooting natives, like angry hornets everywhere at once. "Karlsefni and his men . . . realized . . . that although the land was excellent they could never live there in safety or freedom from fear, because of the native inhabitants. So they made ready to leave the place and return home."[22]

They had one last encounter. Sailing before a southerly wind they reached Markland, where they surprised a family group of five Skrælings, a man, two women and two children. They caught

20 Ibid.
21 Ibid.
22 Ibid.

the children "but the others got away and sank down into the ground."[23] They took the little boys on board, taught them to speak Norse and baptized them, and the children became friendly enough to talk about their people. They were ruled by two kings, they said, named Avaldamon and Valdidida, and they had no houses but lived in holes in the ground. Among other bits of information the children described a country "across from their own land where the people went about in white clothing and uttered loud cries and carried poles with patches of cloth attached. This is thought to have been Hvitramannaland, White Man's Land."[24]

This casual passage opens an exciting range of provocative possibilities as to who actually were the first white people to explore and settle in the North American continent. Hvitramannaland was a legendary Irish preserve generally associated with Asia, somewhere north of India. But some medieval sources connect it definitely with the western part of the Atlantic. In *Landnamabok* there is reference to Hvitramannaland "six days sail west of Ireland." In the *Hauksbok*, a codex of sagas and other learned writings compiled in Iceland in the fourteenth century, this land in the western Atlantic is referred to as "Greater Ireland." The Irish themselves have in their literature, as we have seen, cloudy, mythical allusions to "a land promised to the saints . . . to the west across the sea, which knows neither death nor decay, only simple human joys going on perpetually without care . . ." and an only slightly more concrete reference to a place found by Saint Brendan in his forty-day journey across the Atlantic: ". . . warm, fruitful, bathed in . . . autumn sunshine," from which the monks returned to their boat "laden with fruit."[25]

It is a pity that Karlsefni "had no wish to stay there any longer and wanted to return to Greenland."[26] It would have been a historic confrontation. One can imagine the consternation of the Irish anchorites, if such they were, keeping up their spirits with

[23] Ibid.
[24] Ibid.
[25] *Navigatio Sancti Brendani*
[26] *Eirik's Saga*

parades and banners and shouted prayers, when they beheld the many oars and striped woolen sails of their hereditary *bête noire*. To escape the predacious Norsemen they had fled Ireland in their thistledown curraghs; to their cliff-walled Iceland retreat the enemy had once more penetrated. The devil himself could not have been more persevering than this same obtrusive people turning up to surprise them at their devotions under the alien glacier at the very edge of the world.

Karlsefni and Gudrid went back to Iceland with their little American son, to the farm in the north which Karlsefni had never given up. There he recounted all these events, which were written down by scribes, and there, in the fullness of time, he died and his widow became a nun. Three of their descendants were illustrious bishops. "Many other great people in Iceland are descended from Karlsefni and Gudrid, but not recorded here. And here this saga ends. May God be with us. Amen."[27]

The North American adventure was short-lived compared with the tragic Greenland undertaking, but it did not end absolutely with Karlsefni's flight. Sea travel was as easy from Greenland to Markland as from Iceland to Greenland or Europe, and journeys for timber to North America's forests continued at least into the fourteenth century. A map of the North American coast drawn in 1590 still used the old Norse names, even though Spanish, English and French explorers had already bestowed their own appellations on the lands they considered theirs by right of original discovery. But along with the forfeiture of their political freedom and the deterioration of their literary genius, the Icelanders evidently lost their taste for seagoing enterprise. They never tried again to live in Vinland. The locations of the landings became blurred by time and the old nautical directions, transmitted by word of mouth, became confused. At last the world forgot that a lovely piece of land along the North American shore had for thirteen years been a Norse preserve. Only the annals kept the record, a misty record at best, full of details at once grotesque and tantalizingly realistic.

[27] Ibid.

THIRTEEN

The Thulean Island

THE NORTHWEST PENINSULA, the region of Iceland most alluring for seafarers, is a product of the abyssal upheavals of the Eocene epoch that fifty million years ago brought the basalt floods of the Thulean Province, the land bridge between Greenland and Europe, out of the earth's interior. As the northern seas in later ages inundated the sinking subcontinent a few peaks remained above the surface, among them the Faeroes, the Hebrides and a group of hilly islands, the forerunner of Iceland. The mountainous Northwest Peninsula is one of these ancient basalt islands, incredibly still there despite the ravages of ocean, ice and volcanic holocaust.

It is deeply scarred. Its mountains have been sheared off flat by the glacier of the Pleistocene epoch, some of which still exists in its interior. Its many river valleys, born of volcanic earth fractures and descending to the sea in all directions from the central highlands, have been widened and deepened into fjords by glacier action, so the ocean pours in from every side almost to its heart. The glacier further scoured out the river valleys into chasms with nearly vertical walls. Between its crumpled mass of mountains, its sheer-sided river gorges, its remaining glacier and its superabundance of fjords, most of the Northwest Peninsula is impassable by land.

It must be approached by sea or by air. We went by air in a twin-engined seven-seat plane from Akureyri, in the mid-north, over the great northern fjords, Eyjafjord, Island Fjord, Skagafjord, Jutting Fjord, and Hunafloi, Bay of the Young Bear (this wide inlet, open to the Denmark Strait, was the easiest route for polar bears coming in from Greenland on the floe ice in colder years). The country between the fjords is corrugated; dark narrow valleys creep among rocky, sometimes snow-topped mountains. All the peaks here were cut off at the same height as the glacier scraped heavily down the countryside. From above they look clean-edged, as if the ice had just passed.

The cumulus clouds, mountainous above, are flat-bottomed as if they had risen from seats on the earth mountains. As we near them valleys open in them and they suddenly sweep out to engulf us. Then they are no longer majestic mountain figures but invisible attackers, cold and wet and dark, hurrying on us from all directions at once, not so much attacking as surrounding, swallowing us in wind and sleet. We cannot see the earth or the sky, and our little machine seems helpless. Then we are out in the sun again, moving smoothly once more, no shield of mist between us and the brilliant sky. Between the tunnels of stormy mist and the unfiltered sunlight outside them we are dazzled and dizzy.

Past Hunafloi the cloud cover suddenly seems to be beneath us. It is not cloud but the snowfield of Drangajökull, the Northwest Peninsula's Pleistocene remnant, Iceland's fifth largest glacier. Its area, seventy-seven square miles on maps of 1911 to 1914, has today receded to about sixty-five. Sailing close by its 3,035-foot summit we can see the gray crevasses in the aged ice. At its western side is a fjord in the process of being created. A deep rectangular valley has been carved by ice down through an earth crack to the sea. Sharply delineated cliffs line it in a straight road from glacier to water. At the upper end of the valley the earth is bare and gray; nothing has yet taken root there where the ice has only recently melted off. At the lower end a long finger of the ocean has come in, making a fjord named Kaldalon, Cold Inlet. Mud and standing water all through the valley indicate that the melting ice is still deepening it and that the ocean steadily invades farther.

Beyond Kaldalon is the great hooked inlet of Isafjardardjup, Deep Frozen Fjord, forty-eight miles long, that cuts right through to the center of the Peninsula. Along its cliffy shores a dozen smaller fjords pierce the land. Glama, Moonland, where their rivers have their sources, is wrinkled and brown like old wrapping paper.

The town of Isafjord, Icy Fjord, the Northwest Peninsula's chief and largest town (population 3,000), is deep within one of these narrow fjords, Skutulsfjord, Table Fjord, probably named for the square-topped mountain that closes it off at the head. A spit has been formed in Skutulsfjord, as in many other fjords, by earth and rock deposits brought down by its parent river. Isafjord is built on this spit, right out into the middle of the fjord. Towering cliffs like medieval fortress walls rise hundreds of feet on three sides of it. The sea is calm here, deep inside the inlet, and the spit, jutting crookedly across the water, has made an almost landlocked harbor. Protected by its ring of mountains and closed off by its spit, Isafjord's harbor is almost never disturbed by wind or ocean waves. It is a perfect situation for a fishing and ship-building port.

We land on a narrow airstrip under the cliff wall at the head of the fjord. The airstrip only goes one way. Either you land and take off that way or you don't fly. It depends on the wind. It is generally surer to enter Isafjord by sea. Across the fjord from the landing strip the town appears to rise straight out of the water. Walking its streets one sees the harbor shining at the end of every block. Almost every window looks out on the fjord. It is a clean, pretty town with some houses that date from the eighteenth century. Though their wooden sidings have been reinforced with metal their lines, steep-roofed and gabled, have the gracious simplicity of that age.

Boats are Isafjord's chief reason for being. Fishing boats line its wharves, mostly cod and haddock trawlers and shrimp and scallop draggers. The cod boats have wide-meshed blue-green nylon nets piled on their decks, topped with the heavy wood and metal doors that drag the bottom. Some of them have lines on their after-decks strung with rows of small cod drying in the sun, leathery tidbits esteemed by Icelanders as special delicacies.

The scallop boats are small, built only for bay and coastal fishing. Their nets are of iron mesh with coarse rope net over it. These are attached to an iron frame about five feet wide with a scraper on its underside. The contraption is lowered to the bottom and dragged behind the boat; the scraper digs the shellfish out of the mud and the mesh net behind scoops them up, after which it is pulled tight like a purse seine and hauled into the boat by winch. Scallops are a specialty of Isafjord: bay scallops with shells three inches across, finely ridged, with concentric lines, white and bright orange deepening to purple-red at the hinge. The only part of this large soft-bodied mollusk generally eaten is the firm little cube of muscle that holds the shell together.

When alive the scallop is not among the most intelligent of animals. In fact, along with the other bivalves, it is the least advanced in brain of all the mollusks. But it possesses a startling attribute: eyes of remarkably sentient appearance, one hundred of them all around the mantle, each with cornea, focussing lens and retina. Although those humanoid eyes peering out of the slightly opened valves appear to regard the world with bright intensity, all the scallop can actually see are motion and light. It is a fairly good swimmer, unlike most mollusks, propelling itself forward by beating its valves open and shut and taking in food, microscopic floating plants, as it goes. When alarmed it snaps the shell shut and shoots backwards, a line of bubbles streaming out behind it. Mostly scallops live on the bottom slightly buried in silt, helpless against the scraping nets of their human predators.

Isafjord has two industries connected with fishing: boatbuilding and net-making. A large trawler is in the making inside the factory on one of the wharves. It lies, monstrous, suspended between floor and ceiling, while men swarm over its body with welding torches, steel beams swing through the air, and the sound of riveting hammers echoes under the high roof. Outside, a newly finished boat is at anchor, an all-metal, air-conditioned, carpeted trawler, the *Surtsey*, built at a cost of about $300,000, 80 percent of which was government loan. She is destined for ravaged Heimaey.

Gudmundur Sveinsson, who owns the net factory, had two winters of schooling when he was thirteen and fourteen years old, walking five miles to Isafjord's one school, a little green building that still stands though today it is supplemented by a fine large modern high school. His father's house, at the head of the fjord, was of sod and turf, heated by an iron stove in which they burned peat, driftwood when they could find it or coal when they could afford it. From a poor childhood he entered a struggling manhood, making a living as farmer, sailor and fisherman and somehow picking up an education along the way. Now he is well-read, speaks

The town of Isafjord, in the Northwest Peninsula, is built on a spit of land in the fjord and seems to rise straight out of the water. Its surrounding mountains, among the oldest in Iceland, are flat-topped, sheared off in the Ice Age.

safjord's main business is fishing, and boats line the docks of her nearly andlocked harbor. Fishermen hang out strings of small cod to dry in the sun as supplement to their boring diet while at sea.

233

English easily, knows as much about world affairs as we do and owns a prosperous net business.

The net factory is a large, airy two-story building by the water. It has only one office, Gudmundur's, partitioned off from the big light room where the nets are. Ropes cross the room and the nets hang from them like stage sets, many shades of green from light blue-green to the deep green of the sea bottom. At the floor the nets are draped over sawhorses where the work, a crocheting process with flat narrow wooden blades, is carried on. Most of the netting comes from Japan; in Gudmundur's factory it is cut into the required lengths and shapes, and ropes, weights and floaters attached. The finest mesh is shrimp net, delicately pale green. It is fastened all around with heavy rope of manila hemp two and a half inches thick, soft and furry to the touch, more like wool than rope. A broader mesh is used for the cod nets, long cone-shaped purse seines closed at the narrow end, roped at the wide end. These are used during the spawning season in March and April, when the fish congregate in immense schools off the southwest coast. The cone nets are towed behind the boat through the dense shoals, then the rope at the wide end is tightened and the net full of fish pulled on board like a big bag.

In a corner of the warehouse, on the floor below, are acres of folded nylon seine nets for herring, piled to the ceiling, some of it old and grayed by water and weather, some black and shining, all with floats and ropes attached ready to go out. They will never go out again. Though they were made in his shop, Gudmundur said, they do not belong to him. They have been stored there by the fishermen who own them, and the rotting heaps are mute evidence of tragedy. In the late 1960s the herring failed, the fish that was Iceland's biggest catch. The boats to which the nets belonged lie at anchor now, useless until the cod and haddock season starts next winter. Isafjord was one of Iceland's main herring ports. There is enough industry to keep it going — margarine, glass, paint, plastics and weaving supplement the income from fishing — but the failure of the fish has removed a large source of income and the town is shrinking. The cod is weakening too, says Gudmundur. Over his kind and cheerful face comes an unwonted shadow of worry. Every year they are smaller and the boats come back only partly loaded.

Though the town of Isafjord seems on the surface still to prosper, the smaller villages of the Northwest Peninsula starkly reflect the decline of fishing. All are shriveling; some have been entirely abandoned. The great fjords, with their many tributary inlets, were as inviting country for small-boat fishing as they were for earlier sailors with wanderlust, and they are dotted with clusters of houses and docks. The fishermen found plenty of fish in the calm, nearly landlocked waters, without having to chance the rough ocean. With the coming of the gigantically efficient deep-sea trawlers that fish out everything from the smallest cod to eighty-year-old lobsters there was not enough left in the fjords to give the small fishermen a living. Some of them changed over to shrimp and scallop dredging; these animals were not hurt by the over-fishing of the ocean. Many left, going south, getting work on the trawlers, working in the fish factories. The recent failure of herring was the final blow. This water-oriented country that nourished the sea dreams of men like Erik and Thorfinn Karlsefni is today a place of deserted houses and rotting docks. It is beautiful in its loneliness but it is very sad.

Two journeys along the deeply indented shores of Isafjardar-djup show what is happening to the once thriving water lanes. The first trip is to Hesteyrarfjord, Horse Fjord, named for a horse-shaped crag at its head. It is a small fjord, about five miles long, in the peninsula's northernmost cape, beyond the wide mouth of Isafjardardjup, just below the Arctic Circle. To reach it we have to get the taste of the North Atlantic in a small boat. There is no other way to get there. We are taken by an old fisherman, Petur Petursson. His boat, named *Sigurvon, Victorious Hope*, is about thirty feet long. Built in Isafjord, it has the long low lines of the fishing boats of fifty years ago, designed for maneuverability but alarmingly vulnerable in heavy seas. Petur no longer competes in the dwindling fishing business but makes a small living taking visitors out on the fjord and ferrying fellow townsmen to other fjords and villages. *Sigurvon*, therefore, makes a concession to comfort by possessing benches along the afterdeck and a small cabin. Petur's granddaughter, Veiga Gunnarsdottir, who speaks English, accompanies us. This is partly for our sakes and partly because Hesteyrarfjord is the place she loves best in the world.

In the beginning the water is calm with a gentle swell, giving bent reflections of sky and cloud in shining, ever-moving circles. We are surrounded by birds: puffins fly straight beside us, unmindful of the noisy motor, intent on getting their fish back to the nest burrows; razorbills and murres beat the water with their wings and run along its surface or sink to swim underwater, as we approach; fulmars soar low, caressing the swell; eiders in small flocks of parents and young, the young not ready to fly, the adults molting and unable to, swim fast away from us. Seals swim toward us inquisitively, and a porpoise arches nearby and disappears. Along the shores of the fjord the glacier-flattened mountains, all the same height, ascend dark, wrinkled and precipitous out of the pale water. Their sides are terraced and eroded, giving them the look of tiered ruffles on a skirt.

Soon we are out of the lee of the mountainous shore. A wind from the open ocean hits us and at the same time the water turns very rough. We are crossing a riptide where the North Atlantic is torn apart, its waters dividing into the two great fjords, Isafjardardjup and Jökulfirdir, Glacier Fjord, which penetrates to Drangajökull's northwestern end. The spray turns into full-sized waves breaking over the bow, and we all have to go into the cabin until we pass the bad corner of Geirsfjall, Seabirds' Mountain, where the two fjords meet. Beyond Geirsfjall is a pretty harbor, Grunnavik, Shallow Bay, with green fields coming down to the water between the mountains. There is a village with a church nestled in a corner of the hillside, all deserted.

In the lee of the hilly North Cape the wind dies down, and the waves become ripples as we enter the pleasing inlet of Hesteyrarfjord. Long ago, before the whales gave out, there was a whaling station here. A single stone chimney remains. We land at a beach of soft dark sand covered with clam and mussel shells. A field of long grass scattered with buttercups, purple geraniums and pink cuckoo-flowers slopes down to the beach. Through it flows a little singing river. There is a village of six houses. The one nearest the beach is newly painted, with a bright red roof. It was the store. The only other building in repair is Petur's house, a trim two-story cottage, ground floor and attic, beside the river. Hikers, stranded sailors or fishermen, anyone looking for a night's shelter, are invited to use these two dwellings. All over the Northwest Peninsula one can find such shelter, wherever the owner lives near enough to keep a house in shape. On the door of Petur's house is a sign in Icelandic which reads: "Welcome to all. There is enough wood and oil. Please close doors and windows and clean up when you leave." The kitchen shelves have dishes, cups, flatware and pots, also a few supplies: cocoa, tea, coffee, salt and sugar. Beside the small iron stove is a pile of driftwood. A wooden trestle table has benches built onto it. The living room is not furnished but upstairs the attic bedroom contains two spring beds with coverlets. (A spring bed is an unusual luxury in the rural districts, where the beds, as they were in Viking times, are wooden shelves fixed to the walls. Petur and his wife like their comfort.) The last comers did not observe the sign; the cups and spoons are dirty. Without complaint Veiga brings water from the outside pump to wash them while Petur makes a fire in the stove for cocoa and tea. We eat the bread and cheese we have brought from Isafjord, while they open a basket with dried fish, a bottle of milk, and murre eggs. The beautiful, pointed eggs are about three inches long, pale green irregularly spattered with dark brown. Inside they are not beautiful. They have been three-minute-boiled, and they are unattractively gelatinous. The yellow is deeper than that of a hen's egg and the yolk looks like a jellyfish. We are offered a taste but decline. They have a strong smell. Murre eggs are sold in Isafjord's grocery stores in three grades of freshness. Petur's and Veiga's eggs are grade three, very ripe. Each contains a sizable chick. That is the way they prefer them.

Petur keeps his house neat, not only for chance guests but for his wife. She spends much of the summer here in her old home. When the fishing failed them they had to move to Isafjord and she still finds it noisy and over-busy (quiet little Isafjord!). Here the only society is that of sea birds, seals and snow buntings and the only noises are the purl of the little river behind the house and the whisper of ripples on the shore and the sounds of the birds. For occupation she tends a small vegetable garden and makes ornaments out of the shells of the beach. Veiga comes to stay with her nearly every weekend, helps around the house, walks over the hills or swims from the sandy beach when the sun is out. The water is not cold, says Veiga. She is ready for university, and after her first year she will study abroad. But she will return to Iceland when she is through, and always she will go back to her grand-father's house in Hesteyrarfjord. Wherever she is she will see it in her heart.

Veiga is not alone in her love for this country of fjords and mountains. Gudmundur Sveinsson has three brothers, one a doctor in Keflavik, the other two running a cooperative in Egilsstadir in the east, who join him every July for a holiday. They spend their time out in the hills. Tomorrow Petur will take them to the tip of the North Cape, Hornbjarg, Horn Cliff. From there they will walk across the mountains to Hesteyrarfjord, where he will pick them up three days later. They will not miss this journey; they will walk whether the sun shines or the rain falls. Down in Reykjavik a busy government man, a member of the *Althing* and Director of Surtsey Research, spends every holiday with his wife and children here, walking from one deserted village to the next and camping out when necessary. We never saw the manager of the little hotel where we stayed in Isafjord because he was spending his holiday building a house on the North Cape. He and his brothers had farmed and fished in one of the more distant fjords. They had given it up and moved to Reykjavik, couldn't stand the pace there, moved back to Isafjord, found even that too exciting. Now they are raising a house in a place even more isolated than their original home.

A road leaves the village and climbs the hill beside the river. It is a well-made road, stone-lined and bedded with cement. About thirty years ago a lot of traffic passed this way. During the war the Americans had a radio station at Straumnes, Tidal Race Head, a point of land on the west side of the cape jutting north into the ocean. It is a dangerous point to approach by sea, being surrounded by submerged reefs, and the Americans built the road so they could get to their station from the calm harbor of Hesteyrarfjord. Only Arctic foxes live here now, and an occasional mink gone wild. Arctic poppies, yellow and fragile-appearing, grow between the stones, clumps of plumy boulder fern line the sides, and gnarled stems of creeping willow crack the concrete of the roadbed. Above the fields that line the shore the ground is roughly pebbled, with patches of mossy bog here and there. Around it the old gray mountains rise, seamed with rivulets. The empty electricity poles of the Americans march up through the stony wilderness, over the saddle and down the other side to the wild blue ocean on the west, where nothing remains today but an automatic lighthouse.

The *Fagranes, Fair Ness,* named for one of the Peninsula's multitudinous headlands, is the mail and supply ship that twice a week circles Isafjardardjup to keep the outlying settlements in contact with the world. The twelve-hour sailing is a good way to see the remains, hilly, watery, deeply eroded, of the Thulean Province. *Fagranes* is a small, massive ship, low in the water, made for bay travel only. Most of her is open deck space for cargo, and she is heavily loaded, with five passenger cars wedged among the bales, boxes and piles of lumber and pipes. The few passengers occupy benches around the stern or settle among the bundles on the cargo deck. It is a bright day of sun and wind-driven clouds. Feathers of mist fly over the flat-topped mountains and the calm water is streaked with silver and dark gray.

The first stop is Vigur, Spear (because it has the shape of a spearhead), a green island a mile and a half long and about a half mile at its widest, near the southern shore of the fjord. At its pointed south end, beyond a shelving beach, is a cluster of red-roofed white houses with a church spire among them. In the north the fields widen and rise to a broad wedge of grass-covered rock. The mowing has just been finished and the swathes of drying hay send their sweet smell over the water. Cattle graze in enclosed pastures near the houses. There is no dock for *Fagranes* to land, and two rowboats come from the shore. In one are two young men, in the other an old man and a child. The boats are home-made, as are the oars; all are cumbersome and hard to handle. The old man, his back bent and his face screwed with effort, loads on twenty-five or thirty concrete pipe sections which weigh his boat right down to the gunwales, while the child holds on to the side of *Fagranes*. In spite of the strain the old man laughs and jokes continuously. The two young men hand up about a dozen full milk cans and receive empties in return. At the end two bulging sacks come up. They are full of dead puffins, the product of Vigur's rocky northern end. A month earlier, we learn, the rowboats carried sacks of eiderdown from the island's many nests. Vigur, with its alternative sources of income, has evidently not suffered too badly from the dearth of fish, though the presence of the hardworking old man may indicate that at least one son has found the living softer somewhere else.

Ögur, Little Creek, the name of its river, looks like the other end of nowhere. Its three decrepit houses are uninhabited. Bleak hills devoid of vegetation rise behind it. A narrow dirt road winds down through them to its terminus at the surprising new cement dock. The road is the reason for its being. It circles two capes, then goes inland, skirting Glama, the central rocky plateau, which used to be a glacier about three times the size of Drangajökull. By 1900 it had all melted away, leaving a forbidding desert. The circuitous road is one of the two that provide access from Isafjardardjup to the south coast. (The other is even more roundabout.) It is also vital for the few farms that exist in a green stretch far in the interior, watered by rivers from the heights of Glama.

The five cars are offloaded here, hoisted from deck to wharf on metal treads hung from four ropes attached to a boom on the ship's mast. Most of the passengers debark too, to travel in the cars across to the south coast, thence by boat again over Breidafjord to Stykkisholmur on the Snæfellsnes Peninsula, from where they will drive to Reykjavik. It takes the better part of three days to get from Isafjord to the capital this way. The two-by-fours are also taken off here, along with cans of paint and sacks of cement, to be piled on two tractors. Bags of potatoes follow, a crate of butter, some automobile tires, three oil drums and eight empty milk cans. The little caravan creeps off through the dust, carrying civilization over the brown hills to an unimaginable oasis where someone is bravely building a new house.

Ædey, Eider Island, just off Isafjardardjup's north coast, is a little bigger than Vigur and is slightly more modernized, possessing a new wooden dock. It has no fields slanting easily to the water's edge, but a coastline of rock piled on itself in layers of pillows. Soil and grass cover the rock away from the shore, so Ædey's produce as well as its needs are similar to those of Vigur. One vehicle, a tractor pulling a trailer, waits at the edge of the rock while its passengers, two boys in their early teens, deliver the milk and pick up Ædey's cargo. Their load is small; either few people live on the island or it is self-sufficient. The latter is hardly possi-

ble. The only passengers to disembark are a very young woman
with two small children, all dressed up. They are probably visiting
grandparents. They all go in the tractor, which is driven off by
one of the boys. He looks too young to drive.

Bær, which means Farm, is simply what its name signifies,
one farm. It lies above a curve of gray basalt sand backed by
sloping fields. Two streams tumble through the fields on either
side of its neat houses. It rates a visit by *Fagranes* because, like
Ögur, it is at the end of a road. It is also the last stop of the bus
from Reykjavik. The road, even smaller than Ögur's, a mere
rutted track, curves around the shore to Kaldalon, Drangajökull's
young fjord, and beyond it to other farms on the coast, and
eventually joins the road from Ögur. On the south shore of the
peninsula it joins a slightly larger road which goes circuitously
in and out of fjords, finally arriving at Reykjavik. It is about a
twelve-hour trip and, with the primitiveness of Iceland buses and
the aboriginal state of her country roads, not a comfortable one.
The road begins at the top of the hill, and there the bus waits. No
one gets off the ship here. A few passengers from the bus embark
and we sail away, leaving the empty bus all alone in the middle of
the field.

Now we sail close to the shore past the inlet and glacial valley
of Kaldalon. It is severely bleak. Large black rocks brought down
by the melting ice protrude from the water. The valley is stony,
and in protected places bits of gray glacier remain. On either side
cliff walls lead straight back to Drangajökull, high and dazzling
behind.

A pair of white-tailed eagles nested here last year. These enormous raptorial birds, with a wingspread of about eight feet, prefer
the wildest of open spaces near water, salt or fresh (but not open
ocean, which is too rough for their hunting methods). They nest
on cliff faces, on the tops of rock pinnacles, occasionally on the
ground on a spit of sand and rock far out in a fjord. They feed
largely on fish, catching them on the wing at the surface, sometimes making a brief dive. They will also take birds, even ducks.
In northern Europe they have been known to catch roe-deer, and
no doubt they take lambs when, as in Iceland, the sheep graze in
places far from the tracks of man. They used to be plentiful but
they were widely hunted and the numbers decreased. Iceland was

242

the only country that still had an appreciable population. In 1913 they were put under national protection, but the numbers continued to dwindle. Now the population has sunk below the point whence it can recover: there are only ten breeding pairs left, most of them on the Northwest Peninsula, a part of the world which seems to have been made expressly for white-tailed eagles. Not only are they protected but large fines are levied for disturbing them on their nests by photographing them. With a bird as hugely obvious as an eagle the locations of the nests cannot be kept secret, but the inaccessibility of their territories precludes most hunters and photographers. They have picked a proper spot in Kaldalon, its shores guarded by cliffs, its harbor by rocks.

Beyond Kaldalon is a long stretch of rolling green farmland, rich with the minerals brought down by Drangajökull's glacial streams, and big enough to support two large farms. Horses range along the shore, cows and sheep graze back on the hills. Between the farms is a private airstrip for small planes. At the dock of Melgraseyri, Lyme Grass Banks, twenty-seven milk cans are put aboard, far more than at any other stop. This is the most prosperous spot we have seen outside of Isafjord. Among the supplies unloaded are boxes labeled "Crumble Creams" and "Chiquita Bananas," a sure sign of the affluence of Melgraseyri's farmers. There are very few of them on the peninsula. The region is the poorest in Iceland agriculturally. There is a lot of arable land, but it is here and there, up fjords surrounded by cliffs, on seacoasts backed by inaccessible mountains. Communication and trade are almost impossible over land, and farmers have not been attracted. Fishing has brought the peninsula its only real wealth.

At Reykjanes, Cape of Hot Springs, white plumes of steam rise out of the green fields surrounding a large yellow building, a boarding school. There is nothing else at all on this narrow headland. One family goes ashore, a young couple with two children. They are going to work and teach at the school. No one is there to meet them but they seem cheerful. They stand on the dock waving as we depart, in the midst of a heap of string-tied boxes and aged suitcases. It is not unusual for Iceland's schools to be in out-of-the-way places. Most of them are far off the beaten track, on lonely lakes, mountain slopes or ocean shores. Spots, it seems, are picked for beauty rather than accessibility. The great sweep of fjord, the towering glacier, the far mountainous shores, are probably considered more conducive to the discipline of education than city streets.

Around the corner from Reykjanes is an inlet named Mjoifjord, Narrow Fjord, which it is. In the center of it is an islet which from a distance appears to waver and change shape. Closer, we see that it is covered with puffins, flying, perching, parading, crawling in and out of burrows. The islet, a good spot for a puffin colony, being low to the water on all sides, consists of grass-covered rock ledges rising in shallow steps to a central ridge not more than thirty feet above sea level. Glaucous and black-backed gulls wheel slowly above it, searching and waiting, while the adult puffins fly unconcernedly back and forth and the young hide inside until the sun goes down. Sometimes they don't hide long enough. Chicks deserted by their parents will occasionally emerge, full of hungry complaint, before night has fallen. Sitting at the mouths of the burrows to exercise their feeble half-formed wings, they are plump targets. When a gull dives they can sometimes escape, launching themselves into the sea, close by on every side, not frighteningly far below as in many puffin colonies, and swim underwater long enough to confuse the pursuer.

Another pair of white-tailed eagles, or more probably the same that nested at Kaldalon last year, had a ground nest here in May, right in the middle of the puffin colony. The eaglets must have been almost too fat to fly when the time came to leave the nest.

Out in the main fjord again we start on the way back. The full circle of Isafjardardjup takes twelve hours. The sun has swung from low in the northeast to low in the northwest and the great square mountains are black above the sharp silver dazzle of the water. We go faster now. There are few stops along the south shore of the fjord, though all the little fjords invite. Some have green shores mildly sloping to the water, others have waterfalls at their heads and guardian cliffs. There is not one that frowns, that repels the sea venturer. But their harbors are empty and their houses are falling down. The ancient Thulean island, chiseled by water and ice, smoothed by time, has the loveliest coast in Iceland, and the loneliest. The sea first enticed the Norsemen here, then beckoned them to unexampled feats of exploration. Now the sea has failed them.

FOURTEEN

The Dark Years

AFTER KING HAAKON's takeover of Iceland in 1262 there came years of peace when nearly everyone was pleased by the Norwegian occupation. The fighting stopped magically. No longer were the wealthy and educated families decimated by retaliations in the endless seesaws of family feuds. The common people could go back to their farming and fishing without fear of peremptory calls to arms by their embattled chieftains. Justice was no more a matter of private killings but a subject with which a newly centralized government concerned itself, and revenge became a public crime rather than a personal prerogative. The *Althing* was made purely legislative, and acted in conjunction with the king. Two chief magistrates administered justice centrally. Each district had a royal official who embodied both executive and judicial powers. He dispensed justice locally and collected taxes, being responsible to the king's chief representative, the governor, who in turn had to act in concert with the magistrates. Final authority, of course, rested in the Norwegian crown. In the beginning the king interfered little with the running of his new territory, and aside from the strengthening of the central government, which they badly needed, the Icelanders did not suffer any severe strain from being owned instead of independent.

In time the euphoric sense of security curdled. With the chieftains' loss of power the *Althing's* importance waned. Since they were not concerned directly, everyone, from former *godi* to ex-slave tenant farmer, stopped being interested in the affairs of his country. No longer did the countrymen throng from the most distant valleys to congregate for the summer's merry two weeks of Law-Giving. The old *Althing* was dead, and so were the games, the public storytelling and singing of poetry, the exchange of knowledge and ideas, the meeting of old friends and the making of new ones. The people began to stagnate. Though they still entertained each other through the dark winters with the old stories, they were not making any new ones.

Another factor in the loss of vitality was the disproportionate strengthening of the Church. When the wealthy *godar* first began to convert to Christianity many of them, entering the Church as priests, gave up their worldly possessions to their new master, which amassed enormous tracts of land. But the Church, for the time being, remained under secular control, staying in its place as a religion and not aspiring to political power. However, increasingly in the twelfth and thirteenth centuries the Church's ties with Europe strengthened, and the bishops worked toward achieving the same kind of total authority enjoyed by their brothers over on the Continent. In 1297, thirty-five years after the Norwegian take-over, they got it. All the estates and patronage rights were put into their hands, and they quickly became the ultimate arbiters, able to wield power on the spot far beyond that of the king across the sea. By the time of the Reformation the Church owned about half of all the landed property, and the power of the bishops was nearly absolute. Most of the people had become serfs of the Church. Tithes and taxation were cruel, as many of the bishops, tyrannical and greedy, were out to extract all they could from their fat livings.

As if it were not enough that the bishops took the food out of the mouths of their flocks, the land itself began to fail. Three centuries of free grazing on the fine upland pastures had finally killed the protecting cover of birch and willow and heather. With persistent overgrazing the soil had no chance to recover, and there came drifting sand where the rich grass had grown. The deterioration of the climate exacerbated the trouble. Cattle and sheep, unable to find forage, died in large numbers over the increasingly

246

longer and colder winters. This meant not only a shortage of food but the diminution of one of Iceland's most important exports, homespun woolen cloth.

Iceland never having had much to export, and now even less, foreign trade slowed almost to a stop. With nothing to exchange for the necessary timber and iron the Icelanders could no longer keep their ships in repair or build new ones. This in turn affected the fishing, not yet an important industry but a vital source of food.

The little country badly needed whatever trade Norway could give her, and with the loss of her shipping fleet the Norwegian king could dictate his terms. He did not yet presume to exercise a trade monopoly; that was to come much later. But the Icelanders had to beg in order to get the favor of six ships a year from the mother country to bring in the fundamental necessities.

In the late thirteenth and early fourteenth centuries the trade outlook temporarily brightened. The prestigious Hanseatic League gained ascendancy over Norwegian commerce and the German merchants found a readier market for Iceland's stockfish and fish oil than for her homespun. The trade balance swung in Iceland's favor as German and later English merchants began to bypass Norway, sailing directly to the fish source. The people turned away from farming to enter the growing fishing industry, and the importance of agriculture in the economy waned. As a farming community Iceland had been more or less self-sufficient. Her new major industry made her entirely dependent on foreign demand. This was dangerous, for she had hardly any ships, and no means of controlling the course of her trade with the outside world.

Though money was once more coming into the country most of the people saw little of it. Many one-time independent farmers now worked for a master, to become part of a growing class of laborers. The new wealth was concentrated in a few hands, and the people had to endure again, as they had before the Norwegian takeover, the irresponsible greed of their rich superiors. Yet there was plenty of food and plenty of work, and no one really suffered.

But nature intervened again. The fourteenth century was a time of disastrous volcanic eruptions and earthquakes, destroying fields and killing livestock. Foodstocks became dangerously low.

247

Then a holocaust hit Europe and the trade failed. From 1348 to 1349 the Black Death killed one-third of the population of northern Europe. The busy German, Scandinavian and British ports were nearly abandoned; there was no one to man the ships.

In 1387 Margaret, wife of the king of Norway and Sweden and mother of the king of Denmark, succeeded to all three thrones under the title of Queen of Denmark, known by reluctant admirers as "The Lady King." Though the three countries were only loosely united, Denmark became the dominating force under Margaret's rule as an able despot; consequently Iceland was now a tributary state of a new, tougher country. Margaret, concentrating her energies on uniting her three blustery kingdoms, took no interest at all in her little realm across the sea except for the revenues she could collect from the brutally heavy duties she imposed. Iceland languished. Trade with Scandinavia ceased almost entirely, and the only remaining trade contact was with England. All but a few of the rich merchants lost their standing. The majority class of independent free farmers, already decimated by the fishing industry, degenerated into a cowering peasantry, oppressed by the Church, diseased, underfed, hopeless. It had taken only a little over a hundred years to reduce a nation of proud freeholders to a sorry copy of every pre-Reformation country in Europe.

The Reformation did not bring any relief. While most of Protestant Europe began to look tentatively toward the beginnings of economic development and freedom from tyranny, Iceland was still in thrall to Denmark. Regarded by her harsh mother country as a nation of wretched inferiors, Iceland represented nothing to the Danish crown but a source of income. The increase in royal power all over Europe that went with the takeover of Church lands meant to Iceland only an exchange of oppressors.

A further source of misery were the pirates of the sixteenth and seventeenth centuries, an uncontrollable menace to a defenseless country like Iceland. English, Spanish and Algerian buccaneers ravaged the unfortified seaports, pillaging, burning what they could not carry away, taking hundreds of prisoners, most of whom never got back home again from the slave markets of the Near East, on account of the lack of money for ransom.

In the sixteenth century two bishops tried to help their people against the rapacity of the Danish monarchy. Gissur Einarsson, a skilled and tactful politician, gained some concessions from the king, among them an agreement that the income from the monastic estates, now owned by the Crown, should be used for schools in Iceland. The agreement ended with the death of the bishop. Jon Arason, one of Iceland's greatest leaders and, in the old tradition, a poet besides, fought all his life to get the ancient rights of his people restored. Though beloved by the common people he was a Counter-Reformationist, arousing the ire of the strong new forces of Protestantism, and in the end he got his head cut off without trial, on orders of the king's agent.

After the Reformation the king of Denmark owned one-sixth of the landed property in Iceland. His appointees were all Danish, and nearly every penny that was collected went into the royal coffers. Looking to see what more they could squeeze out of their little tributary, the Danish kings started to freeze out the English and German merchants and restrict trade to Danes. In 1602, under Christian IV, a complete trade monopoly was achieved, establishing a relation of mother country to colony in the same unfair ratio as that of other European countries with their settlements in the Americas.

The monopoly lasted until 1787, and in all that 185 years no merchant could trade with Iceland unless he was licensed by the king. Now emerged the defects of a one-sided economy. As long as there had been abundant traffic and free competition the country had not suffered materially. But the few licensed merchants now supplying most of Iceland's needs, including a large part of her food, could charge what they liked. Imported goods were scarce and expensive, while the prices of Iceland's products stayed the same or fell, depending on the market abroad. Farm labor continued to be drawn off to the fishing grounds, where there was more money, and the state of farming was increasingly depressed. Fishing was chancy at best. It was carried on by handlines from open boats, and the loss of life was appalling. Many were the destitute widows and orphans thrown on the mercy of the community. But the community too starved if there was a failure of fish, as farm produce no longer sufficed. Add to this the exploitation by

249

the Danish merchants and the *laissez-faire* policy of the Danish crown, and by the late eighteenth century the Icelanders were in a condition of shiftless apathy very near to total despair.

In the fourteenth century had begun a progressive deterioration in the world's climate now known as the "Little Ice Age." The lowest temperatures were reached in the middle of the eighteenth century, Iceland's economic nadir, adding immeasurably to her misery. Snow fell until July, sometimes until August, shortening the grazing season and drastically reducing the hay crop. The Greenland Sea was frozen nearly all year round and the fjords were choked with ice, giving the fishermen only a few weeks in summer when they could get their boats out. Polar bears walked over from Greenland to ravage the sheep flocks. "The ice," wrote a Swedish observer, "generally comes in January and goes away in March. But sometimes it only reaches the land in April, and, remaining there a long time, does an incredible deal of mischief. It consists partly of mountains of ice which are sometimes sixty fathoms high above water, and announce their arrival by a great noise, and partly of field-ice of the depth of öne or even two fathoms. . . . The ice caused such a violent cold in 1753 and 1754 that horses and sheep dropped down dead on account of it, as well as for want of feed; horses were observed to feed upon dead cattle, and the sheep to eat of each other's wool."[1]

Further catastrophes added to the sufferings of the eighteenth century. In 1703 a census showed a population of just over 50,000 (of which eleven out of every hundred were paupers.) In 1707–9 an epidemic of smallpox killed 18,000 people. A few belated efforts by the Danish government to relieve the wretched conditions caused a rise in population to about 75,000 in 1780. Then the worst disaster in Iceland's history struck: the 1783–4 flood eruptions of Laki in the south, some of the results of which we have seen while following *Njalssaga*. When the Laki craters poured out their lava about ten million tons of sulphur dioxide were released. The heavy gas, of a pungent, suffocating odor, crept over all of Iceland, covering it with a bluish haze.[2] Grass and other plants

[1] *Letters on Iceland*, Uno von Troil, 1780

[2] This destructive gas is one of the components of the polluted air that lies over many of our cities.

withered, became brittle and turned to powder under a man's foot. Even when the grass began to come back the tainted soil poisoned it so that cattle could not graze and died of starvation in the midst of apparent plenty. A further source of affliction from the eruption was the dust fall, which contained a fluorine compound; when animals grazed the contaminated vegetation the membranes of their joints were damaged so they were unable to walk. A kind of malignant scurvy similar in its effects to leprosy attacked men on account of the lack of vegetable food. Fish deserted the polluted waters of the coastal fisheries, and fishermen could not go farther out after them because of the clouds of dust over the ocean.

Dust, gases and poisoned vegetation killed 76 percent of the horses, 77 percent of the sheep and 50 percent of the cattle. The resultant famine, known as the Haze Famine, ultimately caused the deaths of about 25,000 people. At this point Denmark had had enough of her infelicitous colony. It was proposed to take the remainder of the crushed population out of their wasted country and resettle them in Jutland, Denmark's western section. But the shattered Icelanders clung to their fjords and mountains with a remnant of pride. They preferred to starve among their own barren rocks than live on a dull flat plain on sufferance of a hated landlord.

In 1787, finally perceiving that one of the chief causes of Iceland's deterioration was the grip of the trade monopoly, the Danish government relaxed its strict rules, extending the right to trade without special franchise to all subjects of the Danish king. But it was from the Icelanders themselves that the first real moves came to ameliorate their frayed condition and start the long crawl back to self-respect and eventual freedom.

During the eighteenth century several fine men had arisen, who studied and implemented Iceland's resources and exerted some influence in her government. Skuli Magnusson, the official in charge of economic affairs, worked for reform in farming, fishing and the woolen industry. He was responsible for the building of a woolen mill in Reykjavik, subsidized by the Danish treasury. This helped to break the power of the Danish merchants. He also built a Government House on Videy, an island in Reykjavik's harbor, using a mortar of Iceland stone and lime, a portent of the future, to show

251

that his country need not depend entirely on imported building materials. Bjarni Palsson and Eggert Olafsson studied Iceland's geological formations, hoping to find resources for development of new industries. In the course of their travels they wrote a *Travel Book* which was for decades the best source of information about their country. Eggert Olafsson was a fine poet as well as an outstanding horticulturalist and naturalist but he died at the age of forty-two. Bjarni Palsson studied medicine and became the first state physician in Iceland, a doctor dedicated to improving the primitive rural medical services. Jon Eiriksson, an Icelander in the Danish treasury, was instrumental in having acts passed to improve the state of the roads, introduce agricultural reforms, institute a mail service and provide for the resettlement of abandoned farms. Magnus Stephensen, Chief Justice of the Supreme Court, aroused dormant interest in concerns of culture and intellect, founding the Society for National Enlightenment, an institution for Rationalist studies. He also obtained possession of Iceland's two printing presses and established a printing house which, as well as publishing books of educational and literary worth, brought out the first popular news magazine in Iceland.

Though the accomplishments of these men and other eighteenth-century scientists and humanists seem very small in a country which needed everything, they were vital sparks. The early nineteenth century saw Iceland with new knowledge of her spiritual and natural resources and a glimmer of hope for the restoration of her ancestral dignity. She was ready for the next step, political liberation.

National freedom was in the air all over Europe. In Iceland the movement was led by Jon Sigurdsson, 1811–1879, regarded as Iceland's modern savior, the father of his country. He was descended from Snorri Sturleson and Bishop Jon Arason, but his immediate background was humble. The son of a country parson, he grew up working on his father's farm, struggling with the twin strictures of eroded soil and primitive farming methods. He understood the burdensome trials of the farmers, and unlike his prideful progenitor his later life was dedicated to improving their lot.

252

His political program as acknowledged leader in his country's first moves toward independence was ambitious: complete restoration to the *Althing* of legislative authority and financial control, abolition of all trade restrictions, and improvement in education and public health. Total independence from Denmark was as yet too radical a concept; Jon Sigurdsson knew the limitations of his weak country.

In 1843 the *Althing* was reinstituted, but only as an advisory board. In 1848 a constitution was granted, which stipulated that Iceland was to have representatives in the Danish *Rigsdag*, Parliament. These gestures toward self-administration were disappointing but they were the edge of the wedge.

In 1854 free trade was introduced, the prelude to financial stability. In 1855 freedom of the press was granted. In 1874 King Christian IX, along with many delegates from other countries, visited Iceland for the celebration of the thousandth anniversary of the Settlement. Aside from the pomp of the occasion the king of Denmark's gift to Iceland was real: a constitution with teeth in it. The *Althing* was given legislative power conjointly with the Crown, and at last it got domestic autonomy and full control of national finances. There was still to be a Danish governor, but he was responsible to a new Minister for Icelandic Affairs, an Icelander who was to live in Copenhagen.

During the forty years of his leadership Jon Sigurdsson saw nearly everything he worked for achieved.

At the beginning of the twentieth century a more liberal Denmark became sympathetic to Iceland's long yearning for independence. In 1901 a progressive ministry effected some changes, including a Minister for Icelandic Affairs who would live in Reykjavik instead of in Copenhagen, and who would be answerable directly to the *Althing*. The Icelanders now began quarreling among themselves, some desiring a free and equal union with Denmark, others complete separation. Agreement did not come until 1918, when the Act of Union gave Iceland equal status with Denmark. The two countries were united in the person of the king, by this time no more than a figurehead, who collected salaries from both nations. They shared their coinage, the Supreme Court, the foreign office and the protection of fishing rights off Iceland's coast. In every other way Iceland was an independent sovereign state. The union was to last for twenty-five years, at the end of which time either country had the right to change it or end it.

During World War II (in which Iceland was neutral though she sympathized with the Allies) a plebiscite showed the Icelanders overwhelmingly in favor of severing these last ties. In 1944, on June 17th, the birthday of Jon Sigurdsson, the people flocked to the ancient gathering place in the rift valley of Thingvellir to hear their thousand-year-old republic formally and ceremoniously reestablished. Seven centuries of misrule and oppression ended without a shot being fired.

There is no open bitterness today. Iceland is ostensibly friendly with her cousins across the sea. But there is a deep and abiding reserve. The Icelandic language is Old Norse, the language spoken by the Scandinavian peoples before the tenth century. Though closely related to the modern Scandinavian tongues, it is not even faintly similar in sound or spelling. For centuries Iceland has had a second language. Until 1944 every child had to learn Danish in his earliest school years (now it is English), and today everyone over forty knows Danish almost as well as he knows Icelandic. Yet when my husband, who is half Danish, asks a question in the language of his mother he is answered only with a straight look. They do not frown or mutter or drop their eyes. They simply do not speak.

Iceland began her struggle back to dignity and freedom only about a hundred and fifty years ago. In that time she has jumped straight into today out of the Middle Ages. In the early nineteenth century the population was only 57,000. The roads were pony trails and there were hardly any bridges. There were no real harbors, and the coastline of cliffs, reefs and treacherous shallow sands had not a single lighthouse. Agriculture was archaic. The only handicraft was woolen manufacture, and that was for home needs alone. The houses were dark, damp and unsanitary, the fishing fleet consisted of open boats, there was no regular coastal service to those settlements made inaccessible part of every year by snow or flood, the postal service was almost nonexistent. There was only one secondary school and a theological seminary. The only city was Reykjavik, which had five hundred inhabitants.

The character of the people reflected the meanness of their lives. The pride and spirit of the early years, the quickness to anger, to love, to fight, the swift, biting humor, had given way to a mild, apathetic acceptance. Crime and vice were unknown because there was no luxury to corrupt or attract. (Only in Reykjavik, said foreign observers, was there iniquity, and that came straight from the Danes.) "Being of quiet and harmless dispositions," wrote an English traveler, "having nothing to rouse them into a state of activity, but the necessity of providing means of subsistence for the winter season; nothing to inspire emulation; no object of ambition; the Icelanders may be said merely to live . . . They are negligent with respect to the cleanliness of their persons and dwellings . . . If they give little it is because they have little to give."[3] "They are of a good honest disposition," observed another, "but they are, at the same time, so serious and sullen, that I hardly remember to have seen any one of them laugh."[4] What a dismal representation of the heirs of the sagas!

After the *Althing* got back its legislative authority in 1874, and control of finances passed into Icelandic hands, the transition to modern times went quickly. Decked fishing vessels were built, the fleet grew, and towns were established on the shores nearest the fishing grounds. The extensive herring fisheries began to be exploited and a whaling industry started. A nautical school was opened in Reykjavik. It took longer for modern techniques to penetrate to the depressed farm areas. A few agricultural schools were built and country districts founded agriculture societies. Construction started on roads and bridges. The first bank was founded in 1885. Commerce was gradually taken over by the Icelanders, aided by the organization of consumers' cooperatives, which today are Iceland's main trade outlets. By 1870 the population had increased to 70,000 but thereafter a wave of emigration to Canada, lasting until about 1900, kept it down. The sons of the footloose Vikings have never shown much inclination to move about. Out-

---

[3] *Travels in the Island of Iceland,* George Steuart MacKenzie, 1812
[4] *Letters on Iceland,* Uno von Troil, 1780

side the Greenland and Vinland attempts there has been little interest in emigration. Even at their lowest ebb the farmers cleaved to their stony fields. The Canadian outflux came when the nation was already creeping back to health. It was mainly a farmers' move. While the fishing industry was strengthened and modernized, life on the farms was still antediluvian. Young men saw escape as their only future, and youthful, growing Canada attracted them. But they did not find at once what they sought. The shores of Quebec were gentle and inviting, the broad plains of Ontario were fertile beyond their dreams. But they kept moving until they came to the bleak shores of Lake Winnipeg, in Manitoba. There they found another Iceland.

The twentieth century saw even more rapid progress. Steam trawlers and motorboats revolutionized fishing, which was further stimulated by a new bank dedicated primarily to the industry. The harbor at Reykjavik was built during the First World War. The Icelandic Steamship Company was founded in 1914 and Icelandic ships once more began to carry Icelandic cargoes. Telegraph and telephone brought Iceland into immediate touch with the rest of the world; even more important, they brought home to the isolated country people that they did not live, as they must sometimes have thought, on another planet. The coming of electricity brought new life to the farms, and agriculture at last came out of the Dark Ages. Research stations were instituted in Reykjavik and Akureyri; dairy farms and slaughterhouses were built; schemes were developed for reforestation and reclamation of eroded lands. New hospitals were built and rural medical services extended to the most isolated communities. Today Iceland is one of the healthiest countries in the world.

Education and the arts found fresh vigor. Many new schools were built and in 1911 the University of Iceland was established. The book trade grew as literature thrived again. For the first time ever, in the new, aware Iceland, painters and sculptors flourished.

The depression of the 1930s seemed particularly cruel to Iceland, hitting her just as she was emerging from centuries of exploitation and neglect. All the exciting and necessary work on roads, bridges, harbors and factories was halted, and the generation of farmers' children newly moved to the towns found themselves jobless, while their fathers at home had not enough labor to produce food for a suddenly destitute country. Commerce slowed almost to a stop, merchants went bankrupt, banks were forced into liquidation. As in other countries, public works assistance for unemployed laborers and loans to farmers brought some relief. It was not until after World War II, however, that Iceland really recovered.

In May 1940 British troops occupied Iceland. This naturally produced screams of outrage from a people so recently liberated. The British paid no attention at all. Intelligence had informed them that they were only a hop ahead of the Germans, and Iceland was too important as a mid-Atlantic base to let drop to Hitler. Its protected fjords provided excellent cover for warships, while its peninsulas stretching far out into the ocean served as landing fields for planes and watching stations for radar. Since that time Iceland has not been entirely free of foreign occupation, though it rests lightly on her. In 1941, before the entry of the United States into the war, the *Althing* came to an agreement with the Americans for the protection of the country. After the war the United States was reluctant to abandon the island as long as no peace treaty was concluded with Germany. In 1946 it was agreed to allow the continuance of troops there, though the decision led to a fierce conflict and the fall of the government. In 1951, at the height of the cold war, Iceland was considered too useful for submarine spotting to be left alone. She was persuaded to agree to the establishment of bases by NATO, to be manned mostly by Americans, for aircraft, ships and a small military detachment. The most important of these bases is the complex at Keflavik, south of Reykjavik.

The new building and the stimulus of American know-how coincided with a general postwar economic boom, and real wealth started coming into the country. Purchasing power rose enormously, as did demands for goods, and the standard of living reached a high Iceland had never known. There was money now for new projects and a glimpse into the future as the potentials began to be realized of the country's two most abundant natural resources, water and heat. Greenhouses rose in hot springs areas,

257

Reykjavik's wonderful smokeless heating system was built, a web of hotwater pipes throughout the city, a new power dam was constructed at Burfell near Hekla, hot springs ran an aluminum factory outside Reykjavik and a diatomaceous earth factory at Lake Myvatn in the north.

Constitutional changes kept pace with Iceland's emergence into the modern world. Started under Danish rule in 1874, parliamentary authority has been the accepted principle in Icelandic government. Her present constitution is based on that of the United States, though in some ways it more resembles the British. Legislative power rests jointly with the President and the *Althing*. Executive authority is vested in the President and other officials of state. Judicial authority is separate, and lies only within the courts. The President is elected for a four-year term by direct ballot, suffrage having been made universal in 1925 to everyone over twenty-one.

The *Althing* is composed of sixty members elected for terms of four years in a system of proportional representation. The President convenes the assembly; he may also dissolve it, demanding a general election which must be held within two months of the dissolution. The *Althing* is usually divided into an Upper and a Lower Chamber, the Upper having one-third of the members, elected by a proportional system from the total membership. The two chambers are equal in powers and prerogatives. The *Althing* is mainly a legislative body, but it has considerable power as it controls the budget. The general budget requires its sanction; no spending of public funds can be made without its approval; its authority is necessary to impose or alter taxes, tolls and customs, initiate state loans, dispose of public property; it must annually approve the national accounts. As in the United States the *Althing* may bring actions of impeachment against the President or any other minister.

In legislative action, bills may be brought before the assembly by the President or by any member of either chamber. They are subject to debate in both chambers, then go to the President for signature. A bill may be vetoed by him; it nevertheless becomes

258

law but must be submitted to national referendum by secret ballot. The President may issue provisional laws by himself when circumstances make this necessary at a time when the *Althing* is not in session. These laws must lie within the constitution, and only remain valid if they are approved by the *Althing* at its next session. A change in the constitution requires approval of both chambers, after which the assembly must be at once dissolved and a general election held. If the new assembly sanctions the amendment it is signed into law by the President. The Lutheran Church is the established church, and the constitution requires the government to support and protect it. Any changes in ecclesiastical organization must go through the assembly and then be submitted to national referendum.

According to the Constitution the President has no direct executive power. He chooses his prime minister who in turn selects a cabinet of ministers, the Council of State. This, while it originates all the mandates of government, is immediately answerable to the *Althing* for its acts. This divided responsibility is an excellent safeguard against the possible capriciousness of one individual set above the others. The Icelanders suffered too long from the arbitrary dictates of a king to allow any chance to creep in for undisciplined use of power. The President can in special circumstances stop the course of legal proceedings against anyone charged with offenses against the law. He can also grant free pardons and declare an amnesty. Aside from these prerogatives he is essentially one of a group, and must act in concert.

The administration of justice is entirely separate from the executive and legislative branches of government, and it is strictly protected against any chance of tampering by the others. Its offices are not elective by universal ballot. The judges are appointed by the President but their conduct is supervised by the government. No judge can be dismissed unless he has been convicted of a legal offense, nor can one be transferred to another post against his will. The courts have final authority in a case of doubt as to an executive decision. They also must decide whether any law is at variance with the constitution. Having only the law as their guide, the judges can never be influenced by the executive.

259

Local courts are presided over by the district or town magistrates, who also act as chiefs of police, except in Reykjavik whose police chief has no judicial function. A case may be appealed from the lower courts to the Supreme Court in Reykjavik, which has a bench of five judges. A number of special courts include the Maritime and Commercial Court, the Ecclesiastical Court and the High Court of State, from which there is no appeal. This is composed of the five justices of the Supreme Court, two *ex officio* members of the legal profession and eight other members elected by the United *Althing*. Its only task is to hear cases brought against ministers of the government on grounds of misconduct while in office.

There is no trial by jury. No layman has anything to do with the administration of justice either with the determination of guilt or the imposition of penalty. A judge can — sometimes must — call in specialists on technical problems, who will hear the case with him, for instance in maritime cases. In this instance the case is heard before the president of the court, who is a trained lawyer, and two maritime specialists.

Before a civil action is brought before the court it is submitted to a conciliation board which attempts to settle it by mediation between the parties. A great many unnecessary cases are thus kept out of the courts. There is no overcrowding of court calendars.

The constitutional rights of the citizens are based on the French Rights of Man: freedom of the press is guaranteed, the right to hold public meetings, freedom of association and freedom of religion. Though there is an established church everyone can do as he pleases so long as he is not immoral or disorderly about it. There can be no arrest, no confiscation of property and no entry into a dwelling without warrant. Industrial freedom, relief for the old and disabled, and the maintenance and education of destitute children are guaranteed. No privileges can be conferred of nobility, title or rank.

Among the responsibilities of the citizens, every male who can bear arms is liable to be called in his country's defense. But Iceland has no military forces.

Socially, the nation is organized with awesome efficiency. It is no longer a poor country, but nothing is left to chance. In the matter of insurance the country approaches the design of a welfare state. Social security legislation covers all types of insurance and every single citizen has a network of schemes to support him in the event of every conceivable eventuality. Health, hospital, unemployment, accident, old age, social assistance, widows' grants, children's annuities, employment disability: no possible catastrophe is overlooked. Medicine is socialized, though not yet totally. Everyone is entitled to an old age pension on reaching the age of sixty-seven, regardless of personal income or property. Family allowances are paid for all children below the age of sixteen. Every woman receives maternity grants.

The national income, from being abysmally low in the years of the trade monopoly, has risen continuously though unevenly since the economy has been transformed from one of subsistence to one of exchange. The standard of living, as a result, is among the highest in the world, and this applies not only to a few but to the total population. Wealth is spread more or less evenly, with no large underpaid labor force and no outstanding fortunes. As an index to the generally high standard, there were in 1970, per thousand inhabitants, 185 cars, 160 television sets and 330 telephones.

Housing, from being about the worst in Europe, has in two generations become the best. Because the native stone is largely unworkable and there is no native timber, the houses of the poor had to be built of sod and thatch. They were damp in summer and cold in winter, with no heat but peat-burning stoves and very little light because of the necessary smallness of the windows. In the beginning of the twentieth century many of them were replaced with timber covered with corrugated iron. Now, with the widespread use of concrete, a new age has opened for housing. The new houses are spacious and bright and many are architecturally imaginative. The few sod houses left have become picturesque museums. Practically every house in Iceland in use today has been built within the last fifty years.

A similar reconstitution is overdue with the roads. Automotive traffic is fairly new in Iceland; consequently highway and bridge construction have lagged. To be sure, they had a long way to go. At the beginning of the century there were only 150 miles of roads suitable for motor vehicular traffic. Now there are some 7,000 miles, almost all surfaced with gravel or dirt. Quantity has of necessity been produced at the expense of quality. First, roads have to be built; only later can the expense of concrete and asphalt be justified by increasing traffic.

The discomfort of road travel is offset by the convenience of plane hopping, a recent development and a sign of the country's growing affluence. The building of the airport at Keflavik made possible Iceland's entry into the modern air world and brought her totally within the European-North American community. Her overseas line, *Loftleidir*, Icelandic Airlines, is the cheapest way to cross the ocean and is popular with today's youth. Every flight is jammed with students, hikers and youth hostelers of many nationalities; though uncomfortably overcrowded it is very gay. Internally Iceland is served by *Flugfelag Islands*, Icelandair, which runs charter and regular flights by one- and two-engined planes to every corner of the island. No one is isolated any longer. The domestic planes carry not only passengers but mail and cargo, even including remotely produced agricultural products. There is also a regular air ambulance service. Iceland's new reliance on air travel is only partly a consequence of the primitive state of her roads; it reflects the fact that people have a lot of money. In a peak year more than half the total population flew from here to there within the country.

Iceland is less isolated from the world than she would like. The presence, first of British occupying troops during World War II to keep the Germans out, then, from 1951 until the present, American air and naval forces for NATO at the Keflavik air base and a few other places, is a continuing source of abrasion. It is not that anyone is virulently anti-American; on the contrary, the bias of the nation is generally pro-West in spite of strong Communist representation in the *Althing*, and the Americans are for the most part behaving. But the merest taint of occupation is vexatious to a people who have so recently sloughed off a long and painful burden of subjugation. The Americans are loath to phase out the NATO base, which is considered essential for the patrol of the ocean corridors between Scotland and Greenland. There is no other locality from which Soviet submarines can be so efficiently monitored as they navigate these narrow channels to make their forays into the Atlantic. NATO maritime aircraft also use the base at Keflavik to keep a watch on Soviet surface ships and long-range bombers. It could all be done, claim the Icelanders, from Greenland. But it would be impossible, reply the Americans, to cover this vital ground with the necessary vigilance from such a distance. Who cares, answer the Icelanders, in effect. A country with as little contact with the rest of the world as Iceland had until the twentieth century cannot be expected to exhibit much interest in the *realpolitik* of international military power maneuverings. The lack of an army and navy accentuates this indifference.

There are 3,000 Americans in Iceland, 2,000 naval personnel, 1,000 air force and two army men. Most of them are at the base at Keflavik, Bay of the Cut-off Land, an appellation that seems apt to the aliens, a barren contorted piece of land at the tip of the Reykjanes Peninsula, which looks like the bottom of the ocean, as indeed it is. A few thousand years ago the earth cracked under the sea here and the ocean floor, torn by floods of lava, heaved itself above the waves in a grotesque extrusion of twisted rock. Against this backdrop the complex of NATO barracks is incongruously painted pastel shades of pink, green and yellow and named after American battles from Bunker Hill to Coral Sea. A gigantic radar antenna that looks like attenuated modern sculpture rises at the edge of the dark ocean. The men are presumably kept content by a cinema, a theater, a field for outdoor sports, an indoor swimming pool and handball courts, with television and radio in all the living quarters.

The Americans, however, are not happy in their glossy quarters. Most of them hate the misshapen scenery with which they are surrounded. They are only allowed off base one day a week, and that is the day that all the stores in Reykjavik are closed (probably on purpose). A young American air force pilot we met lounging on the dock in Reykjavik with nothing to do claimed the Icelanders hate them, and throw things at them when they see them in uniform. There are a lot of "Commies," he said, who want them out. During the war and shortly after it, we learned later, there was bitterness against the alien culture the British and Americans brought with them, particularly the way they regarded every pretty girl as fair game. Possibly the girls didn't mind but the men were irked. This is no longer a problem, as American personnel have strict orders to maintain a very low profile off base. The leftist fringe element occasionally makes trouble but in some cases the Americans bring it on themselves. Our informant (who was in civilian clothes) said he enjoys sweeping over the sea in his fighter plane, which flies with the speed of sound, and darting down to buzz the fishing boats.

In spite of friction and leftist agitation most Icelanders are vaguely in favor of the continued existence of the base. At present they do not want to terminate their membership in NATO. They would like, however, to replace many Americans with Icelanders and have fewer personnel altogether, which, it is claimed by experts, would seriously undermine the efficiency of the base. Actually, Iceland is out of focus on the whole situation. She knows neither exactly what she wants nor why, and the various political parties are continually battling over it. The swift and unstinting assistance which American air force personnel and technicians were able to give during the Heimaey eruptions helped considerably to ameliorate the tensions. But the situation is still fluid. When the 1951 Defense Agreement with the United States, which gives NATO the use of the vital base, runs out there will be a "review or termination," which may or may not end the ambiguity.

This is one of the few sources of discord in a regime mostly harmonious despite Communist representation in government. Iceland is too wealthy and too well organized to have serious fears of social change in the near future. She steers a middle course between capitalism and socialism by means of a vast conglomerate of cooperative societies. Aside from the export of fish, fresh, frozen and dried, most of which is controlled by producers' sales associations, the cooperatives cover nearly every aspect of commerce. The societies, started near the end of the nineteenth century as a rural movement to help the farmers, have become through their organization, the Federation of Iceland Cooperative Societies, the largest single factor in Iceland's economic life. All the agricultural exports, which consist of dairy produce, mutton and other sheep products, are in their hands. Almost all retail trade in rural areas and much of that in the cities is run by cooperatives. Since World War II the Federation has branched into many other fields including manufacturing, shipping, insurance and banking.

Iceland is a healthy country physically and spiritually. The death rate is 6.9 per thousand, the lowest in Europe. The infant mortality of twenty per thousand is the lowest in the world. The crime figures are spectacular: there is less than one murder a year. There are only about one hundred law enforcement officers in the country, four-fifths of them in Reykjavik. The most numerous arrests are for drunkenness, which is the only serious national vice.[5] There is nowhere an overconcentration of population; there are no slums and no unemployment, no mine-blighted areas, no pollution. The air is as clear as morning and the water comes fresh out of the ground with the taste of a mountain spring.

Equality is not only written into the Constitution, it is born and bred. Since there is hardly any poverty, since Icelanders are homogeneous in background, since great wealth cannot be amassed under a semi-socialist regime, there are no classes. Equal dignity belongs to all and opportunity is a national fact. A fisherman can become a minister of state. A farmer can publish a book of poems or a monograph on Hymenoptera. A small and refreshing indication of the national self-esteem is that there is no tipping, anywhere, of anyone, for any service whatsoever.

[5] An attempt is being made to deal with this by allowing only 3.2% beer, which is sold in food stores, and limiting the purchase of hard liquor to government package stores, which are meagerly scattered. Hard liquor, for instance, is sold in Reykjavik and Höfn but nowhere in between, a distance of 270 miles. The next package store is at Seydisfjord, a fishing port and government center 145 miles up the coast on the east. The only ones victimized by this, however, are foreign visitors. Icelanders have all the liquor they want delivered by mail.

The quality of life is extraordinarily amiable. Iceland's leap from the Middle Ages to the 20th century might have brought, as it has elsewhere, tensions causing mental and physical breakdowns or at the very least a national restlessness. Somehow this has not happened. The sense of easy relaxation is pervasive. Nobody hurries, everybody is friendly. Strangers talk to each other on buses. You inquire the way in a strange town and you are taken on a tour of the high spots. You ask a favor and get invited to dinner. For outlanders from an unquiet world Iceland seems the last outpost of an uncluttered civilization.

FIFTEEN

A Harvest Too Prodigal

THE MAIN SOURCE of Iceland's wealth is fish. Ninety-two percent of her exports are fish and fish products, and 20 percent of the population is engaged in catching and preparing these. About 850 vessels with a total gross tonnage of 78,000 carry some 6,000 fishermen, most of them to the waters off the southwestern coast, one of the richest fisheries in the world.

It is only within the last seventy-five years that this wealth has been efficiently tapped. Before the development of the internal combustion engine the fishermen braved the Atlantic in open boats propelled by sails and oars. The usual boats, built locally of imported oak, were about thirty-five feet long with two masts, one center and one forward. They held twenty men and were rowed with long, heavy, narrow-bladed oars. The fish, caught on handlines, were strung by the gills and dragged behind the boat, a prey to sharks all the way home. The low-slung, overloaded boats offered scant protection from the heavy seas that rolled offshore even on calm days, and the mortality was grievous. The work and the danger were not over when the fishermen reached port. Even though many of the harbors were protected by cliffs the tides raced through them and on windy days waves broke over the rocky shores. Few harbors possessed beaches, and if the boats reached port safely the men still had to drag them up over the rocks out of the reach of tide and waves.

When the twentieth century brought steam trawlers and improved harbors fishing, for so long a dangerous and uncertain livelihood, came into its own as Iceland's chief means of support. Other countries too discovered the bonanza in these roiled waters, and fishing vessels came, and still come, from all over Europe, to fish with every kind of gear. The larger ships use the otter-trawl, a coarse-meshed net attached to heavy double plates of wood and iron that drag the bottom and close like doors, indiscriminately trapping everything that lives there. Smaller ones have the cone-shaped purse seines for cod that we saw being made in Isafjord. The smallest, which have no room for nets aboard, use longlines. We have seen these ashore: miles of quarter-inch line looped in fat strands around wooden posts and strung with thousands of hooks. Some carry as many as 20,000 hooks, running ten miles behind their boats. We couldn't figure out how they got baited.

The port closest to the fisheries is Heimaey, and until Helga-fell's eruption it was by far the country's most important fishing center. In addition to Heimaey's own fishing fleet, numbering eighty, from open forty-foot dories for lobster fishing to 1,000-ton trawlers for cod and pollock, there were usually even larger ships from other parts of Europe, mainly Germany, Denmark and England. Even before the eruption European ships had stopped using the port except in emergencies. A sinister change had occurred, threatening Iceland's future. The main catch had been herring, accounting for 56 percent, and most of the boats went out in summer and fall with purse seines, converting in the winter months to cod and other bottom-feeding fish. Up to the mid-1960s the catch was so massive that even the voluminous purse seines could not contain it and the fishermen had to release streams of fish as they drew in the overladen nets. With every boat, large and small, chasing them the herring had no chance. Continuous pursuit reduced the fish to the point of no return. For ten years herring no longer spawned in Icelandic waters. Though the fish are trickling back, Iceland's enormous herring industry has not recovered.

Cod is the second biggest catch and now its future too is menaced. Iceland is the last stronghold of the cod, the world's most ubiquitously useful fish. The island lies in the middle of a great mixing area, where the Gulf Stream meets the Polar Front. The confluence of cold and warm currents makes for a luxuriant upwelling of salts, phosphates and nitrates, food for diatoms, one-celled algae which are said to constitute 99 percent of ocean plant life, Light favors their growth, and during Iceland's long summer daylight they float upward and multiply enormously. At the surface they are devoured by copepods, almost invisible marine insects with rounded bodies, jointed tails and oarlike legs (which give them their name) to propel themselves in a lurching manner. Copepods are the basic animal population of the sea, food for most marine life. In spring and summer the well-fed insects reproduce in uncountable billions and are in their turn eaten by young fish of all kinds. As a result Iceland's territorial waters, particularly off the southern coast where the Gulf Stream is strongest, are a vast nursery. Sixty-six species of fish are known to propagate there.

The cod, one of the fish at the top of the predator triangle, follows its prey, herring and capelin, both plankton feeders, to this rich spawning area. The fishermen follow the cod. The latest trawlers are as efficient as vacuum cleaners, and the over-fished cod are getting smaller, averaging only six to twelve pounds. They cannot live long enough anymore to grow to the twenty-five-pound size of thirty years ago or the sixty pounds of the turn of the century. Other cod fisheries — Massachusetts, the Bering Sea, the Newfoundland Banks — are nearly fished out. Until the year 1972 Japanese, Russian and western European ships were flocking to Iceland's still healthy grounds, and the ocean-isolated country, dependent on imports for most of life's necessities, was faced with the possible extinction of the industry which earned most of her hard currency.

In September 1972, Iceland officially extended her twelve-mile fishing limit to fifty miles. The International Court of Justice at The Hague argued the legality of this and came to a decision against Iceland. The little country, which possesses no army or navy but has a thousand-year-old tradition of defending herself with spirit, ignored the decision and sent Coast Guard ships to intercept European fishing boats. These were mostly English, other countries having withdrawn their vessels in deference to Iceland's need. The English have fished in Icelandic waters for centuries, and the British government, egged on by irate fishermen, took it as a personal insult when the coast guard ships cut the lines of the fishing boats that refused to retreat when warned. The bitter fight, known as the Cod War, which went on for over a year and occasionally erupted into open violence, nearly resulted in Iceland's quitting NATO and demanding the closing of the vital air base at Keflavik. In October 1973, the dispute was settled with a two-year compromise. The English were to be allowed to send into Icelandic waters fewer and smaller vessels, and the annual catch was to be reduced by one-fifth. Iceland was not happy with the compromise and the government tottered under the onslaughts of Communist members of the *Althing*. But in the main both countries were relieved that the Cod War was ended. In 1975 Iceland again extended her fishing limits, to two hundred miles, the first European country to do so. By then, however, the drastic need for conservation in the oceans had become generally recognized, and to this date no new clashes have occurred between Iceland and her fishing neighbors.

In the summer of 1972, Heimaey's last summer before the long dispute soon to start and the holocaust already boiling up below the island's roots, the life of the fishing port had a peaceful rhythm. During the days the harbor was deserted, a quiet place given over to gulls and terns. Slim small kittiwakes, white-headed, backs and wings delicately gray, with wingtips sharply delineated in black, banked and soared with clean grace over the smooth harbor water. They looked like idealized models of birds. An outflow of waste came from a fish plant and the elegant birds converged, quarreling coarsely, to clean up the pollution and take it to their young in the ledges of Heimaklettur's lava cliff. Arctic terns skimmed over the water, now and then rising high and stopping, to hover in one place with wingbeats almost as rapid as a hummingbird's, then plummeting straight at the water for the briefest of dives, to emerge with or without a small fish in the beak. The terns ignored the garbage. They ate only live fish.

Toward evening boats started coming in to unload, and life came back with a rush to the empty quays. Trucks drove out of the factory bays and backed up to the boats while they were still tying up. Metal baskets were winched in and out of the holds and fish began to pour down chutes from deck to truck bed. There would be a pause as a nearly full truck started forward then stopped with a jerk, shaking itself so that the fish could slide toward the front and balance the load, making room for more. Other trucks brought shaved ice, which was shoveled down into the now empty holds. Such was the hurry that some of it missed, and the decks were dusted with snow. Tank trucks delivered diesel oil, grocery trucks dumped crates of food and beer on the dock, trucks from the net factory brought immense trawling nets folded and bulging over their sides. When these were offloaded the net trucks departed with the torn nets from the boats which were to be mended before their next return. If a net was not too badly ripped it was winched onto the dock, where it lay like a thick spiderweb. Three or four crewmen waded among the heavy strands, to sit on overturned boxes and crochet the rents back together, plying their broad wooden needles with swift efficiency. The nets were faded blue-green nylon with bright orange floats. The lines mooring the boats were of hemp, thick as a man's arm, and furry. They looked as if they had lain at the bottom of the sea for years.

The boats themselves were rusty and dirty, in great need of overhauling. Though the main cod-fishing season is January and February, when the fish come down from the Arctic to spawn in the warmer waters off Iceland's southwest coast, there were still plenty of fish around in June, and the fleet was busy all the time. At the end of June most of them would go into dry dock for painting and repairs. When the herring still ran this had to be done in a hurry, as the boats went out with the seine nets in the summers and were therefore in continuous use. Now the summer had unfortunately become a leisure time for many Icelandic fishermen, and the boats would become cleaner than usual.

The weather-worn boats looked useful and much-lived-in. Some had clean clothing hung out to dry on the rails, most had a dozen strings of small cod strung by the gills outside the after cabin drying in the cool ocean wind, to supplement the boring ship diet of canned foods and hard bread. On one deck there was a gutted mackerel shark, a fast, dangerous ocean killer about eight feet long. This would provide a delicacy unaccountably beloved by Icelanders, shark meat aged underground for several weeks. One seaman took a few minutes away from the organized frenzy. Scooping up a handful of dark red shark liver he left the boat and walked to the side of the dock. He sliced chunks of the liver and threw them over the water, and the beautiful kittiwakes flocked, screaming, to seize the pieces with their clean yellow beaks. He dropped some bits beside him and a bolder gull landed, then another and still another. He coaxed them closer; one ate from his hand. But then the liver was finished and he had to go back to work.

In two hours the labor was finished. The late evening sun of June threw the long shadows of the masts over the water as one by one the boats sailed out through the harbor's narrow opening for another light night and day of fishing. The last truck rumbled into the fish factory. The wives of the fishermen backed their cars around and drove their children home to supper. Silence fell again but for the harsh cries of the terns and the gulls.

The next morning the focus of activity had shifted to the fish factories. On the ground floor of the freezing plant, an immense open shed where the trucks had dumped their loads, lay the heaps of fish, still buried in snowy shaved ice. There were cod, silver and green with a pale stripe down the side; pollock, in the cod family, plump and olive-colored; ocean perch, a red-gold fish that gives birth to live young; ling, long and slender; plaice, a dark flatfish like a big flounder, about two feet long; a small pile of clawless lobsters caught, not in traps like New England lobsters but by bottom trolling from small open boats. Men with long forks separated the fish according to species and threw them on a big conveyor belt that took them upstairs. They landed first in a room with three large machines that skinned the bigger fish. The plaice went to a smaller machine with a cutting edge that had to be sharpened every two or three minutes so that it would take only the thin skin and not mangle the delicate flesh. Then the belt took the fish around the edge of the big barnlike main room, where young women and boys, wielding large knives, quickly gutted, cleaned and filleted the cod, pollock and plaice, throwing the entrails on another conveyor belt beneath the first, which carried them to the fertilizer plant, in an attached building. The ocean perch had their tails cut off, the only part of the fish considered edible. The rest of the bright, beautiful fish disappeared down the belt into the fertilizer plant. The livers of the cod went on a separate belt, to be cooked and rendered into oil, which was then stored in several large tanks down at the seawall.

The big fillets were sliced thin, cut into shorter pieces and packed in pretty blue cardboard boxes labeled "Icelandic cod" (or "pollock") and weighing five pounds each. These were piled into metal flats, fifteen packages to a flat, and taken by forklift to the freezers. There they were quick-frozen at minus 15–35 degrees F. for a few minutes, then returned to the packers, who wrapped them in transparent paper and sealed each package with a small electric hand iron. They were then put into cardboard cartons of ten packages each, stencil-labeled with the country of destination, and taken by another forklift back to the freezing room, where they would be kept until shipped out by freighter. The lobsters, also quick-frozen, were packaged in the same pretty blue cartons. (These small, tender crustaceans are the best we have ever eaten, far superior to the similar South African variety which appear to have cornered the United States lobster-tail market.)

The factory was a busy place but not a nervous one. Forklifts scooted rapidly around corners, their drivers laughing as they narrowly missed a pretty girl. Young boys slid the big fish with easy nonchalance from belt to table, girls handled their long knives with awesome efficiency. But they were relaxed. They had time to stop and chat, to go to a window and watch the quiet harbor as they sipped coffee or smoked. They were on weekly wage, not piecework as in countries where labor is not so highly organized, and this accounted in part for the lack of tension. This thoroughly unionized, semi-socialist nation would not tolerate the conditions that result from the throat-cutting competition of piecework. Part, also, was the relaxed and cheerful nature of a people who have few external pressures. Not war, nor poverty, despotism, foreign competition, pollution, nor most others of mankind's modern ills darkened their lives. Iceland, a rainy country, has a sunny people.

Most of the fish caught is frozen, but there is a good market for dried fish, known as stockfish, and about 20 percent of the cod caught in the winter months goes to the outdoor fish racks. On Heimaey they were south of Herjolfsdalur in the steep, flowered meadows where the cows and sheep grazed. The twelve-foot-high networks of weather-whitened wooden poles were hung with cleaned whole fish until April, when the sun's rays begin to be too direct. The drying fish have to be cold; as soon as the weather gets warmer flies lay eggs in them. Stockfish is a big export to countries that have little fish of their own and cannot spend much on imports. Nigeria is a market, as well as the Cameroons and other parts of West Africa. We saw a large Danish freighter in port at Heimaey that was loaded to the scuppers with fifty-kilo bales of pressed stockfish bound with enameled wire and wrapped in Hessian cloth, intended for the Cameroons: protein for at least a year. The fish is so thoroughly dehydrated that it keeps for a long time in hot climates. A slightly better, higher-priced grade goes to Italy, Yugoslavia and Greece, where it is soaked and filleted, then cooked with herbs, spices and vegetables. A variation of stockfish called hardfish is kept for home consumption. It is eaten as a delicacy, torn into narrow strips and spread with butter. Highly nutritious it undoubtedly is, but it takes more chewing than effete Americans are used to. The flavor is unassuming, faintly fishy.

Whaling is a very small part of Iceland's fish industry but in recent years it has been attracting more disapproving attention than any other of man's organized hunting. Pelagic whaling (the circulation of a factory ship among the whalers to process the catch on the spot) being prohibited by international agreement, Iceland's one whaling station is land-based. It is at the head of Hvalfjord, Whale Fjord, which we visited on our journey up the west coast to Snorri's country.

Hvalfjord is not named for the station but for the whales that used to play and blow in its calm deep waters. Seventeen species found Iceland's coastal seas to their liking, to the extent that the gentle mammals were even considered a danger. A sixteenth-century traveler noted that "There be seen near unto Iceland huge whales, like unto mountains, which overturn ships, unless they be terrified away with the sound of trumpets, or beguiled with round and empty vessels, which they delight to toss up and down."[1] The ocean then held few threats for earth's largest creatures. Boats were too small and men too few to menace its peaceable way of life. Today whales no longer sport near shore; the trumpets to frighten them off have been replaced by the sound of motors and the whine of the explosively charged harpoon. At Hvalfjord's whaling station are processed all of the four hundred whales caught yearly by Icelandic whalers in accordance with the international quotas set in a self-serving manner by the whaling nations themselves. Iceland is one of the three countries, the others being Russia and Japan, which resolutely hold out against any diminution of their annual whale catch. (Eighty percent of the whaling, it must be noted, is done by the two larger countries; Iceland's modest catch is not considered a serious threat except that as the whale population dwindles every whale killed is cause for very real alarm.)

From the 1880s to 1915 most of the whaling around Iceland was done by Norwegian ships. They were so efficient that the whales in that area almost disappeared, and in 1915 all whale-hunting was prohibited in those waters. By 1935 it was considered safe to start again. Now Iceland has four whaling boats, which range for the four summer months one or two hundred miles out at sea, catching mostly finback whales.

There is a finback whale at the station when we arrive at Hvalfjord, in fragments on the cement dock. One man saws the head into pieces about a foot wide, using a steam-driven saw. Two others slice the ivory-colored blubber with flensing knives, sharp, heavy, curved blades at the ends of sticks. As they cut each piece they pick it up with a large hook and throw it on a pile. Other men cut the pieces smaller and put them on a moving belt that conveys them to the cooking room below, where the skin is taken off and they are rendered into oil in enormous stainless steel pressure cookers. Under the blubber the meat is dark red. It is being cut into monster steaks a foot square and four or five inches thick, which go into another vat and down to the cooking room. Strong-smelling steam comes up from there through vents

[1] *Voyages and Historie of Island and Grœnland*, Dithmor Blefkens, 1563

in the floor. In a corner they are cutting up the vertebrae, which follow the meat and the blubber into the steam pots. Everywhere is blood, brains and matter. The men wear heavy boots with long sharp studs on their soles to keep them from slipping. The slaughterhouse smell is penetrating but it is not a smell of putrefaction. No one seems to mind it. Music comes over a loudspeaker. The men chat and laugh as they work, and no motion is fast. The whole leisurely process is unspeakably removed from the sense of the ocean's noblest creature, now lying all over the dock in flattened, jellylike heaps.

One tries to put the whale back together from the fragments. The back was dark gray and the belly white, for camouflage. Seen from above the back blended into the gray-blue of the Atlantic; from below it was light as the sky seen through water. The throat was folded in long undulating pleats, which permitted it to expand to take in great mouthfuls of the euphausids, copepods and swarming little fish of the zoöplankton. In spring these whales come north from their winter breeding grounds in the South Atlantic to feed on the vast multitudes of tiny animals that proliferate in the upper layers of Arctic and sub-Arctic waters in summer. They strain as much as two tons a day through the baleen fringes, the hairy-edged bone plates that hang in curtains, three hundred of them on each side of the mouth, graduating from about eight inches long at the outer edges to four feet in the center.

The brain that spills out from under the motor saw was, in life, large and fine. Whales are thought to be more intelligent than chimpanzees. They talk, in words that to us are wild as the songs of wolves. What those words mean we can never truly know. They recognize facets of their world which are outside our ken, as ours are beyond theirs. Their intelligence, recognizable as such to a human intelligence, goes in entirely different directions. We may someday fathom a small and simple part of what whales can do and say and learn, but we will never be able to perceive the subtleties.

Besides using its voice to communicate the whale, to compensate for weak vision, emits staccato sounds continually as it travels, listening for the echoes. The high-pitched clicks can be precisely aimed, and with these sound arrows the whale determines the size, motion and direction of objects in its path.

The oil that has poured out of the lungs, to be caught in big basins and processed below, was the whale's safeguard in the changing pressures of its environment. It dove deep and fast and ascended with equal swiftness, breaking the surface of the water with the speed and sound of an express train. The oil absorbed the nitrogen that would otherwise get into the bloodstream and make bubbles that would cause the disease of the bends.

Of the body's strong grace there is no longer a sign on the bloody dock. The tail fluke, which could push the whale into the air or down to the depths, as well as act as a sensitive rudder for balance, lies split near the vertebrae. The body that twisted and leaped out of the water, that could attain a speed of thirty miles an hour when pursued, the fastest of whales, that enabled the finback more than all others to turn and fight when attacked, is spread over the dock, all fifty tons and sixty feet of it, in unrecognizable piles of meat, muscle, fat and bone.

The butchery is unnecessary. Every part of the whale that is used can be replaced more plentifully, cheaply and efficiently by other products. The bones and offal are made into bone meal for chicken feed and fertilizer. A very small part of the meat is frozen for human consumption. Most of it becomes bouillon cubes and pet food. Vitamins are extracted from the liver. The baleen, in this age of freedom from corsets, is thrown away except for the small fringes, sold as souvenirs. The blubber oil, which used to be the world's lighting and cooking fuel, has little use today. Some of it is made into cooking oil, some becomes lubricating oil for fine tools.

The whale was a happy animal. It played and sang and loved. It mated for life after a long and tender courtship. It was disease free except for a few external parasites. It had no enemies but killer whales and an occasional swordfish. It was also a highly efficient animal, perfectly adapted, with all its bulk, to its varied, far-ranging ocean life.

The whaler is more efficient. His narrow, rakish boat can go faster even than the fleeing finback. From his tall mast he can recognize the spout and gauge the size of every kind of whale. His flexible gun can swivel at a touch, and implant a harpoon with an explosive head. When the struck whale tries to escape the head explodes, causing four long barbs to open out inside its body. The shot, from a pitching boat at a moving target, rarely kills at once, and the whale sounds, running with the boat sometimes for many hours, vomiting and bleeding, the barbs tearing at its flesh. It tires at last, is winched in and killed with a second shot. Then its body is pumped full of compressed air to keep it afloat, and a flagpole is driven into its upturned belly to mark it for the shore tender that circumnavigates the area to tow the carcasses back to the station. The whales that are not sighted singly or in shoals from the mast are spotted by helicopter. They have no chance. Their only hope is in man himself.

Though Iceland's second source of income is agriculture, it accounts for only 6.1 percent of her exports. (All her other industries combined bring in only 1.9 percent.) Oddly the labor figures are not too far below those of the fishing industry. About 17 percent are engaged in farming, compared with 20 percent in fishing, and in the last two centuries, while farming has declined in importance, the actual number of farmers has changed little, being today about 5,500 as against 6,000 fishermen.

Since the short summers preclude a growing season for most grains and vegetables the main outlets are dairy products and wool and other sheep products. Hay is the chief crop. A few vegetables can be grown but they are only for local consumption. Most farms have patches of turnips and potatoes. Rhubarb grows everywhere. In protected valleys there are beets, onions, radishes and other root vegetables, also a few leafy vegetables such as lettuce and cabbage. Lately hot springs have been tapped to bring heat and steam to greenhouses like the big ones that surround Hveragerdi, and the Icelanders can now supplement their diet with vegetables from warmer climates, as well as decorate their tables with fresh-cut flowers all year round.

Most of Iceland's cultivated land, which is only 1 percent of her total area (78 percent can never be productive) is under grass, and even much of this has had to be reclaimed. Near the ocean, where the majority of the farms are, there are wide areas of swamp, river delta or land once ocean which has been inundated by mud and sand in glacial bursts. Above them the talus (rock debris) which covers the slopes becomes water-saturated and creeps down in streams of stone to spread over the level land below. Rivers of lava wind broadly and impassably over the countryside. Even the friendliest of the fields are full of hummocks and rocks. One of the worst problems is a man-caused one: erosion due to deforestation and overgrazing.

Before the modernization of fishing made it Iceland's most important industry, farming was the only means of subsistence, and lands had to be cleared painfully and slowly by hand, with the help of the native strong little horses and occasionally of a team of oxen. Today a lot of this work is done by tractor and the farmers' lives are much easier than they were only fifty years ago. They are still not easy. We have seen farmers laboriously carrying squares of turf to make the *sandur* bloom. We have seen them digging out the hummocks and rocks and piling them along the edges of the fields to make walls, then leveling the fields with giant stone or iron rollers. We have seen the immense acreage of reclaimed bog along the southern coast, great green squares lined by ditches. All this land is well worth restoring. The soil has an abundance of biologically important mineral deposits from the layers of volcanic tephra blown by the wind. The boggy areas, in addition to minerals, have a rich surface layer of organic matter.

When one sees how the farmers used to live — in fact how nearly everyone lived from medieval times until well into the twentieth century — the suddenness of the leap into modern times is astonishing. The farms were the sod-walled passage houses, an example of which we have seen at Keldur while following *Njals-saga*. Though the farm at Keldur was built in the eleventh century the style lasted until the twentieth with only slight variation. At Laufas, Leafy Temple, on the green shore of Eyjafjord, Island Fjord, in the north, is a nineteenth-century passage house built not of stone but of wood and turf. The five little attached houses, their roofs all grown over with grass and field flowers, barely rise from the meadow. The earthen bricks of their walls are arranged in opposing diagonals, a pattern in warm browns. The gable ends are of white-painted wood and unlike the houses at Keldur, most of which are underground, they have very small windows, two beside each door, one above. At the roof peak of the middle house is a carved and painted wooden ornament of two figures arbitrarily attached. A small head of a woman thrust forward like a ship's figurehead is surmounted by a garland of leaves with a platform on it. On the platform sits an eider duck much larger than the figurehead, with two eggs under her breast. Figures on a rooftree were said to attract good luck to the house. Perhaps the farmer-fisherman piled his farm symbol on top of his boat symbol to gain extra portions of luck, some at sea, some on land.

At Skogar, Woodland, on the south coast, another passage house has been preserved with its furnishings intact. Skogar is a farming community in a lush valley beneath Eyjafall Glacier. The glacier has retreated, leaving a small hanging valley with a perfect semicircle of rock beneath it, down the center of which falls a heavy cascade, Skogafoss, Woodland Falls. It is evident that the cascade was originally much larger, for the stone is pitted with smooth holes where the erstwhile water ate away the softer deposits. Most of Iceland's rivers and waterfalls have beds much larger than themselves. The warming trend of the past seventy years has melted the inland ice cover to the extent that there is conspicuously less water. Though much reduced from former times, the thunder of the three-hundred-foot-high cascade sounds through the town; you can hear it even through the foot-thick walls of the half-buried passage house.

The house is smaller than the one at Laufas, having only three rooms, storeroom, kitchen, and living- and bedroom combined. There the family slept, on wooden shelves too short for any but children (and they were, still are, tall people) under heavy woolen covers woven with beautiful intricacy. The women worked in the same room at their carding and spinning. All their implements hung on the walls out of the way when not in use. For carding they used long-toothed wooden combs to sift out the long hairs. Besides the foot-operated spinning wheels they had hand spindles for both horsehair and sheep's wool. The raw wool was brushed between two big brushes of stiff lyme grass bristles until it was finely separated. Then it was drawn with the fingers of one hand onto the spindle, which, its point resting on the floor, was spun like a top with the other hand. We saw this done at

Skogar; it was a noteworthy exercise in manual dexterity. The weaving looms were in the storeroom, which also held wooden pails, churns and saddles, sacks of woven horsehair and ropes made of the roots of the lyme grass. Lyme grass, or wild wheat, which grows wild all over Iceland, was the farmer's friend. From the grain was ground coarse flour; brooms, brushes and baskets were made from the stalks, thatching from both leaves and stalks.

Through the long dark winters both men and women had time to devote to ornamenting their poor lives. Besides the beautiful weaving and knitting, which still are world-famous, they covered everything with carved designs: food bowls, bedboards, chests, tables and chairs. They told stories, sang songs and played the two-stringed *langspil*, a primitive fiddle. They used to dance, but after the Reformation dancing was forbidden by the Lutheran Church. All these activities were performed by the light of the whale-oil lamp, a stone dish with a wick twisted of swamp cotton floating in it. The children had time to play outdoors in the winter, and they had ice skates made of the shinbone of a cow.

The kitchen was small, dark and smoky. The stove was an open hearth with a grate over it. It was not attached to the chimney, which was but a hole in the roof above it. The food consisted mainly of variations of fish and milk, with occasional mutton and a few native vegetables. Most of the preparation of food was based on the premise that ten months of the year there would be nothing to eat but what had been kept over from the other two. So the menus bristled with things sour, dried, smoked and pickled. There were many ways to diversify milk. *Skyr*, their most popular dish (still popular, and delicious), was the curds, separated from the whey in wooden buckets with filters of horsehair or wool. This was preserved all winter in casks. For lack of straight sugar it was mixed with crowberries or juniper berries and eaten with heavy cream. Sour butter, another favorite, was sometimes kept for twenty years before being eaten. The older it got the more value it had; one pound of well-aged butter was worth as much as two pounds of fresh butter. While they churned the butter they poured off the buttermilk, warmed it, then added rennet (the contents of the stomach of an unweaned calf) to make it curdle.

They separated this, ate the curds and kept the whey to drink, or to boil and make into cheese. Some they kept until it became as sour as vinegar, when it was used for pickling.

Most of their fish was smoked or sun-dried, and it was eaten with butter but without salt. From shark meat was concocted a curious dish greatly esteemed by Icelanders but by no one else, called *hafkal*, sea cabbage. The flesh was smoked or pickled, then aged in the earth. Reactions of foreigners differed only in the words they used. "When it made its appearance our noses were assailed by so horrible an odor, that we were glad to have it removed as soon as possible."[2] "It looked like rusty bacon, and had so disagreeable a taste, that the small quantity we took of it, drove us from the table long before our intention."[3] They still eat *hafkal*. We had some and found that it tasted exactly like what it was: an animal long dead. An odor of ammonia hung about it. The shark, a primitive animal, has no circulatory system to carry urea and other wastes from its body. These it gets rid of through its skin as it swims. When it swims no longer the urea cannot be shed and it breaks down into its components, one of which is ammonia. The knowledge of this did not add to our enjoyment of the dish.

Fresh mutton they usually boiled, making a thick soup with cabbage, turnips and potatoes, the only vegetables they could grow. In winter they ate it dried or hung. The bones and cartilage of the sheep they boiled in sour pickling whey until they dissolved; they were left to ferment for a few months, then eaten with milk.

With the rare flour they could import expensively they made thick cakes one foot in diameter, boiled in water and whey, then dried on a hot stone. Wild vegetables besides lyme grass included *fialgras*, Icelandic moss, of which they made flour; the leaves of mountain avens and speedwell, which they made into tea; *söl*, dulse, a red seaweed which they ground into flour or boiled in milk; *hvön*, angelica, a heavy-leaved, thick-stalked flowering plant which grows on damp hillsides, of which they boiled both the leaves and the stalks.

Though they decorated their furnishings lavishly they did not extend this attractive vanity to their clothing, which was plain to

[2] *Travels in the Island of Iceland*, George Steuart MacKenzie, 1812
[3] *Letters on Iceland*, Uno von Troil, 1780

an extreme. They made their clothes from what they had: cow leather, sheepskin and wool. Wool was worn all year round, indoors and out. In particularly cold weather farmers and fishermen wore sheepskin pantaloons and coats. For wet weather they had a one-piece leather garment that covered them from the neck down to the wrists and the ankles. Under this was a heavy sweater of gray unbleached wool. On their hands were gray knitted mittens and over the head was worn a leather hood with a woolen lining. Their working shoes were made of one piece of cow leather, sheepskin or sealskin, without a heel. The skin was scraped and stretched, then cut to the size of the feet and soaked in water. The man drew these over his feet still wet, pulled them tight with a leather thong attached to the edges all around and walked around in them until they dried and hardened. They were said to be extremely comfortable but they look like cardboard boxes. The women knitted pads or embroidered bits of wool cloth to make the insides of the shoes warmer and more comfortable. These linings, which no one ever saw except the man when he put his shoes on in the morning, were brightly colored and gaily patterned. They were the only part of his clothing that was adorned.

The women's dress was equally somber, being almost entirely of black wool day in and day out. She was married in black, with the variation of a white shirtwaist of starched linen, a white silk apron and a white veil on her head. If her family was well-to-do she wore a coronet of silver over the veil, and silver filigree fastened the black bodice. Ordinary days she wore a broad scarf around her neck, tying its ends together in a bow in front, and another wool scarf on her head when she went outdoors. When she wanted to be elegant she wore a little round cap of black cloth, plaited her hair in two braids, and looped the ends under the cap. A wool or silk tassel threaded through a silver tube hung from one side of the cap down over her shoulder. The wives of wealthier farmers owned an apron of colored silk and a wide silk belt with a silver buckle; some belts were composed entirely of silver links.

Poor as were the people who lived in Skogar and Laufas, they gave freely of what they had. Hospitality was an unquestioned custom. "Geirrid . . . came out to Iceland. She had her hall built across the common travelled way, and all were [invited] to ride through it. There was always a table there with food on it, which was given to all who wished to eat."[4] The generous welcome of the saga days continued through the poorer centuries. Anyone who came by a farm hungry or tired was expected to stop. His horse was fed and watered and he was invited into the house, where he shook hands all around. Then he was asked to sit down, to talk and eat and drink, but his business was not discussed unless he volunteered it. When he left he was given something to take on his way, food or a gift.

The lives of these people, as we see, were not without grace. From a modern nostalgic viewpoint there is charm in an existence as harmoniously attuned to the earth and its seasons as that of Iceland's farmer-fishermen. Attractive as it seems from a distance, however, none of us today could stand the arduous physical labor that rarely ceased, the moldy, cramped discomfort of the houses, the poverty of the food, the unending uphill struggle just to stay alive. The Industrial Revolution passed Iceland by and her people remained peasants, a downtrodden serf class in thrall to rather than in tune with the earth, while the rest of the Western world experienced the heady new taste, brought by machinery, of leisure and freedom.

They have caught up. Though Iceland's farmers cannot be called exactly a leisure class, machinery has brought them to the same level of ease as most other people of the working classes today. Cattle and sheep form the backbone of the industry, and these grazing animals do not require a great deal of work. The fertilizing and manuring, the mowing and curing and the transport of the summer's two hay crops are all mechanized. The milking, a cooperative venture, takes place with electrical equipment in airy sterilized barns. Factories run by farmers' cooperative societies produce the butter, cheese, *skyr* and other dairy products the farmwife used to spend all summer preparing with her home-made equipment.

The dairy town of Selfoss, Cow-Shed Falls, south of Reykjavik, is the biggest center of milk production in Scandinavia. It

[4] *Eyrbyggja Saga*

lies in the valley of Floi, Marshy Fen, Iceland's richest dairy country. Floi is rolling, gentle farmland. Cows and horses lie or browse comfortably on cropped fields; sheep graze in rougher, hummocky pastures; newly cut meadows have rows of fresh haystacks. It looks as far as possible from earth's youngest country. It could be Pennsylvania. But the grass- and flower-covered humps here and there are not smooth old glacial boulders but volcanic excrescences, dark red and jagged where they are exposed. And all around the horizon beyond the wide meadows is an anarchic pattern of mountains that do not look like conventional mountains. They are stark and sharp-edged, haphazard productions of volcanic upheaval in every shape but that of a pyramid.

Selfoss, in the middle of all this, is modern, clean and plain. Its central street, broad and paved, is lined with pretty new concrete houses, and there is a large shopping area at a mall in the center. Around the edges of the town are the milk processing plants, immense flat-roofed buildings of concrete and glass. Laufas and Skogar are in another world. The cattle responsible for this prosperous and efficient setup are unbeautiful and nonpedigreed, colored black, brown, white and combinations of these. There are more than 57,000 of them in Iceland, of which 41,000 are milk cows. Though each cow consumes twenty-two to thirty-three pounds of hay each day she responds by producing 5,840 pounds of exceedingly rich milk each year. The cows are of mixed background, bred only for this outflow, which continues until they are very old. At the end they are slaughtered for food, the tough, inferior meat being useful only for ground beef and stew. Some of those in the fields around Selfoss have udders so big and swollen they are slung in nets like oversized brassieres to keep them from sweeping the ground. The cows exhibit unbounded patience though they cannot be comfortable.

The sheep stock, hardy, agile and thick-fleeced, goes back to the animals brought over during the years of the Settlement. An attempt to introduce foreign strains in the 1930s resulted in a virus disease that spread all over the country, severely decimating the flocks. That was the first and last time outside breeding was attempted. It is now against the law. The population built up again and now there are about 820,000 sheep, more than four for every Icelander, nibbling away at Iceland's dangerously depleted ground cover. Both sexes have horns, those of the rams long and curled several times back off their foreheads, the ewes' shorter but also curved and sharply pointed. Their faces are thin, like the faces of goats. Their coats are long and silky, of unlimited combinations of white, brown, black and gray. A white lamb will have a coal-black saddle; a brown one a pure white head; some are brindled all over. They are as sure-footed on rocks as chamois. Everywhere you go there are sheep. They will find the two blades of grass in a field of cindery lava. They will tread the quagmires at the ocean's edge, grazing placidly among the hunting skuas. They are to be seen on ledges beneath overhang cliffs and down in sheer-sided gorges, nosing up the weeds at the edges of cascades. They will get through the fences erected around the few remaining stands of trees, and chew off the tops of the farmer's potato crop. Every barbed wire fence seems to be made partly of sheep's wool. They are a menace. But they are important. The splendid sweaters and blankets and rugs made from their untreated, undyed wool are famous all over the world, and the export of their meat, second only to that of dairy products, is an economic necessity to a country which has so few natural resources.

Horses are no longer needed on the farms. Yet they are still raised, for local riding and for export, and about 30,000 graze along with the cattle over the best fields. From the Settlement to the tardy industrial revolution they were the country's most valued animals. The original settlers and all those who followed them used horses for every purpose: for travel, for herding cattle and sheep, for clearing and plowing and haying, for pulling heavy loads. They largely took the place of dogs and oxen. Just at the city line of Reykjavik, when you come in from the east, is a stone statue of a horse, heavy-laden and patient. He was the vital link between the farmer and the city, bringing wool, skins and butter to town and taking back wood and flour and every supply needed to sustain life.

Besides being work animals they were unquestionably man's best friend. A Viking burial usually included his faithful horse, with accoutrements as elegant as those of the owner: the bronze-mounted "chair," a collar-harness which lay over his neck, through which ran the braided leather reins; the finely carved wooden saddle with its gaily woven blanket; the iron stirrups inlaid with silver and copper. Every Icelander of whatever rank could shoe a horse. Iron was so scarce, however, that generally only the forefeet were shod, and in times of real need they used the horns of rams.

The Iceland ponies are unmixed descendants of those brought by the settlers in the ninth and tenth centuries, and they are the closest living relatives to the first domesticated horses of Europe. It is thought that their original background was Arabian and North African and that over many generations of selective breeding and survival in the northern countries they became smaller and developed heavier coats. They stand about thirteen hands and are sturdily built, with deep chests, short backs and necks, broad faces and alert small ears. Though they are not heavy-footed — their hooves are remarkably dainty for a workhorse — they are sure on every kind of rough terrain from swamp to block lava, and fearless in the face of torrents of water or shifting sands. Their color varies extremely, from bay or dun through piebald to pale chestnut with white manes and tails. A few are all white, and they give birth to black colts that turn white after a year. Their tails sweep the ground, their manes are long and thick, their forelocks hang over their eyes. They always look young, probably because, no longer having much to do, they are sleek and healthy all their lives. Their only task is to carry humans on their backs, and their riders seem to have been born on horseback. No western cowhand ever handled his horse with more ease than a farmer's son of nine or ten rounding up the sheep in a mountain col and bringing them home down over the rocks and rivers. He never rises from the saddle, his body turns with his horse, he sits to a trot, a gallop, a sudden turn or a jump as if he were part of his animal.

I rode on a farm in the north that is more than twice as big as the Grand Duchy of Luxembourg. It has to be, for it encompasses fields of lava in gigantic hardened blisters, quaking bogs with the mud bubbles of hot springs, hills of sliding gravel. The animals have to travel far to find enough to eat and they are so scattered that, riding for many miles, you hardly see a living creature. My guide was a boy of eight who rode a very young, very gay horse. He took me over roadless heath at a steady trot which usually broke into a gallop going downhill. There were no fences and no trails except sheep tracks. Sometimes we traversed scree slopes of loose pebbles, sometimes we ran across fields full of hummocks and holes and rocks, sometimes we careened down into tight little valleys with muddy streams at their bottoms. The horses were neck-trained and docile, but when you are traveling behind a small boy you do not want to be caught slowing down. Once his horse shied at a ptarmigan and threw him; he somersaulted twice, jumped up and mounted the animal, which had politely stopped when his rider fell. The ptarmigan was a mother with a flock of six round, fluffy, unfledged young. She staggered in front of us so realistically that I thought my guide's horse had stepped on her. But as soon as she was out of the way of the hooves she straightened up, corralled her chicks, and scurried under the thin ground cover where she melted invisibly into the mottled brown background. They were the only living beings we saw. It was a footloose and carefree ride. The sun was warm on our heads, the heath was lonely and limitless, the horses were unfalteringly eager. Besides the trot and the gallop they had two other gaits, the pace, which is a soothing side-to-side rack, and the *tölt*, a running walk with which these sturdy animals can cover great distances without tiring. When we got back after an hour of running they were not even breathing hard, and the breeze had dried the sweat on their thick coats.

In order to support the animals which form so large a part of her livelihood, Iceland must unceasingly reclaim land that is being wasted through overgrazing, wind erosion, floods, glacial bursts, volcanic dust. It is a continuing struggle, and still the losses exceed the gains. The worst offenders are the grazing animals. More than half the rangelands are being overused, and the sizes of the herds continue to increase. This ominous development, like the ravaging of the oceans through overfishing, has up to now been irreversible. Iceland has lost far more land through misuse than through natural causes.

There are two main areas of reclamation: fertilization and reseeding of the denuded pastures, and reforestation. Everywhere we went we saw tired meadows being rejuvenated, sand dunes held in place by new planting, fields of tephra freshly coming up green. Most striking is the planting around the base of Hekla and on Heimaey, where the thin shoots of wild rye, fescue and blue-grass are vivid against the new black ash.

All the grass seed in the world, however, cannot put back into the soil what was destroyed by wholesale deforestation. Not only is the treeless land continuously subject to erosion, the wind blowing the porous, unprotected soil from the heights into the valleys, the rains washing it down to the sea, but the composition of what remains is chemically poorer. The destruction started with the first settlers, who cut off the ground cover for fuel and let their cattle and sheep graze where they would. In winter the animals, unable to feed through the snow, ate the leaves off the trees and in spring they devoured the new shoots. In time the trees were eaten right down to the ground and lost the power to regenerate themselves.

Icelanders are used to having no trees. Though they know that their ancestors found a country densely wooded all around the coasts, from the lower mountain slopes to the ocean, their bare landscape has been familiar to them for so many centuries that the idea of forests is surprising and not necessarily beautiful. It is only recently that they have begun to realize that the cosmetic effect is the least advantage and that the health of the soil, in fact its very survival, demands a forest cover.

A forest in Iceland is not what we think of as a forest. Most of the trees hardly exceed ten feet and the woodlands look from a distance like overgrown meadows. With the exception of the rather rare native mountain ash the indigenous trees — three kinds of birch, three willows and dwarf juniper — constitute forests that are usually no more than a knee-high ground cover. But their spreading root systems are vital to hold the earth together, and their destruction has left deserts. All of Iceland's volcanoes have not devastated as much land as her deforestation by man and his animals.

Iceland belongs in the world's coniferous forest belt, and fossilized remains in the Eocene mountains of the north show that before the Pleistocene Ice Age the remainder of the Thulean Province had a forest cover similar to that of Scandinavia. The ice scrubbed the land bare, and when it retreated, leaving a newly risen Iceland innocent of flora and fauna, most of the pre-glacier species never reached it across the ocean. It is possible for better trees to grow in Iceland than grow there now. It is recorded that the settlers cut wood for building, and though the forests must have yielded but inferior timber, at least the ninth-century birches must have been more than ten feet high.

Before it was discovered that you cannot plant a tree just any-where, there were discouraging experiments with various kinds of northern trees. Typical of these was the endurance trial of the first apple tree. Planted in 1844, it lived for many years and in 1909 it finally bloomed, producing five apples. Then it died. Now the Forestry Service is planting trees which need not function so heroically. Generally it is found that the vegetation of high altitudes is similar to that of high latitudes, so seeds and seedlings are being imported from countries both mountainous and northern, which have Iceland's types of flora.

From Norway are coming Norway spruce and Scotch pine. From Alaska there are Sitka spruce, white spruce, mountain hemlock and western hemlock. From British Columbia comes lodgepole pine. From an elevation of 9,200 feet in Colorado comes Engelmann spruce, and from a 5,200-foot elevation in Oregon alpine fir. Deciduous trees include Siberian larch from Arkhangelsk, Pacific poplar from Alaska and Norwegian elm from Norway. All these trees are theoretically capable of surviving in Iceland. The experiment is very new, and it will take years to find out whether the foreign trees can attain their full growth in this land of much wind and little sun, and establish the forests Iceland so desperately needs. In the meantime the Forestry Service is rigorously encircling the native copses with fences so that the small remainder of indigenous growth will not go the way of the rest of the pre-Settlement tree cover.

These ancient woodlands show a different, softer Iceland, more like the temperate zone on the edge of which she lies. There is one in the Fnjoskadalur, Valley of the Touchwood River, in the north. We drove up the valley from Eyjafjord, where the river empties through a deep sandstone gorge. From the Settlement until the eighteenth century Fnjoskadalur was one of the two centers for the production of bog iron, an inferior ore found in marshes, which was used until the balance of trade allowed import of a better grade. One of the requisites of bog iron production is extensive birch forest, and there was a lot of that in Fnjoskadalur. Now it is a bare brown valley with the shining river visible along all its length until the road crosses the water over a high arched bridge. The Fnjoska's bed is broad and deep here, and the river is no more than a rapid trickle at the bottom of a sandy cleft. It is evident from the height of the bridge that at some seasons the little river becomes ferocious.

At the other side of the bridge is the beginning of Vaglaskogur, Beam Woods, so-called, presumably, because the trees were large enough for building timber. This is all that remains of the extensive woodlands that were cut over to produce iron. It is very small, only about three miles long and one mile wide, but when you are in it the outer world is lost. A sunny mist hangs in the net of birch leaves, still gleaming from recent rain and breathing out their sharp-sweet smell. Wild geraniums and dandelions and buttercups grow tall from a green carpet of horsetail. These primitive forerunners of tree ferns have no leaves and no flowers but a spray of jointed stalks with spore-bearing cones at some of their tips. Along with the more advanced tree ferns they covered the earth 300 million years ago, growing sixty to ninety feet tall and forming from their decayed remains great beds of cannel coal and jet. In the shadow of Vaglaskogur's small birches the horsetails' brushy heads are a dense mat no more than six to eight inches high.

Young redwings, in the family of thrushes and blackbirds, seem to fall out of the trees in alarm as we approach, barely managing to alight in low branches. Their feathers are mottled brown, their voices harsh squawks, their flight clumsy and uncertain. Their parents, sleek brown with streaked breasts and bright chestnut flanks, fly anxiously in the green canopy above and sometimes a short fluty song floats through the leaves. Redpolls, small finches, flutter through the branches as if blown by wind, with constant metallic chirping. These northern birds need deciduous forest for their seed food and their nests, of twigs, moss and feathers in the forks of branches. They have to go far to find homes in Iceland, but wherever there is a small leafy copse like this one the

291

sociable little birds congregate, never silent, never in repose. Sometimes the sweet trilling courtship song rings through the woods but mostly they just talk. Two fat snipe walk ahead of us in the path, backs striped with red and brown and black, heavy long bills pointed earthward. Aware of us, they turn with deliberate slowness into the horsetails and are gone. These birds, elsewhere very secretive, are quite tame everywhere in Iceland, probably because no one hunts them. However, it is impossible to find their nests. They walk into ground cover no higher than their backs and vanish entirely.

It is briefly hard to remember that just beyond the river, whose ripple we can hear through the wind's murmur, is the scarred earth of exhausted fields, and that a few miles away over the next range of hills is a savage desert, the most actively volcanic place in the world.

Another woodland has been saved in Fljotsdalsheidi, Heath of the River Valley, in the east, one of Iceland's most fertile valleys and, unlike most, undergrazed. Through this gracious rolling country flows the Lagarfljot, Smooth, or Orderly, Flood. In contrast to most of Iceland's short and restless rivers this one, flowing a full eighty miles from its source in Vatnajökull to the sea and collecting water from a host of tributaries out of the valley's guardian mountains on the way, is calm as a lake and as much as one and a half miles across. East Iceland is all pre-Pleistocene, like the Northwest Peninsula part of the ancient basalt flood surrounding the newer central volcanic section. Its old gray rocks protruding from the velvet of the grass are low and smoothed over by the glacier. Its mountain summits, instead of peaks, have depressions hollowed out by ice. On the east side of the long valley rises a ridge of these gouged mountains. Winter is all year round here. Pools of mud, water and old black ice alternate with fields of boulders and gravel where nothing grows. Snow lies on the ground, some grayed and porous, some fresh. Everywhere is water, running under the snow, standing in pools by the road, tumbling out of the ice. These mountain-top basins have very recently been glacier.

On the other side of the valley the land ascends in rounded terraces to heights that resemble the tundra of the high Arctic.

Up there, hidden behind layers of folded hills, is a wild and secret waterfall, Hengifoss, Hanging Falls, more romantic than most because it is almost unattainable. The way to it is a climb of about two hours, steeply up over pasture so thick with mountain avens, moss campion and cinquefoil that trying not to step on the cushions is like attempting to avoid the grass. Near the top a straight green gully leads upward. Under it flows a little river. We can see the water spurting out of rock farther up; then it disappears underground. Occasionally there is a hole in the gully and down there the stream shines and gurgles. At the end of the gully a series of sandstone escarpments bulges outward above the tremendous yellow-gray river far below. You feel the wet cold wind off the falls before you can see the water. Then around a last bluff, a last slithery traverse of mud, sand and shale, there is a great circle of horizontal red and black bands tipped upward toward the south, with the water of Hengifoss thundering down it, five hundred feet into its dark basin. Covering one side of the basin is a mushroom of old gray ice that looks as if it were left over from the Pleistocene. Around the ice a little garden of flowers grows in the brightest yellow-green moss, and above this a rainbow swells and fades as a shaft of sunlight comes and goes, piercing the cloud of spray. The place has a magical privacy. Even sheep have not been here, though their hoofmarks were with us until the last traverse.

High over the falls, where we look down on them another day, the still rising land is flat, hummocky and marshy, the source of many rivers. A snow bunting flies up before us, then flutters down with cascades of song. Golden plovers stay with us, sometimes one, sometimes a pair, calling plaintively as they fly from mound to mound. It is their land, as lonely as the Arctic.

With marshy tundra on its western heights and melting glacier on its eastern the protected valley is uncommonly lush. Looking down from these heights its green is intense and unreal, like a theater set. The shadows of clouds and patches of sunlight look painted on. A hill slope in the distance is a rectangle of darker green, soft and furry. That is the forest of Hallormstad, Town of Snake Hill (an appellation the derivation of which it is impossible to conjecture in a land of no snakes). The river runs straight as an

293

arrow down the center of the stagy fields, widening and narrowing as it goes, and gleaming silver-white, so dazzling that one can hardly look at it. It too appears motionless as a river in a backdrop.

It is obvious that there should be trees in this wide, benign valley watered and shielded by its mountain castellans. For the first time we miss them. Hallormstad's little forest, three and a half miles long by one mile wide, comes as a relief. It is densely shady, sweet-smelling and full of birdsong. Native birch and mountain ash are augmented by larch, pine and spruce. Little trails wind through it, climbing into the open over picturesque cliffs and descending into shady dells full of moss and mushrooms. Everything is small-size. Coming out of this miniature pleasure garden, the valley seems too bright and bare.

But on both sides of the river groups of girls and boys are planting future forests. Each one has a sack of spruce seedlings about twelve inches long, and a shovel. They plant rapidly, digging a hole with a single sweep of the shovel, putting in a seedling with one hand and patting the earth around it with the other. The trees are set out about four feet apart in each direction, which will make about 2,700 seedlings per acre. There is a critical flaw here: a planting all of one kind of tree is far more prone to attack by fungus, bacteria and insects than a varied planting. A further disadvantage is that even after thinning it will be a forest in rows, like cornstalks, without the attractive disarray of the natural woodland. The regular grids will form an incongruous overlay on Iceland's haphazard and untrammelled scenery. One wonders how the people will react. To look into the distance, to see the unruly sweep of mountains, the shapes of the rivers, the ice, and the shore of the ocean, this is part of the place they were born. The original forest cover was low and clung to the ground like fur. All the outlines, though blurred, were still visible. The new plantations are necessary, to overcome the damage the people themselves have done. But it will be years, maybe centuries, before they become a true part of the land they have been sent to heal.

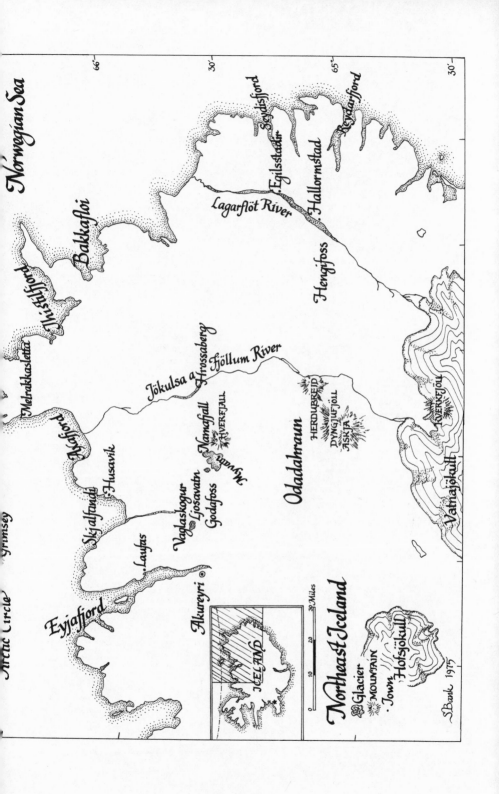

Northeast Iceland

Glacier
MOUNTAIN
Town

S.Bank 1975

Norwegian Sea

Arctic Circle

Grimsey

Eyjafjord

Melrakkaslétta

Thistilfjord

Bakkaflói

Skjalfandi

Husavik

Laufas

Vaglaskogur
Ljosavatn
Godafoss

Myvatn

Namafjall
HVERFJALL

Akureyri

Aðaldalur

Jökulsa a Fjöllum River

Hrossaberg

Odadahraun

HERDUBREID

DYNGJUFJÖLL
ASKJA

KVERKFJÖLL

Vatnajökull

Lagarflöt River

Egilsstaðir

Seydisfjord

Hallormstad

Reydarfjord

Hengifoss

ICELAND

0   10   20   30 Miles

Hofsjökull

66°

30'

65°

30'

SIXTEEN

Words and Music

FISHING AND FARMING provide the hard cash that keeps Iceland comfortable. In education, in the arts, in the life of her cities, the nation shows a spiritual vigor that reflects her physical well-being. There is a tradition of mental cultivation. When the Latin alphabet arrived along with Christianity, cultural education quickly became a prime consideration in the teaching of the young, esteemed equally with the Viking heritage of accomplishment in the manly arts. During the years of medieval feudalism Iceland was one of the few European countries — the only one in the north — where knowledge was held in esteem and where many were learned in philosophy, natural history, mathematics, astronomy and to a lesser extent divinity. They knew Latin well, so well that young men in the bishops' schools often read forbidden texts: a bishop catching a young student reading Ovid's *Ars Amatoria* struck it out of his hand in fury. But they were independent scholars. They translated everything into Icelandic and adapted Europe's learning to their own ways. Lay poetry and romance became well-known along with works of scholarly erudition, and by the thirteenth century ordinary Icelanders were reading the legends of Merlin and Arthur and the history of Charlemagne.

Even before the invention of the printing press most Icelanders knew how to read and write. Reading out loud in the long winter nights is an ancient pastime still popular today. In 1530 Jon Arason, the beloved Catholic leader who lost his head for backing the wrong side after the Reformation, brought the first printing press, making Iceland one of the earliest users in the Western world. Paper was a greater boon to the people. The printing press was mainly used in the service of Church and State. The farmers wanted more than Bibles, hymnals and the Book of Laws, and they copied out secular books on the new cheap and plentiful medium with such zealous devotion that there were as many books in manuscript as there would have been in print.

Through the centuries of misery and oppression the passion for reading and education solaced the people. Even in the terrible eighteenth century, when the only schooling for children took place in the home under the guidance of the local parson, most of the population was literate. Year after unhappy year the children learned the old stories and songs and poetry, and the generations, reminded of their brave history, kept faith in themselves.

Education in Iceland today is among the best in the world. There is no illiteracy. From the age of seven to fifteen school is compulsory. To graduate from secondary school a child must not only be able to read and write but to have proficiency in two languages and the ability to swim. (The latter is not so much a holdover from Settlement times, when physical skill and toughness were necessities, as a must in this ocean-directed country where drowning used to be a fact of life in nearly every household.) Without a degree one cannot get any but the most menial jobs, nor apply for any further training.

Twenty-seven percent of the national income goes into education, and all tuition is free. There are 206 primary schools, 113 secondary, 96 technical and special schools, five grammar schools, or gymnasiums, and the University of Iceland, with an enrollment of over 3,000. All this in a country with a population of only 210,000!

Most of the primary schools are day schools. But some parts of Iceland are still so inaccessible that school buses cannot reach them. To these remote farmsteads come traveling teachers, spending two to three weeks on different farms to teach whatever children can walk there from neighboring farms. Boarding schools are beginning to take the place of itinerant teachers. So far thirty-nine have been built in isolated areas and more are planned. These schools are organized cooperatively by several surrounding counties, and judging by the one we saw at Kirkjubærklaustur, school for these farmers' children is no hardship. It is a broad two-story building of textured concrete, with wide, shallow staircases and enormous windows. Instead of a dormitory with iron cots in rows there are little rooms, every one different, each sleeping from two to six children, with wooden shelf bunks, eiderdown comforters, bright curtains at the windows and contrasting carpeting. The cheerful contemporary decor has the warmth of a home, not an institution, yet the educational equipment is complete and absolutely up-to-date. The great windows look out on one side over Kirkjubærklaustur's little hillside forest, on the other to the magnificent ice towers of Vatnajökull.

Most Icelandic towns have secondary schools where children spend two, sometimes three years until they receive the required degree to go out to work or to continue in the more strictly academic grammar schools. In 1900 the first two boarding schools were founded, based on the idea of the Danish Folk High School movement. Now there are eight of them, providing two years of instruction with the emphasis on Icelandic studies, physical training, swimming, music and technical studies. Most of them have been built in hot spring areas so the buildings can be heated with hot water and there is outdoor swimming all year round. They have the same chaste elegance of architecture and interior design that distinguishes the primary boarding schools.

There is one at Hallormstad, a wide low building of wood, concrete and glass, built on two levels into the hillside, with the entrancing woodlet behind it, lakelike Lagarfljot before and the wild Arctic mountains rising beyond. In the schoolyard is a large stack of sawed logs from the little forest, the astonishing luxury of firewood. The living room and dining room have stone fireplaces. Carpets, curtains and upholstery are clear blues and greens to reflect the colors of forest and river. The bedrooms, singles and doubles, are comfortable, roomy and light. Nothing here is ornate; the beauty is of simplicity and good taste.

These boarding schools become hotels in summer. In a country where tourism is very new, where most people outside the cities don't know much about catering to the tastes of strangers and the usual hotel is an exceedingly simple guest-house on the main street, these lovely buildings provide welcome hostelry.

The University of Iceland occupies several large plain concrete buildings at the edge of Reykjavik. It has no campus, although around it the land is bare of houses, with nothing on it but a few plots of grass and a soccer field. Two modern white buildings alongside the older traditional gray ones house a Manuscript Institute and a Science Institute, the latter comprising research departments in physics, chemistry, mathematics and geophysics.

The University was founded in 1911, when the theological seminary, the school of medicine and the law school, all started in the middle nineteenth century, were merged into one. To these three faculties was added the faculty of philosophy, which specialized in the study of Icelandic philology, history and literature. Today the university has seven faculties, having added over the years those of economics, engineering and science. Baccalaureate, master's and doctor's degrees are conferred. It is largely a self-governing body, its management being divided between a rector and an academic council composed of the deans of the faculties, with ultimate responsibility to the minister of education as the supreme authority. A member of the students' council sits as a member of the academic council, and can speak and vote as the others do. But he may only join the meetings when the council is considering questions concerning the students of the university as a whole. A student can be expelled on the decision of the academic council if found guilty of improper behavior. But since there is nowhere else in Iceland for him to receive his higher education, and expulsion may destroy his career, he can appeal to the Supreme Court against the decision.

In the Manuscript Institute, one of the two new buildings, now repose the manuscripts of Iceland's antiquity, the original vellums of the Eddas, the sagas and the histories. During the seventeenth century Scandinavian scholars from the mainland began to take an energetic interest in Icelandic literature, so closely tied up with the history of their own ancestors. They started to collect the old manuscripts, which were scattered over the country in inadequate storage places. Iceland was in such a sad state of physical and moral depression that the precious relics were in danger of falling apart in careless hands or simply rotting away in damp unheated huts. The scholars, with the active cooperation of prominent Icelanders, began to remove them. During the period of 1650 to 1670 all of Iceland's literary treasures were transferred to Copenhagen (which was, after all, the capital of Iceland), to be stored in the vaults of King Fredrik III. When Iceland became an independent republic in 1944 the return of the manuscripts was requested. It took nearly thirty years of negotiation to persuade the Danish scholars that the historic documents, however willingly their owners had originally parted with them, belonged in their country of origin. To Iceland the possession of these treasured parchments was as much a symbol of her status as a nation worthy of her proud cultural heritage as a national treasure of incalculable value. In 1972 they began to come back, to be housed in the new building erected for them.

An integral part of this cultural heritage resides in the continued purity of the Icelandic language. The earliest Norse language was spoken in all the northern countries until the eighth century. During the Viking Age there was a break between the eastern and western segments of Scandinavia. The language of the Norwegians evolved into West Norse, that of Sweden and Denmark into East Norse. The settlers of Iceland spoke the Norwegian variant and that language, with little change, is what they speak today. Through the centuries it stayed pure and free of dialect, with no difference between the spoken and written word, because of Iceland's smallness and the mobility of her citizens. Many farmers were nomadic, moving with the grazing needs of their stock; the *Althing* brought hundreds to Thingvellir every year; in the fishing season great numbers went down to the sea; there was usually a floating population working seasonally on the farms. In addition few people left and almost none came in. Only a hundred or so Danes and a handful of Norwegians and Germans have arrived in the past several centuries, to swell the population by about one percent.

Present-day Icelandic has a larger vocabulary and different pronunciation from the old, but the spelling is the same, their alphabet containing three extra letters and lacking five of ours, and ordinary

Icelanders can read their own twelfth-century literature. The language, called Old Norse, is as near to the modern Scandinavian languages as are Middle English and Latin to modern English and Italian. It is considered a historically valuable language, having preserved more words from the Indo-Germanic period than any other language but ancient Greek. It has a lilt, like the other Scandinavian tongues, and is musical and expressive to listen to. But most Scandinavians cannot even read a Reykjavik newspaper.

The Icelanders cling to their lovely and impossible language, and resist the intrusion of foreign words. A group of purists founded in 1918 an organization called the Technical Association, nongovernmental, to repel these invaders and to invent and recommend new words to replace Latin-based or other derivatives. Many foreign words have never found their way into the language, Icelandic alternatives having been used from the beginning, such as *berklaveiki*, the barking sickness, for tuberculosis.

Despite the possession of a vivid and fluid language seemingly designed for song, Icelanders lost the spirit for literary creation after the thirteenth century, when the writing of the medieval sagas tapered off. For some six centuries no fiction of note appeared, few poets' voices were heard, no drama raised the heart of a dispirited populace. It was the middle of the nineteenth century before prose writing began to come out of the long sleep, and it was not until the present century that a few Icelandic novelists took their place among the world's great writers. The very popular Jon Thoroddsen, 1818–1868, is considered to be an Icelandic Dickens, though his novels lack the bitter social satire of Dickens' and are rather stronger on the romantic side. Unhappy as the people of Iceland were, their conditions, mostly those of rural poverty, could not approach the nadir of misery reached by England's urbanized lower classes in the polluted industrial milieu of that country; there were no excesses of cruelty, crime and exploitation, contrasted with extreme wealth, to sharpen the tongues of her writers. Romanticism prevailed until, for a short period after 1880, naturalism became popular, and romance gave way to realistic narrative, humor, some social criticism, and tragic endings.

The present century is producing extremely interesting writers, most of them, for lack of translation, not yet widely recognized outside of Iceland. An exception is Halldor Laxness, born in 1902, an *enfant terrible* whom the Icelanders half deplore, half adore. This extraordinary novelist, using a flexible, impressionistic style in revolutionary defiance of the classical orthodoxy of his contemporaries, enraged his people by exposing to the world what he considered their abominable state of rural backwardness. At the time he started publishing, in the depressed early 1930s, Iceland was a rather miserable place. Most of the new, long overdue projects designed to bring her out of her long medievalism had to stop, and she was abruptly thrust back into the mire of poverty from which she had so lately emerged. At the same time thoughts of independence were very strong, and she felt the need to impress the world, not only as Europe's first democracy but as the heir to one of Europe's oldest and brightest cultures. Along came this fiery young novelist full of rage at materialism and of pity and anger for the hopeless ignorance and wretched lives of the farmers and fishermen, the nation's mainstays. He laid bare his country's afflictions in ruthless, brutal, exciting prose, and Icelanders were horrified at what they saw as unfair exposure at a very sensitive time. In the shocked beginning most of the critics were bitterly unkind to him. Later they began to recognize his remarkable genius and, discounting his political bias, paid due homage to the impassioned blend of anger and compassion, lyricism and satire, sensitivity and coarseness, that inform all his immensely varied work. He received the Nobel Prize for Literature in 1955, and has had ten books translated into English out of his fifty or so published works, which include novels, short stories and essays. He remains a prolific writer, in his seventies still hard at work in his big white house on a lonely hill not far outside Reykjavik.

Like narrative writing, drama is a latecomer. Its origins date back to the late eighteenth century, but it was not until the 1860s that the first memorable play, *Skugga-Sveinn*, a drama of an outlaw, by Matthias Jochumsson, 1835–1920, was written and performed. Though not a great work of art it is original and genuinely, freshly Icelandic, loved and still performed today. The two greatest Icelandic playwrights were Johann Sigurjonsson, 1880–1919, and Gudmundur Kamban, 1888–1945, but both of them made their homes outside Iceland, Sigurjonsson in Copen-

301

hagen, where he wrote for the Danish theater, Kamban part of the time in the Danish capital, part in New York and other cities. Sigurjonsson, with his strong, philosophical plays such as *Galdra-Loftur*, an Icelandic "*Faust*," was the first Icelandic author to be fully recognized outside his country. Kamban, equally renowned, dealt with contemporary problems, varying from the romantic to the satiric and the tragic. With the death of Sigurjonsson and the decline of Kamban's powers drama, after its promising start, languished. But recently a National Theater has been founded, with a striking new building in the capital, and it appears that this is beginning to stimulate a new generation of dramatists.

Poetry was the only literary form to survive through the centuries, though not at all in its complex medieval forms. As the fascination with heroism, battle and death waned the poets dropped along with it their obsessive involvement with kennings, meters and internal rhymes. The one aspect retained was alliteration, which is still commonly used today. Poets continued to be revered through the dark centuries, but they were no longer the coddled scions of great houses. Instead they were, most of them, educated in the Church, and their poetry tended rather to religion than to love and war. The greatest of them, the seventeenth-century Hallgrimur Petursson, had a deep love for the common people, who suffered most through the years of poverty and depression. His secular poetry was often satirical, mocking the ostentation and pride of the rich; or merry, describing in extravagant burlesque rustic activities and tastes. His religious poetry is still loved today, particularly his *Passiusalmar, Passion Hymns*, and his beautiful meditation, *On the Uncertain Hour of Death*, which is still spoken over the dead. Poetry thrived through the Age of Enlightenment and the nineteenth-century romantic reaction, during which poets turned increasingly to the writing of hymns. Religion and patriotism joined in the second half of the nineteenth century, when Iceland began to wake up. In 1874 Matthias Jochumsson, the nineteenth-century dramatist and hymnist, wrote the national anthem, a gentle and moving prayer. The secular poetry of the time was sweet and homely, simple in language and rather over-facile in meter. Poets became somewhat bolder in the twentieth century, allowing their imaginations free rein and daring to express passion. But even the modern poetry has a rural sound to it, the easy flow of folk music, and much of it is directly concerned with Iceland's stern and stirring beauties. This is what people want. The new poets, proponents of a school known as "atom-poetry" whose chief characteristics are absence of rhyme and alliteration, and which attempts to abolish the boundaries between the conscious and the subconscious, have not found favor. Icelanders love to read poetry and to listen to it read aloud, and for them the old-fashioned lyrical, songlike style remains the best. Poetry has as yet no Halldor Laxness to shock it awake.

The visual arts are Iceland's youngest, having no backlog of tradition at all on which to draw. The beauties of nature do not appear to have attracted Icelanders in the past; there is no visual sensitivity in the old literature, except in some of the illuminated manuscripts of the thirteenth and fourteenth centuries, where the inspiration was religious and the pictorial representations have a gauche and entertaining charm. The natural scene is hardly noticed in the secular writing, with one notable exception, Gunnar's two short sentences as he looks back at the fields from which he has been exiled: "How lovely the slopes are, more lovely than they have ever seemed to me before, golden cornfields and new-mown hay. I am going back home and I will not go away."[1] This terse and moving description is unique. Most mention of nature is in connection solely with its practical connotations. "It is beautiful on Hvitarvellir," says the farmer, "when the fishing is good." Nature was fair when bountiful, ugly in most of her Icelandic guises. Volcanoes, glaciers, the lifeless desert of the interior, storms at sea, the long dark winters, all were alarming enemies. Superstition and folklore sharpened fear: the volcanoes were the mouths of hell, the ice was the home of the gods of storm, the desert was the abode of ghosts and giant-sized outlaws. In the far past men and their ponies, undismayed by their rugged countryside, had fearlessly made tracks all over the land to visit one another and to attend the *Althing*. During the Occupation and its attendant spiritual deterioration these paths were forgotten and the neglected country took on an evil aspect to its frightened and subjugated

[1] *Njalssaga*

inhabitants. No one wanted even to look at that wild and rude scenery, let alone to picture it.

Iceland stagnated artistically until the eighteenth century, when thoughts of independence began to open windows in men's minds. The French Revolution was a gale of fresh air, not only politically but in its appeal to individualism and the dignity of personal freedom. The freedom of nature, too, people began to see, was beautiful, and they looked at their land of fire and ice with new awareness. It was but a step from philosophical awareness to concrete expression. But it took a long time for the most recent of Iceland's arts to find acceptance. Artists had to go abroad to study, and even after receiving foreign commendation they met only bored inattention at home. Education had not proceeded to the point where people could see any virtue in looking at pictures of their own scenery, so recently abhorred. Gradually this changed, and by the time of Iceland's first great landscape painter, Asgrimur Jonsson, 1876–1958, appreciation had advanced to the degree that the *Althing* actually voted him a grant to study in Italy, of as much money as the salaries received by the nation's highest-paid state officials. Asgrimur, from being a painter of straight landscapes, came to be much influenced by the French painters of his time, particularly van Gogh, and his paintings changed from pure scenery to subjective impressionism.

Asgrimur and his predecessors depicted a vast, empty Iceland. Johannes Kjarval, 1885–1972, was not so much concerned with the distant mountains and the shapes of storms as he was with texture and structure close at hand. Mosses, sharded lava rocks, wind-torn grasses, form the compositions of his paintings, not only their backdrops. Into these subtly colored, intricately textured pictures he often weaves mysterious figures from legend and history, picturing in nature a shadowy re-creation of Iceland's past, and blending reality and fantasy into an imaginative whole.

Jon Stefansson, 1881–1963, worked mostly indoors, carefully, logically and slowly. His early paintings, chiefly still-life studies, nudes and portraits, are strongly reminiscent of the first great influence in his life, Cézanne. Later he too became fascinated by the scene of Iceland, presenting it, not as did Kjarval, in sculptured microcosm, but in great powerful blocks, wielding color

304

dramatically. He did not find it easy to paint, struggling for months, sometimes for years, with a single idea, on occasion to reject in the end as imperfect what he had been long working on with intense dedication. Yet in his paintings, particularly the later ones, the painful discipline is not obvious. They are immediately appealing; they look like the spontaneous creations of an unfettered mind.

Iceland was even less receptive in the nineteenth century to sculptors than to painters, and her first sculptor, Einar Jonsson, 1874–1954, turned away from any possible inspiration around him to take his themes from the late nineteenth-century penchant for romantic fantasy. He worked mostly with religious motives, creating human figures and surrounding them with small, beautiful symbols from Norse, Greek and Oriental mythology. Most of his work is in a castlelike studio-museum he built himself. The aura, both of the work and its setting, is ecstatic and mystic, far removed from the realistic expressionism of twentieth-century art.

More in tune with the times is Asmundur Sveinsson, born in 1893, who, in the late 1920s, began to change from the classical style he had been taught in Sweden to more cubist forms. In common with many Icelandic artists and writers he often chooses themes from folklore. One of his favorites, the subject of his earliest turning away from the classical, in 1927, was the story of Sæmund and the devil. Sæmund the Wise, the twelfth-century scholar who collected and inscribed the tales of the *Poetic Edda*, was considered by his contemporaries to be a practitioner of "white magic," a warlock with the good of mankind in his heart. The master, studying in the Black School in Paris, found he had no way of getting home. He called up the devil, who offered to change himself to a seal and carry Sæmund through the ocean, in return for his soul and his service for eternity. When the mountains of southern Iceland came into view Sæmund jumped off and hit the devil on the snout with his Bible. The devil sank and Sæmund swam home free. Asmundur's blend of antique form and cubic shaping in this huge group imparts an eccentric grandeur. He went on to construct grand-scale statues in concrete of the common people at their labors, a universally favorite theme of this period, the Depression years to the Second World War. Since the

305

war he has returned to history and folklore, but now his sculptures are symbolic and abstract as he seeks to draw parallels between the heroic world of legend and the fearsome stresses of the present. His studio, which he designed and built himself with very little outside help, is an extraordinary arc-shaped structure of concrete and glass. From outside it looks like an abstract Greek temple. The inside is simple and airy. From a low outcurving wall painted white the ceiling soars upward, supported by triangle beams of white concrete, to a thirty-foot incurving wall facing north, which is all of glass. Under the cold light of the sky the sculptures have a glowing exuberance. Though Asmundur has a preference for concrete, with its infinite malleability, there are numbers of smaller, more delicate forms in wood and metal. Many of his heavier sculptures stand in public places; others are artfully displayed in his large studio garden, convoluted figures of massive grace.

Icelanders love their artists. They eagerly buy contemporary paintings; they will design a living room around a Kjarval or a Jon Stefansson. The newest sculpture has its place in the garden, where it looks as vividly natural as the lava rocks that delineate the tulip bed. Art appreciation has come to be a national tradition, like total literacy.

Music in Iceland is both very new and very old. The first music, originating in Norway and the British Isles long before the birth of Christ, came with the Settlers. This Bronze Age music, of which no one knows the origin, was an unaccompanied chant, and had been used by the Vikings in singing their lays. The Iceland *skalds* and the narrators of the sagas continued the tradition, intoning their compositions in the old modes. In the early days there were no native instruments. The traveling *skalds* later brought home from Europe a stringed instrument called the *langspil* with which some of them accompanied themselves. It is a rounded hollow wooden box with a long neck and from two to six strings. The upper strings are plucked while on the lowest a pedal point is sounded with a loose horsehair bow. The poets accompanied themselves in parallel fifths in modes unfamiliar to us — not those of the medieval Church. When Christianity came the Icelanders, for the first time in close touch with Europe, started to bring their music up to date. Early in the twelfth century a French scholar was brought to Iceland to teach music at one of the new bishops' schools, and traveling Icelanders brought back liturgical styles. Then came the Occupation, the trade monopoly, the "Little Ice Age," the plagues and the volcanic holocausts. From being one of the most culturally progressive nations Iceland, sadly reduced, became about the most backward. The exposure to European liturgical music had been too short and for seven centuries music evolved almost not at all.

The comments of European voyagers to Iceland in the eighteenth and nineteenth centuries were not complimentary. "They generally sing very bad, without observing time or any other grace, particularly as they have not the least knowledge of the modern improvements in music."[2] "I do not admire the music of the Icelanders . . . They show neither genius nor taste for music."[3] These observers, had they but known it, were listening to echoes to the music of the *skalds*, the Bronze Age chants that had survived in lonely Iceland while the rest of Europe progressed to Bach and Mozart.

In the late nineteenth century, as the other arts advanced in the fresh aura of national consciousness, a few pioneers of the "new music" began to raise their voices. Their compositions, while respectably modern and even somewhat known outside Iceland, did not rise to the level of the best of the European romantics, nor did they reflect the ancient folk music. Composers, it seemed, were loath to draw on their own backlog, finding that music too strange and primitive for successful incorporation in the involved, introspective style of the times. The attitude and work of today's composers is, again, respectable but not outstanding. The musical art of the Western world has been developing for ten centuries. Iceland has been part of this world for only one. What was in other countries an unconscious birthright has been in Iceland a conscious and workmanlike development. She has come into the modern musical world with a leap, and it is too much to expect that

[2] *Letters on Iceland*, Uno von Troil, 1780
[3] *Travels in the Island of Iceland*, George Steuart MacKenzie, 1812

307

an art as deeply dependent upon its antecedents as music, in a country where there are no such antecedents, should yet have come to a true flowering.

But in teaching and performance Iceland ranks high. Choral singing is very popular, and Icelandic choirs tour the world ambitiously and successfully. There are Icelandic singers in the Royal Opera in Copenhagen. The National Symphony Orchestra, founded in 1950 and run with the cooperation of the State Radio and the National Theater on federal and city grants, is busy and always sold out. Icelandic soloists alternate with top performers from other countries. (At least one soloist from outside, the world-famous Russian pianist Vladimir Ashkenazy, found the artistic climate of Iceland so sympathetic that he married an Icelandic woman and changed his residence permanently to Reykjavik.) Though there is not yet a full-fledged opera company the National Theater puts on every year performances of opera and operetta, using mostly Icelandic artists, with a few foreign guests. A Chamber Music Club and a "Musica Nova" club provide their own specialties, and their concerts are always well attended. As with the visual arts music is warmly appreciated and supported to the hilt. It is nationalism in the very best sense.

Pursuit of the arts as lively as that of Iceland's after her centuries of stagnation requires an urban center for the exchange of ideas and for the stimulation that an artist can get only from having an audience. Until the beginning of the nineteenth century there was none. Iceland's capital was Copenhagen, 1,400 miles southeast over the ocean, and Reykjavik was a provincial port of a few hundred people. A painter or musician could study and produce in the distant capital, but until he could communicate his art to his own people he could not call himself truly an Icelandic artist. Even more difficult was the writer's situation, at work in two languages, with no defined audience. Conversely, from the experience of art by the public is built the appreciation that encourages greater dedication, higher quality and increased productiveness.

Reykjavik does not owe its position as Iceland's capital and cultural center to the fortuitous drift of Ingolf's high-seat pillars, though it is conceivable that the first settler gave them an assist, liking better the calm deep waters of inner Faxafloi than the shallow, exposed south coast of his initial landfall. Toward the end of the eighteenth century, when small industries and the fisheries began to be developed, Reykjavik's extremely favorable site in a pocket of the broad bay, easily accessible to ocean-going vessels yet not subject to the storms of the open sea, gave it an edge over other harbor villages. The little town of two hundred souls was selected as a good location for a projected industry and fishery station. On August 18, 1786, it was granted a municipal charter and designated the capital of the country. That date is regarded as the city's birthday.

Some twenty years later the capital was still not an impressive town, according to an English visitor. "Viewed from the sea the capital of Iceland seems of a mean appearance . . . The houses . . . are formed of wood, coated on the outside with a mixture of tar and red clay . . . The church, a clumsy building covered with tiles . . . is in a sad state of dilapidation, the winds and rain having access to every part of it . . . It is not much frequented on ordinary Sundays . . . In the neighborhood of the town there is a considerable number of cottages, all very mean, and inhabited for the most part by the people who work for the merchants . . . The whole population amounts to about five hundred."[4]

The nineteenth century saw very slow growth, as the prospective industrial development hardly materialized and most of Iceland's population remained firmly rural. By 1910 the capital's population had only reached 11,600. The big development has come during the past thirty years. With increased productivity in all fields during and since World War II and the continuous streaming of people away from the farms to urban centers, Reykjavik has at last become a capital worthy of the title, a bright modern city with a social and artistic life as spirited as anywhere in Europe. Today it has, together with its two suburbs, Kopavogur, Seal Bay, and Hafnarfjördur, Harbor Fjord, about 103,000 out of a total population of 210,000. It is by far Iceland's largest city. Akureyri, Meadow Banks, the second largest, has only about 10,500.

Reykjavik, Smoky Bay, is probably the cleanest capital city

[4] Ibid.

on earth. The columns of steam that gave it its name come from underground hot springs, and they provide the city with all its heat. No factories or power plants dim the air with fumes or foul the ocean with waste. The extraordinary clarity of the air is the first impression a newcomer has. Even on a foggy day Reykjavik's many-colored houses shine as clear and bright as the flowers of the fields. Everything looks new. It is as if the city had come up out of the sea, clean-washed and fully formed, only this morning.

The impression of a sea-born city is strengthened by its situation on a point of land cleft by fingers of water, inlets and small bays. The town rises among these, the red and blue and green roofs of its low houses climbing, it seems, straight out of the ocean up a central hill dominated by the white steeple of the new Lutheran Cathedral. Behind it is the barren stony countryside of recent volcanic activity, source of those practicable hot springs. Beyond that the city is widely encircled by a ring of mountains from the white cone of Snæfellsjökill on Faxafloi's northern arm, around Esja, Clay Mountain, and Kengill, Overhanging Crag, in the east, to the unkempt peaks of volcanic Reykjanes, Smoky Peninsula, the southern arm of the bay.

Reykjavik is shiningly new. The wooden shacks and leaky churches have gone. No building in the city is over two hundred years old and most of them have been built in the past fifty. With a few exceptions they are styleless; not ugly, just plain. The prosy architecture is redeemed by greenery and water. Most houses are surrounded by their own gardens, squares and small public parks are full of trees, many streets are lined with plantings of shrubs and seasonal flowers. Right in the middle of the city is a tree-bordered lake, Tjörnin, Tarn, home to ducks, geese, swans and terns, and in the eastern sector is one of Iceland's best salmon-fishing rivers, Ellidaar, Ship's Poop-Deck River (so-named for the shape of the lake from which it flows), a broad rock-filled stream that races along the walls of the new fourteen-story apartment buildings at the city's edge.

The tidiness is remarkable. Boys and girls work in the city in their summer holidays, doing mandatory outdoor labor. In the old days children went home to work on the family farms or out to sea in their fathers' fishing vessels when school was over. Now, with these activities much decreased or taken over by professionals, the government places those who are not otherwise employed in paid outdoor jobs. The youngsters we had seen in Hallormstad planting spruces were doing their summer stints. In Reykjavik they take care of the public gardens, cultivating, planting out annuals, pruning the shrubbery, cutting the grass. They also keep the streets clean. You never see a stray piece of paper blowing down a Reykjavik street. No one drops anything because from an early age they have all been conditioned to the knowledge that they are the ones who will have to pick it up.

The most attractive buildings are the oldest and the newest. The *Althingshusid*, Parliament House, erected in 1881, is a gracious two-story rectangular building with a style reminiscent more of eighteenth-century classical than Victorian gingerbread. It is one of the city's few stone buildings, most of the old ones being of corrugated iron, the newer ones of concrete. The new Lutheran Cathedral, finished in 1975, is named Hallgrimskirkja, Hallgrim's Church, for the beloved seventeenth-century poet Hallgrimur Petursson. Its tall tower of fluted concrete falls in one long graceful sweep to a broad curved front. The National Theater, completed after World War II, is a simple square building of fine proportions, its soaring interior designed after Svartifoss, Skaftafell's waterfall with its circular curtain of organ-pipe lava. Neskirkja, Peninsula Church, beside the campus of the university, constructed of white concrete in successively higher narrow rectangular blocks leading up to a stark slim steeple, looks as if it is about to take off into the sky.

A few of the old wooden buildings still stand. A charming one, on Hafnarstræti, Harbor Street, consists of twin two-story houses with peaked roofs, connected by a roofed one-story passageway, the whole painted red with white trim. Though covered now with metal for preservation, its old lines are still felicitous. A white wooden balustrade runs along its three roof peaks. On the center one is a facsimile of a Norse ninth-century ship, and iron ravens perch on the corners above it. This is the site of the initial landfall of the adventurer Floki, the first Norseman to sail into Faxafloi, guided by a raven. Today it lies well back from the water, due to landfill and harbor improvements.

311

The squares, gay with flowering annuals, are adorned by statuary, some abstract, some representational. On a wide grassy square at the top of Skolavördustiger, School Watch Steps, Reykjavik's central hill, before the new cathedral, is Leif Eriksson, presented by the United States, high on a stylized ship's prow, one foot boldly forward as if to step out onto the new land. In Austurvöllur, East Field, an old-fashioned square planted with shrubs and flowers and surrounded by nineteenth-century stone buildings, Jon Sigurdsson, father of his country, stands on a narrow pyramid thoughtfully gazing at Parliament House, the successor to the building where he led the *Althing* in its earliest claims for autonomous legislative power. The statue was done by Einar Jonsson; it is one of his few nonmystical works.

The general aspect of Reykjavik, as you walk the narrow old streets of the inner city or ride buses along the broad modern boulevards at its edges, is one of modest affluence. The private houses on the quiet lanes of Skolavördustiger and along the shores of Tjörnin, each surrounded by its walled garden, are elegant but not showy. The severely plain fourteen-story apartment buildings going up on the eastern edge are monuments to light and air, with balconies, big windows and long views over the bay to the west and the mountains to the east. The row houses that swell the southern sector, merging into the two huge suburbs of Kopavogur and Hafnarfjördur, are bright little concrete boxes with picture windows and gardens. Since that sector of Reykjavík is hilly, most of these small new houses face the wide sweep of the bay, with the low cityscape rising out of the water in the foreground and white Snæfellsnes beyond.

Thoroughly metropolitan as it is, there are still reminders that Reykjavik is the capital of a fishing and agricultural nation. From everywhere in the town you can see the masts of the fishing fleet at anchor in the harbor. In the sports stadium in the eastern sector at Laugardalur, Valley of Hot Springs, cows graze in the uncut fields around the Olympic swimming pool and the great modern stadium, and sheep nibble at the trees and vines whose branches have curled through the fence of the Botanical Garden. On a hill at the town's eastern edge is Arbær, River Farm, a group of wood and turf houses with a sod-roofed stone church in their midst, all now pre-

312

In Reykjavik's old-fashioned government plaza Jon Sigurdsson, Father
of his Country, gazes thoughtfully at Parliament House where, in the
nineteenth century, he led Iceland's fight for autonomy. The sculptor
is Einar Jonsson.

313

At the edge of Reykjavik an eighteenth-century sod house, Arbær, still stands, now a museum, reminder that less than a hundred years ago everyone lived like this. The sculpture, by Asmundur Sveinsson, represents a woman churning butter, one of the farm wife's never-ending chores.

315

served as a museum to show how Reykjavik's farmers lived not so long ago.

There is always a lot going on in Reykjavik. Since it is the only city of consequence most of the country's artistic life as well as its business and financial centers are here. Yet it is as informal as a small town. Many of its inhabitants are acquainted, and people who visit from the remotest country districts have friends and relatives here. In fact if you speak to almost anyone in Iceland about almost anyone else they are likely to know one another. Such is the homogeneity, due to the small population and the long tradition of visiting back and forth, that alphabetical listings, even in the telephone directories, are by first names. Iceland has few family names. Almost every man bears his given name and the name of his father, as do the women. A married woman does not change her name; throughout her life she is the daughter of her father, not the wife of her husband. Their sons and daughters, in turn take their father's name as their second name. Jon Vigfusson, for instance, is the son of Vigfus Gislason who was the son of Gisli Hakonarson. Jon's daughter will be Thora Jonsdottir, no matter how many times she marries. Outsiders find this confusing but Icelanders know exactly who is who. The easy familiarity makes Reykjavik a cheerful city to visit. It has become the national meeting place, as the *Althing* was in the early years, and it is a perennially busy town, its excellent hotels and beautiful shops always crowded. Busy as it is, however, there is no sense of impatience or overcrowding. Rush hour on its narrow streets is, like everywhere else, a slow time. But you don't hear automobile horns. The faces of the people waiting on the bus lines are serene. On the crowded pavements there are more smiles than scowls. No one appears to be in a hurry and almost never do you see the inward frown of worry.

With an annual inflation rate of over 40 percent, the highest in the world, there should be a lot of gloomy faces. But Jon Sigurdsson, the chief economic adviser to the Government, expresses the national viewpoint when he says, "We have always lived with inflation. People are used to it, not upset by it. They expect it. We even say we have learned to love it." This carefree assurance in the face of the uncontrollable upward spiral works down from the official government attitude to the state of mind of the people. The government tries to see to it, and mostly succeeds, that no one will suffer. Though the need is recognized for wage freezes and import restrictions, these measures are not given highest priority. First considerations are full employment and home ownership. Wages, social security payments and pensions increase automatically with the cost of living, and when this massive compensation goes sky-high the government simply imposes higher taxes. These are mostly indirect, on sales and imports, but plenty comes in from the income tax. The majority of the population is in the highest bracket, paying a rate of 50 percent — which, however, since it is estimated on last year's earnings, is far less than it seems. People uncomplainingly pay enormous prices for bread and butter and clothing and theater tickets. More books are published in Iceland per capita than anywhere else. Seven daily newspapers are published in Reykjavik. The high standard of living and the nonchalant sense of fatality about economic affairs are reflected in the aspect of Reyjavik's people. Though not one of the world's most beautiful capitals, it is probably the happiest.

SEVENTEEN

Heirs of Tomorrow

ICELAND HAS ALWAYS looked to the sea. Her great inland plateau, a wilderness of ice and barren mountains surrounding the most continuously active volcanoes in the modern world, repelled settlement. None but outlaws ever sojourned there. Little of Iceland's human history can be connected with this hostile ground. Yet it *is* Iceland. Without the central plateau there would be no rivers to irrigate the lowland pastures, no minerals to vitalize them, indeed no soil at all. All of Iceland's fertility comes from that unfriendly source.

Something else is there which Icelanders are at the bare beginnings of utilizing: natural sources of energy. One cannot harness an active volcano or subjugate a glacier. But the tremendous amounts of water, heat and steam engendered by these forces can produce enough power for an entire new industrial revolution. Iceland's wastelands have no human past. They may be the source of her human future. Agriculture has become a minor industry. Fishing is in peril. A new, vital life for the little country may come out of those terrible hills.

The active volcanic belt runs diagonally through the country northeast to southwest, from Melrakkasletta, White Fox Flats, Iceland's most northerly cape, to Reykjanes and the Westmann Islands, with a side zone in Snæfellsnes on the west and another in Oræfajökull in the south. It centers at Kverkfjöll, itself almost in Iceland's center, on the inland plateau at the inaccessible northern edge of Vatnajökull. But all along it, under ice, under water, in desert, in pastures, in towns, are volcanoes, hot springs, geysers, steaming lakes and boiling mud pots, a steady supply of potential power from the ever-restless layer of molten rock a thousand miles below the rigid crust of the earth.

This power source is already being tapped here and there along the civilized edges of the country. It is used for Reykjavik's incomparable heating system. People used to walk an hour from the city to wash their clothes at the hot spring Thvottalaugar, Laundry Basin. Anyone lucky enough to have a geothermal area in the backyard baked the bread there, burying the loaves in the hot ground for a day or two. Reykjavik itself, coal-heated, lived under a pall of black smoke. In the 1920s it finally occurred to someone that underground hot water could be brought to the people instead of the people going to it. In 1928 the first bore hole was drilled at Thvottalaugar and hot water was piped two miles to heat the town's new swimming pool, a hospital, two schools and seventy dwellings. This thermal area was not very large, and in the middle 1930s a more generous source was discovered at Reykir, Hot Spring, eleven miles out of town. Then in the 1940s exploration drilling and geophysical observations and measurements discovered thermal areas right in the city. Today there are thirty-two bore holes within the city limits and nine at Reykir, supplying 99 percent of the residents with hot water heat. Some of these go over a mile down, the deepest being 7,200 feet. The water thus tapped is as hot as 275° F. and is kept under high pressure by pumps inserted into the wells, so that it will not boil in the pipes. The wells are not inexhaustible, and the system is so new that no one can say how long it will last. But there is such a vast reservoir under the entire area that if one well runs dry it is believed that one only has to go a little deeper to find a new water-laden layer to keep the city warm into the indefinite future.

Even after it has circulated, the water is still hot enough for household purposes. Not only does it run a lot of washing machines but it supplies this wintry town with private outdoor swimming pools worthy of a Florida resort. Anyone who has the skill and the patience can put up a greenhouse in his garden and grow his own bananas. The water, coming from deep underground where no impure air can reach it, is free of bacteria. This is also true of Reykjavik's cold water. No filters are needed, no chlorines or other purifiers must be added. There is not a taint of sulphur or any other chemical and the water is very soft. Here, out in the grimy world, we have forgotten how fresh water tastes. Iceland's water is an elixir, the very spirit of water.

Hot springs are beginning to be harnessed for another use in Reykjanes down in Iceland's southwest corner. Past the entrance to the busy Keflavik airport the land is immediately lonely, a for-lorn region of crooked hills, black sand and fractured lava bubbles. In the middle of this distorted landscape is a row of smooth red and yellow knolls, and from them comes an unimaginable high whining roar so loud that a quarter of a mile away one has to stop talking. Uneven puffs of white steam rise between the hillocks, and ponds of standing water are a strange muddy light blue. A vile chemical smell hangs in the air, compounded of sulphur and fluoride and other volcanically produced gases. In this nether-worldly hot spring zone an immense pipe has been laid, and it is from this that the steady bellow comes. Water is surging out of it in a fast yellow flood. There is no building here, not even a shed. We learned later that a factory is planned but that the plans have been temporarily shelved. The area is prone to earthquakes, and if a factory were to be built around this pipe it might happen that tomorrow there would be an earth disturbance and the hot springs would be coming up somewhere else — to say nothing of the fate of the factory building. Until they decide what to do, millions of gallons of potential horsepower are importantly bursting out of the earth in a setting of unapproachable lonesomeness. Around them the land is hugely wrinkled from previous earthquakes and beyond their colored hills lava twists away in smooth coils down to a dark beach. There is fog over the ocean and through it a flock of birds veers back and forth over the water showing now black, now white sharp through the mist. They are Manx shear-waters, so-named because they fly so low that their wings seem to cut the waves, coming to nest on this untenanted shore, their northernmost breeding place, from their home on the open sea.

No other living thing is there. Yet someday, surely, this will be a new city.

Iceland's glacier-born rivers race too fast down her mountains and over her coastal cliffs and gravelly plains to be anywhere navigable. Since the Settlement they have been tapped for irrigation, but it is only in the last forty years that any attempt has been made to use their tremendous power. Today Iceland is the seventh country in the world in consumption of electricity per capita. Nearly every farm has electricity, many of them manufacturing their own power from their own speedy little glacial streams. The newest and most spectacular power plant is at Burfell, Bower Mountain, in the valley of the Floi, Marshy Fen, just north of Mount Hekla. Through the Floi winds the broad yellow-gray Thjorsa, Ship's Beak River, Iceland's longest and biggest in volume. It flows 147 miles from its source in Hofjökull, Temple Glacier, a tributary of Vatnajökull, now separated by land as the ice cap has shrunk.

North of the mountain Burfell the Thjorsa is mightily primitive, thundering through gorges, sluicing over the plains, opaque and dangerous. Below the mountain the river's power is 1,265 feet per second, and here is where the dam and the plant have been built. A tunnel through Burfell channels part of the torrent into the dam and through the plant, where the now-tamed water produces 210,000 kilowatts. The rest of the river above Burfell is diverted around the mountain into a lake to catch the ice that is carried down from Hofjökull in the spring break-up, before it can obstruct the tunnel and clog the machinery of the plant. A hundred and ten thousand kilowatts supply Reykjavik's new aluminum smelter, built in 1969 on the road to Keflavik, which produces 60,000 tons of aluminum a year. The remaining 100,000 kilowatts are for other factories and for farmers in the neighborhood.

The power plant was officially opened by Kristjan Eldjarn, Iceland's third President, on May 2, 1970. In a ceremony of pomp and splendor he pushed the button to open the dam and start the machinery. Three days later came the earthquake that heralded Hekla's latest eruption. It was not a major one, and the flow came nowhere near the dam, so the Icelanders laughed. President Eldjarn had pushed Hekla's button, they said. Behind the humor is unease. It is poetic but conceivable that in taming the river man had loosed a force of anger deep within the earth.

Undismayed, Iceland is building two more, even bigger power plants within Hekla's orbit. One, twenty-five miles northeast of Burfell, will harness a massive cascade at Hrauneyjarfoss, Waterfall in the Lava Field. The other will be nearby in the lava stream Sigalda, Sand Wave, residue of a prehistoric eruption of Hekla. If a way is ever found to package electricity and send it around the world to needy areas, little Iceland will find herself a very consequential country.

No roads lead to Kverkfjöll, The Throat, the volcano under Vatnajökull's ice, center of the volcanic plume on which Iceland uneasily rests. This hot spot seethes and bubbles continuously under its cover of ice, sending reflections of its earth tremors all along the country's volcanic belt and as far as 1,000 miles south through the ocean along the Mid-Atlantic Ridge. Thirty miles north of the hidden volcano is the *caldera* of Askja, Box of Ashes, an active volcano in the depths of the fearsome waste of the Odadahraun, Burnt Land of Evil Men, Iceland's central desert plateau. And thirty-seven miles north of Askja, still within the boundaries of the Odadahraun, are the farms of Myvatn, Midge Lake, Iceland's only settlement on the barren interior tablelands.

The forces of vulcanism are very near the surface at Myvatn. The large shallow lake, fourteen square miles and nowhere over nine feet deep, lies in a valley between rows of fissure craters and fields of lava bubbles. To its northeast, beyond a bare yellow mountain, are columns of steam. On the southeast side of the lake is a field of block lava, elongated, distorted shapes rising out of the flat ground like the warriors that sprang up when Cadmus sowed the dragon's teeth. On the west and north shores the little explosion craters pop up every few yards, miniature volcanoes about ten feet high, and hollow. Some are perfect cones, others have caved in and look like ruined bunkers from an old war. Birds fly in and out of them. Following a pair of dunlins I climb one of the low peaks and descend into its chimney. Inside is a surprising garden, an artistic arrangement of ferns, birches and moss around

323

gnarled rocks. The craters, called spatter cones, are products of a series of earthquakes and fissure eruptions two and a half centuries ago in the regions of Blafjall, The Raven, and Leirhnuk, Clay Peak, hills on either side of the lake. As the magma rose, the earth's pressure on it decreased and it suddenly boiled over all along the weak fissure lines. Bubbles of hot rock exploded out of the ground, hardening into rows of cones about the same distance apart and all the same size. The disturbances lasted for five years, from 1724 to 1729, and destroyed everything around the lake except for a small church at Reykjahlid, Slope of Hot Springs, the farm and village at Myvatn's north end. Earthquakes and eruptions are not unexpected here. The region has been bubbling and exploding ever since the end of the last Ice Age about 8,000 years ago, and today it still looks as if you could put your ear to the ground and hear the liquid rock creeping and mumbling right there under the thin, broken crust.

The road, of cracked red lava gravel, is a narrow course between lake and lava fields. The lake is studded with little green islands and its water is yellowish green, startling in the middle of the arid volcanic landscape. A fecund growth of algae colors it, food for tens of thousands of ducks and other water and shore birds. From the thick grass along its shore rise clouds of midges thick as smoke. Across the road, on the dry lava side, there are none at all. The midges, which give the lake its name, can only exist in the ripe, moist, vegetative atmosphere of the lake. Though they do not sting they are terribly in the way, drifting into mouth, nose and eyes, crawling in the hair.

Here at Myvatn is Iceland's first experiment, started in 1969, with the forces that underlie her forbidding central plateau. Two resources join here, diatoms and hot springs. Diatoms, one-celled algae encased in beautiful transparent shells of varying geometric shapes, are members of the golden algae group, so-called because under the microscope they shine with a gold-brown light. They convert minerals and water, with the aid of the sun, into food, mainly in the form of oil. They thus become the lowest link in the food chain of the oceans. The oil of most marine animals comes from their primary or secondary dependence on diatoms. Not only are the little plants vital as food but they, together with the other

Volcanic forces are close to the surface at Myvatn, Iceland's only settlement in the barren central plateau. The contorted lava pillars of Kalfaströnd, products of a recent eruption, rise from the algae-filled water of the shallow lake.

plants of the ocean, of which diatoms are by far the most numerous, enable every living creature of the air to breathe. Photosynthesis, the process of using sunlight to convert the elements into living tissue, reverses the function of breathing. It utilizes carbon dioxide and discards oxygen as a waste product. Between flora and fauna the atmosphere of air and water is kept at a nice balance. Seventy percent of the atmosphere's oxygen comes from the plant plankton of the oceans. Accumulating residues of DDT and other man-made poisonous chemical compounds in the water are slowing down photosynthesis in the ocean's algae — gradually and surely reducing the amount of oxygen released into the air, and tipping that critical balance.

When the diatoms die, the shells in which they are encased drift to the bottom. The flinty silica, a constituent of sand, of which they are made, does not decay, and the hosts of skeletons form a light, soft, chalky layer underlying oceans, lake bottoms and peat beds. This substance, called diatomaceous earth, is used in silver polish and other polishing powders, for high-temperature insulation, and as a filter for sugar, fruit juices, beer and soft drinks. The great deposit at Myvatn goes back to the millennia before Iceland's modern vulcanism, when the Atlantic flowed over most of the eroded Thulean Province and the ocean bottom accumulated layers of the shells and skeletons of marine animals. The diatomite, remains of the ancient ocean life cycle, is being pumped out of the lake by the ton and drawn through a big pipe to a plant over in a valley of Namafjall, Mine Mountain, the yellow hill northeast of the lake, where hot water bubbles up to the surface in dozens of sulphurous springs. The mountain got its name because sulphur was mined here in the Middle Ages. It was used in gunpowder by Denmark in her wars against Sweden to such deadly purpose that in 1567 the Swedish king Eric XIV considered plans to conquer Iceland and turn Denmark's source against her. The plans fell through and so, eventually, did the mines, as sulphur extraction was no longer worth the expense involved. Now the sulphur springs are used only for their thermal qualities. Seven wells have been sunk in Namafjall's flanks, to a maximum depth of 4,000 feet. The steam is being used to dry the oozing masses of slime drawn out of the lake and separate out the diatomite. Some of it is diverted to turn the turbines of a pilot power plant generating three megawatts.

Even on a rainy day Namafjall looks as if the sun were on it. We round the yellow flank to find the source of the steam clouds, and we are at once cut off from the lake and the lava fields, in a craterlike depression with small hills around it. The hills are streaked with yellow and orange and pink-red. Steam oozes out of fissures all over the smooth hillsides. At the bottom of the depression is a mud pond, murky pale blue, with viscous bubbles in it. Everywhere is the smell of sulphur. It is warm back here, the warmth of mud and steam. It seems as if the earth has opened and we are standing, not on its crust but on a bridge over the simmering sludge of its interior. Our bridge, the road of lava gravel, seems frail. On either side of it the blue mud boils slowly.

A little beyond the mud crater, still in Namafjall's ring of steaming hills, is a startling green field of grass, the greenest we have ever seen. It must be that something in this Stygian place is kind to growth. But there is only that one curious field. All around it the pink and yellow slopes are empty of life.

From Namafjall steam is piped to the diatomaceous earth plant, and it shoots in two mountainous jets from ponds beside the factory. The road goes between the ponds, which are of two colors, one bright light green, the other saturated turquoise. Like the colors of Namafjall, these look not of the earth. Even manmade paint could not achieve their intensity. The modern concrete and glass plant is drab beside them.

It must be said that the plant is detrimental to the extraordinary diabolic scenery, as the dam at Burfell has destroyed the barbaric grace of an untamed river. A price, perhaps too high, is being paid for the future.

Namafjall is the only area of Myvatn that has so far been tapped for power, and diatomaceous earth the only product. But Myvatn is eminently livable. Not only are the surroundings striking but the climate is the dryest in Iceland, receiving only fifteen inches of rain annually. The town of Reykjahlid is growing. Besides a beautiful new hotel, one of Iceland's finest, where you eat, among other delicacies, brown trout caught the same day in the lake, it has a host of new little concrete houses in a variety of pale shades, for the factory workers. There are farms here too — there is no part of inhabited Iceland that does not have farms, no matter how far the stock has to wander for pasture. The farms near the lake are small, as pasture is limited to the immediate lake shore. But the farm of Reykjahlid, where I rode horseback, stretches from the lake east and south for over 2,000 square miles. Far up in the deadest-looking mountains, way into the desert of Odadahraun, range its cattle, horses and sheep, searching for the sparse gray grass and nibbling at the little desert flowers.

All around the shores of Myvatn continues the rococo display of volcanic activity. Southeast of Namafjall is Grjotagja, Stony Chasm, a ridge three miles long where the earth has cracked apart in a not-so-ancient earthquake. Along the top of the ridge is a fissure whose angular rock sides are exact parallels. From the rift comes steam and in the darkness below is the shine of water. Walking beside the ridge, which is ten or fifteen feet high, one comes on holes where the rock wall has fallen in. Most are too small to enter but through two of them a man can creep. One of these is for boys, the other for girls, and you can hear shrieking and splashing down there as the children float and play in the warm water, the sexes bathing separately in the nude. Myvatn has not yet become a health spa, but that too is in its possible future.

The water of Grjotagja, close to the surface and exposed to air, is not hot enough for industrial purposes. But the stony field in which the rift ridge stands is smudged with steam. It looks as if the earth were smoldering inside and the smoke creeping out through rock crevices. One would have to dig only a little deeper than the natural chasm to come on a layer of water as hot as those under the city of Reykjavik: natural heat and natural power to be piped away or used on the spot.

Even though the ground is almost visibly rippling from underneath, as if it should be too hot to touch, its earth is productive. A farmer has cleared a space and planted potatoes, protecting his little field from marauding sheep with a filigree fence of the porous lava rocks he dug out of it. Outside his wall, fragrant ground juniper crawls over the ground, its exposed roots, dry and tough,

331

seeking among the stones for the smallest crevices of earth. Bilberry grows low among the rocks, with pink bell-shaped flowers hanging heads down below the leathery red-green leaves.

Southward along the east shore of the lake the lava formations are older by some 2,000 years, but the lava still looks newly frozen in midstream. Birch trees have grown up among the burnt rocks, and moss and wildflowers soften their demented outlines. Dimmuborgir, Gloomy Castles, was a pool of lava that collapsed as it was cooling, leaving columns fifty to seventy-five feet high, eaten out at their bases, awry bridges, meandering caverns: a scene of total surrealism. In the lake across from Dimmuborgir is a similar stagy spectacle, the stacks of Kalfaströnd, Calf's Strand, a collection of deranged arches and pillars reflected blackly in the opaque greenish water.

Next to Dimmuborgir is a little volcano, 1,438 feet high, named Hverfjall, Cauldron. It is the third youngest volcano in Iceland, the newest being Kirkjufell, daughter of Helgafell on Heimaey, and the next that which brought Surtsey into being. Hverfjall burst out of the ground 2,500 years ago, fully formed, within, geologists conjecture, a period of one day. It is a perfect cone with steep stony sides on which nothing can grow for long because wind and rain wash the roots out of the loose gravel. Walking up it is the labor of Sisyphus: up three steps, back two, a half hour of serious toil. Going down is a lighthearted five-minute slide. At the top a narrow rim runs around an oval crater. In the middle of the crater there is another mountain, a tiny, exact replica of Hverfjall. It all looks new and fresh and idealized, an object lesson in volcano-making. It makes one reflect on Iceland's extreme youth. When Cro-Magnon artists painted the caves of southern France, up here in the North Atlantic 150 active volcanoes were just beginning to build an island out of a sea-washed waste of basalt. One day, while Judas Maccabeus was fighting to free the Jews from the rule of Syria, little Hverfjall sprang out of the earth. No one was here to see. The triumphs of man were being fully recorded in an old, already tired world, while unwitnessed miracles were creating a new one.

A few miles farther down the road, at the southern end of the lake, is Myvatn's other village, Skutustadir, Farm of the Rock

Cave, named for lava formations near it. This hamlet of ten or twelve houses is possessed of a dance hall, and here a concert was given one evening by a Danish choral group. They were all very young and very musical, and they sang with engaging fervor a difficult program from fifteenth-century madrigals to Bartók, to a full and attentive hall. The audience was well-dressed, enthusiastic and all Icelandic. None of the hotel tourists was there but us, and Myvatn has no summer colony. They must have been farmers' families and factory workers. Talking with some of the singers afterwards, we learned that the Myvatn audience was by far their biggest and happiest; it was also their only country stop. Perhaps, faced with the continuous reality of a raw and destructive nature, the people of Myvatn turn with greater need to the frail beauty of the abstract. Or possibly they came the far distances over desert and mountain mainly for the social life.

So far people are unimportant at Myvatn. They may be full of ideas and ambitions but these have not materialized to the extent that human presence is more than incidental. The lake belongs to birds. Its shallow, algae-filled waters and the luxuriant vegetation of its islands attract in the breeding season as many as 150,000 ducks, of seventeen species, from the commonest, the scaup, to the rare American harlequin, which breeds nowhere else in Europe. In spite of the prodigious numbers of eggs along the shores, on the islands and in the lava stacks the farmers of Myvatn respect the duck population, taking eggs but leaving four or five in every nest by unspoken law. Particular care is taken of the eiders, as their perpetuation assures the continuance of an important source of income, eiderdown. Eiders have always been precious to the Icelanders. "The eider-bird is . . . useful to the natives, who consider it a kind of treasure; and it is seldom heard that a prudent housekeeper shoots or kills any of them."[1] A farmer will adorn his rooftree with a painted wooden eider as an augur of good luck, and will entice the ducks with mirrors, streaming ribbons, and wind chimes to settle on his land.

The nest, a foot in diameter, is hollowed out of coarse grass, mud and gravel, usually on the edge of a stream leading to larger

[1] *Letters on Iceland*, Uno von Troil, 1780

water so the newborn ducklings can swim at once to relative safety. The female eider plucks down from her breast to line her nest and cover the eggs when she is gone. The dark down serves not only for warmth but for protection. From a few feet away the nest is invisible, as is the duck herself when she is brooding, her mottled earth-colored back level with the earth around her. The farmer takes down twice from the nest, the first time just before the eggs hatch, the second after the young have left. The mother can replace the down only once and the farmer, mindful of the value of his eider families, respects her. About one-sixth of a pound comes from each nest; several hundred nests yield a tidy heap. Most of the down is used for the voluptuous comforters, lighter, airier and warmer than wool, under which every Icelander from farmer to bank president sleeps.

While the female eider is brooding, her conspicuous mate, his wings sharp black, his head, back and breast gleaming white, stays away, the drakes gathering in large rafts in the middle of the lake. When the young have hatched the male is likely to join his brood, even though his flashy plumage may attract predators. Eiders can protect themselves. Even the attacking herring gull is put off by the hissing, quacking and wing-beating of the heavy-set, gooselike eider, while the young, which can dive shortly after they are hatched, have innate ability to dodge and hide. On some shores eiders and gulls nest side by side, the populations remaining constant. In Iceland even humans do not dismay the ducks, as they are never hunted or hurt. The female on her nest is docile when the human hand reaches in to test her eggs. One of the pleasantest aspects of eider life in Myvatn is the confiding manner in which a pair of eiders leads its young parallel to the human walker a few yards away on shore. The couple, clucking softly and constantly as they glide, have in tow a flotilla of twenty ducklings, just hatched and still downy. When the adults dive for food the whole troop follows in a series of little circular flips, up with the head, then down, the tail following the head motion. Coming up, the hatchlings shake themselves all over, water sparkling on their down. To some of the twenty the adult pair is probably aunt and uncle. An eider does not sit on twenty eggs though she has the capacity for more than that. As with all ducks the number she lays is in direct correlation to what she can find to eat, snails and other small marine animal life, and in less direct but just as strong relation to her predators. Her clutch is variable. Where the gull is slow to reproduce, laying three eggs at the most, once a year, the eider, laying two or three times, can go on and on if her first eggs are taken. There are always potentially more ducks than gulls, an example of the continuous oscillation by which the animal world keeps itself in balance between predator and victim. "No predator can afford to be too efficient."[2] Man is the only exception to this natural law, and it is to be wondered how long he can safely continue to deny it.

In the same family, *Anatidae*, as ducks are swans, the Icelandic representative of which is the tundra-breeding whooper, a straight-necked swan with a voice like a bugle. The swans come from heaven, it is told, from the holy *Urdar-brunnr*, Weirds' Spring, under the third root of the ash tree Yggdrasil, whose branches spread all over the world, where the gods sit in judgment and the Norns dispense the fates of men. "Two fowls are fed in Urdar-brunnr; they are called swans, and from them are descended all the birds of this species."[3] The birds of heaven have never been killed even when flocks of thousands gather in migration and destroy the meadows in their search for food. The only use made of them was that swan feathers, when shed, were collected for writing quills. A flock of fifteen frequents Myvatn, always coming in together in a soaring V-shaped flight high above the lake, the ringing trumpets of their voices filling the quiet air of the summer evening, before they descend on great still wings. The word swan comes from the Sanskrit *svanas*, "sound" or "sing," a word of the same derivation as the Latin *sonere*, and it was given originally to the whooper, the most musical of the swans.

The Myvatn area is kind to other families of birds besides the *Anatidae*. Among the shore birds the commonest are the northern phalaropes and the redshanks, both nesting, both very busy. The feeding of the redshank is an occupation that appears to be as feverish as the rest of the activities of this permanently apprehensive

[2] *Voles, Mice and Lemmings*, Charles Elton
[3] *The Prose Edda* of Snorri Sturleson

bird. The birds run jerkily from side to side, jabbing at the ground with anxious haste. Their food consists of worms, snails and small bivalves, invertebrates that have no way of escaping their predators in a hurry, and the birds' overwrought speed seems unnecessary. In fact the redshanks are efficiently finding as much to eat as possible in as short a time as possible, in order to get on with the business of the season, nesting, egg-laying and brooding. Feeding by night as well as by day, these sandpipers are known to consume, at times, 40,000 items of prey every twenty-four hours. Their nests, along the shores of the lake, are depressions hollowed in grass tussocks, exceedingly difficult to spot since the birds' obstreperous clamor leads the searcher all over the lot. We did come across one downy, mottled youngster not long out of the nest. It ran before us on skimpy pale-red legs that kept folding under it, and disappeared absolutely in a small heap of lava rocks brown-stippled like the young plumage. Awkward and neurotic as their behavior seems, redshanks, young and adult, manage their lives with finesse.

The phalaropes, whose reverse housekeeping is in progress along the muddy shores, are in contrast confidingly domestic. They go about their business with nonchalance, some pecking in the dusty road at our very feet, like chickens, others running in circles in the ripples at the lake's edge a few feet away, stirring up the mud. At an invisible signal they all suddenly take off, wheeling and twisting low over the water in unison, then return to their shore stations, tame as before.

On the map parallel dotted lines signifying "track" indicate the way from Myvatn into the volcanic heart of Iceland. It is not so much a track as a direction, marked by occasional yellow-painted cairns. It is used by geologists and hydrographers, each one defining the way a little more. But the wind that sweeps uninterrupted across the plains blows sand over the ruts, rain washes them out, rock slips and snow avalanches in the mountainous areas cover them. Every season the trail is blazed anew. Generally one follows the Jökulsa a Fjöllum, Glacier River of the Mountains (as distinguished from Jökulsa a Breidmerkursandi, the glacial torrent on the southern sands), south to the mass of the table mountain Herdubreid, Broad Shoulders. Skirting Herdubreid one leaves the

336

river, making a right angle turn east, toward the now visible twin mountains Dyngjufjöll, Dungeon Fells (probably named for its sheer walls rising spectacularly from the desert) and the live volcano Askja.

Driving this route is not at any time a matter of following a road; indeed there does not seem the slightest likelihood that a wheeled vehicle could ever have traversed it. The driver is on his own; he heads for the objectives of the two massifs, and for the rest he seeks the lesser pitfalls, intent only on keeping his machine from slipping off precipices, impaling itself on rocks or stalling in midstream. The wear and tear on the vehicle is extreme; it is rock-climbing in an automobile.

We go with Arni Ingolfsson, a skilled driver who looks younger than the seventeen-year-old bus in which he takes tourists around the desert. Our car is a rented Ford Bronco of somewhat more athletic vintage, and we persuade Arni to drive us in this rather than his bus. The Bronco is an uncomfortable car on the highway, its steering wheel loose and its springs hard. Driving it is continuous exercise. It is made only for the kind of work it has to do in the Odadahraun. The looseness of the steering mechanism provides leeway for maneuvers in which the front end of the car is frequently off axis with the back, and if the springs were softer they would soon give way on the crumpled rocks of the lava fields.

The journey begins nineteen miles east of Myvatn, where the Myvatns Oraefi, Myvatn Desert, stretches in every direction beyond sight, a gray plain that looks like the ocean with, instead of white-topped waves, long rollers of dry earth breaking cleanly and regularly. Out of this strange sea rises a single long rock like a crouching animal, Hrossaberg, Horse Rock. It is about half a mile long, flat-topped, and a hundred feet at its highest end. On a ledge near the top, under an overhang, three young gyrfalcons sit close together, leaning against each other. They are light gray and still downy, and they stare at us without moving. Above them, on a pinnacle of rock, perches an adult, pale gray streaked and mottled with darker gray. The bird calls repeatedly with thin squeals. Then it leaves its perch and begins circling us, and the inadequate cries are belied by the effortless strength of this largest and noblest of falcons. It does not dive but circles at about the level of its nestlings, behind the rock, out over the desert, back again, using thermals and hardly moving a wing, its head turning continually to watch us. Near the bottom of its cliff two wheatears, pretty black-masked thrushes, fly in and out of a rock crevice where the fool-hardy pair appear to be building a nest. Today the downy falcon chicks look helpless and cuddlesome, like toys, but tomorrow they will have wheatears for dinner.

Iceland, Arctic Norway and Greenland were the only places where this northern falcon bred that were accessible to medieval Europe. In the eleventh and twelfth centuries, when falconry was a favored sport of knights, royalty and even the higher clergy (priests who planned to hunt after mass had permission to wear hunting attire under their robes, and sometimes the falcon perched on the altar), Iceland's most valued export was the young of the gyrfalcon. The magnificent hunter was reserved for royalty, and every year a ship was sent from Denmark by order of the Danish king to collect the season's crop of nestlings, which the king then presented as gifts to other kings. The nests were legally robbed only by royal agents; other poachers were severely punished. Only wild birds were used. Gyrfalcons were never raised in captivity as caged birds could not develop the hunting skill of their wild brethren. The gyrfalcon became so closely identified with Iceland that in 1921 the Order of the Icelandic Falcon was created, the nation's only decoration. It is a silver falcon on a field of blue, and is conferred on Icelanders, both men and women, and on a few foreigners, as a mark of honor.

As a hunter the gyrfalcon is unsurpassed. In the family *Falconidae*, predatory bird life has reached its highest development, and the gyrfalcon, nearly two feet long, with a four-foot wing-spread, has a tenacity in chase and a crashing power in its stoop that make it even deadlier than the swift peregrine. It catches its prey on the wing and carries it in strong talons to the nest, where it kills it with a stab of the notched beak. Gyrfalcons are useful predators in farm areas, preying heavily on rodents. In the Oda-dahraun, which is not rich in animal life, they feed on the birds of heath and desert, mostly golden plovers and ptarmigan. The wheatears rashly nesting below the falcons' ledge will make a

338

diminutive meal for a bird that can catch a kittiwake in flight and tear it into strips for its hungry nestlings.

We watch the circling falcon for only a few minutes, then walk away to allow it to return to its perch. There is a severe penalty in Iceland for photographing on their nests gyrfalcons, white-tailed eagles and dovekies, three disappearing species, as the birds are likely to be disturbed to the extent of deserting eggs or young. This pair has found a spot so far off the usual paths of human traffic that it might have been considered safe from obtrusive curiosity were it not for the open secret of its lonely nest, conveyed by word of mouth from one ornithologist to another. There are car tracks and footprints all around the base of the birds' cliff, and the parent's nervousness gives evidence of frequent invasion. It does not stay on its perch twenty seconds, but is off again, beating toward us on slow wings, calling querulously, until we have reached our car, half a mile distant.

All around Hrossaberg stretches the desert, sere and flat and inhospitable to life. But it has life, the small flowering vegetation that decorates Iceland, growing on windy beaches and arid mountainsides where one would think nothing could grow, creeping over sand and rock, thrusting roots wide and deep into sliding earth, the leaves needlelike, rolled or furry for protection, the stems intertwined in defensive mats to hold moisture and repel cold. Silverweed, mountain chickweed and moss campion brighten the Odadahraun with their small radiant blooms. *Thymus serpyllum*, wild thyme, spreads a web of prostrate stems with small-leaved branches standing a few inches erect, each with a cluster of purple flowerets at its tip. *Silene cucubalis*, a diminute bladder campion, has furry leaves and delicate notched white blossoms. *Armeria maritima*, sea pink or thrift, raises dark pink cloverlike heads on softly hairy stalks from clumps of grasslike leaves. The roots of the sea pink grow very long. One I measured was eighteen inches, tough and woody. Growing among rocks and pebbles where the soil is thin, its roots, unable to go deep, must spread laterally.

These hardy plants, together with the barrens trees, creeping willows and dwarf juniper, support a small population of birds.

Rock ptarmigan, plump, chickenlike birds, scratch nest hollows in the gravelly earth and eat the buds, leaves, seeds, twigs, even the roots of the desert vegetation. When startled they rise with a noisy flurry of wings and shoot off in a straight line only a few feet above the ground, wings beating so rapidly they are nearly invisible. Against the somber desert the male is shockingly conspicuous, body bright cinnamon-colored, wings white. His mate, folding her white wings against her cinder-gray body, hides against the dun earth when the shadow of the gyrfalcon falls on her, and the predator goes for her showy mate instead. Lacking camouflage, he will sometimes attack. If his threatened mate calls in her grating croak he will hurl himself at the intruder in a startling onslaught of wings and claws, confounding even a gyrfalcon with hungry nestlings.

The golden plover is the most beautiful bird of the desert, its underparts velvet black all the way up the throat and cheeks, a curving white line delineating the change to the intricate gold and black pattern of its back (its Latin name, *apricaria*, means sun-touched). When it returns from its winter home in North Africa and its plaintive two-note call again rings sweetly over the early-blooming plains, the Icelanders say that summer has come back. Boldly the plovers hollow minimal nests in the open on the tops of ridges, where the female lays four large eggs. Though uncovered they are hard to find. Brown, spotted unevenly with darker brown, they disappear among the surrounding pebbles. The male promenades on the surrounding ridges, flying at intruders, while the female lures the enemy away with a creeping run, stopping every few yards to flatten herself on the ground, spread her wings wide and beat them slowly. She accompanies this with an incessant thin crying, looking up at the enemy in a piteously helpless manner. This appealing display gets her nowhere with the gyrfalcon but it presumably works with the occasional Arctic foxes of the Odadahraun, her only other enemy there.

The world of the Odadahraun is too harsh for human habitation. It has always repelled Icelanders, and since the earliest times it has been the subject of curious legends. In its hidden valleys, they tell, lives an older people, the Utilegumenn, Outlaws (from which the name Odadhraun is derived), an evil race, half man and half giant, which inhabited the country when the first settlers came. In other countries similar folktales of abnormally large or small people have been found to be based on the actual existence of primitive races, feared, scorned and misunderstood by the new-comers to the extent that their physical features and powers became grossly distorted. But Iceland had no indigenous people. No one preceded the émigrés from Norway but the gentle Irish monks, whose existence was documented by the settlers and around whom no such legends arose. It is impossible to penetrate the source of these strange stories. They crop up in the sagas, notably in the one that is most closely identified with the interior deserts, *The Saga of Grettir the Strong*, but no hint is ever given of who these sinister and supernatural beings might have been.

In recorded history there have been only two sojourns in the Odadahraun. The first was that of the aforementioned Grettir, a flawed hero of great courage and dangerous temper who, after a run of extraordinarily ill luck, was declared an outlaw. He learned young to exercise his strength and vent his bad temper by van-quishing berserkers, trolls and ghosts, but a ghost was his undoing. Glam the shepherd (his name means "ghost"), a truculent thrall with "large gray eyes and wolf-gray hair," was killed by a devil because he broke the fast on Christmas Eve. His body, "black as Hel and swollen to the size of an ox," could not be dragged to the church and his unquiet spirit haunted the farm where he had worked. He trampled over the roofs at night, breaking them, and of the people who saw him "some were struck senseless and some lost their wits."[4] No one dared to go out at night, and horses and dogs were killed when they went near the farm. The following Christmas Eve all the cows in the cowshed gored each other dur-ing the night, and the new shepherd was found with "his neck broken and every bone in his body torn from its place." Grettir, unafraid, offered to extinguish the wicked spirit. In the moonlight he grappled with Glam, who was as tall as the roof, with "horri-ble rolling eyes." After a long and terrible battle Grettir overcame his opponent and struck off his head; then they "burned Glam to cold cinders, bound the ashes in a skin and buried them . . . far

[4] *Grettir's Saga*

away from the haunts of man or beast." The malignant spirit, before his vanquishment, laid a curse on Grettir: ". . . your deeds shall turn to evil and your guardian-spirit shall forsake you. You will be outlawed and your lot shall be to dwell ever alone. And this I lay upon you, that these eyes of mine shall be ever before your vision." From that day Grettir's luck turned, his bad temper gained the ascendancy and at last he was banished for murder, to spend the rest of his life a lonely outlaw. On account of his violent nature people were afraid to help him; in turn he could not live long alone as Glam's curse had made him afraid of the dark. He occasionally took in as companion another outlaw whom he supported by his strength and skill at hunting and stealing. These partnerships did not last because the price on his head, nine marks of silver, more than any other outlaw had ever had, was too tempting. His life in the desert and around its edges was a twenty-year ordeal during which this Icelandic Robin Hood helped defenseless farmers as well as robbing, fighting and killing when the need arose. During one of his years in the desert he lived in a valley where ruled Thorir, a giant of the old-time race, the feared desert indigenes. Thither Grettir had "turned his steps . . . taking with him a kettle and fuel," to find a "long and narrow valley in the glacier shut in on every side by the ice which overhung it . . . Hot springs . . . kept the ice from closing in above the valley." There were sheep there, kept by Thorir, "under whose protection he remained." As Grettir was undaunted by ghosts, neither did a giant dismay him. He was safe there; no man dared attack him while he was the ward of the genius of the ice-bound valley. But the curse of Glam's ghastly eyes lay on him and he could not stay there. Leaving the lonesome security of the wilderness he took refuge on an island where he was beset by his enemies and killed at last through a woman's witchcraft; but not before, nearly dead, "his thigh mortified up to the rectum"[5] from a poisoned wound, he had run his sword through several of his attackers.

This story of Iceland's most famous outlaw, a biting tale of the Viking hero gone bad, is an extraordinary character study. Grettir's unhappy manhood is foretold in his lonely youth, when

[5] Ibid.

his sharp tongue and cruel tricks alienated even his father. His later fantastic, supernatural adventures, cogently related in the usual cool, detailed, objective saga style, have the effect of symbolizing the man's essential loneliness and wildness. That he is basically good is revealed in his help to farmers in distress and his tolerance of the cowardly murderers who are sent to kill him. And on his death day he is at last brought back into the human fold as his brother joins him, having refused to betray him, to share his fate. Grettir does not die, as he has lived, in haunted isolation.

The second inhabitation of the Odadahraun was by American astronauts before the first moon landing, for the purpose of acclimatizing themselves to moonlike surroundings. Iceland's central desert, with its lifeless mountains, volcanic craters and ragged fields of lava, was considered to be the place on earth most closely approximating lunar terrain. There is even a crater there called Ludent because of the similarity of its formation to moon craters, leading geologists to theorize that the latter were volcanically caused rather than, as early scientists had surmised, created by meteoric bombardment. For several months the Americans tested their equipment in this rough and lonely territory. Presumably in the course of training they also tested their states of mind. But the condition of modern man in the wilderness, surrounded by the sophisticated accoutrements of lunar survival, hardly bears comparison with the problems of Grettir the Strong, haunted, hungry and doomed, with no companion but the rare Arctic fox and the great gray shadow of the gyrfalcon.

Leaving Hrossaberg we meet the Jökulsa, a lazy, shallow river dark with volcanic dust. Its flow is spread so wide over the flat land that bits of it get lost from the main stream, wander off to distend into marshes and ponds, return in a series of scattered trickles. The country is made of lava bubbles here, and Arni twists and turns to avoid the crumbled edges where they have collapsed. Sometimes we go between them, the Bronco on a sharp sideways slant, sometimes we go right over the tops, the car swaying like a boat in a storm. It is like riding over frozen billows. We cannot see the end of them. The horizon seems to have withdrawn into a measureless distance. Though it is cloudy one has to keep dark

343

glasses on against the pervasive glare of the enormous sky. It is a day of rain showers and flashes of sunlight, and the colors are the infinite gradations of sharp black-and-white photography. On the horizon are white piles of cumulus clouds, and above them in layers varying from light to sooty gray the straight lines of the rain-bringers, nimbostratus and altostratus. The land echoes the sky, black rocks, pale sand, steel water in clear contour even out to the distant dark table mountains that now appear on the southern horizon. The quietness is extraordinary though a strong wind blows. Little plumes of sand fly up and behind us our tracks are quickly obliterated. On level ground we can feel the car shake, and outside of it we are nearly blown down. But, having nothing to beat against, the wind whips across the empty land in silence.

To stay beside the Jökulsa we have to cross its tributaries, wide slow streams with marshes on their shores. Sometimes the marshes are quicksand, sometimes they are oases startlingly green in the monochromic landscape. Out of bright wet moss grows *Eriophorum vaginatum*, swamp cotton, a slender sedge whose flower heads, gone to seed, resemble cotton balls. Each downy wisp carries a seed which will float on the wind to a new home. Here in the desert they will have to fly many miles. In former years farmers' wives twisted the cotton into wicks for the shallow whale oil lamps that were Iceland's only indoor lighting. Alongside the delicate swamp cotton, *Heracleum sphondylium*, cow parsnip, is obese. It is a tall, rank-smelling weed with segmented leaves as much as a foot across, two-inch-thick stems, sheaths at the bases of the branches swollen into dropsical bulbs, shaggy umbels of pink-white blossoms. In spite of its ugly smell (which is attractive to the insects that pollinate it) cow parsnip is not poisonous. But it is closely related and somewhat similar to the deadly *Conium maculatum*, poison hemlock. In its austere surroundings it is spectacularly vulgar. Wheatears and pipits flit among its gross foliage and an occasional snow bunting sings, perched on a flower head.

Crossing the streams is a slow and careful process but it is not dangerous. Arni knows where the safe fords are. The dry washes, however, are very bad. Our technique, learned in the deserts of the United States Southwest, would have been to get a start at the top and race through to avoid bogging down. Here we would have found our front wheels stuck between two rocks and the car slewed around in a pretzel. Arni stops, shifts into the lowest of the six gears and creeps down into them. Even at a walking pace the Bronco skids; the hillocks of soft sand often conceal pointed rocks and between them the sand is up to the hubs.

We come to a field of ropy lava, an old volcanic stream from long-extinct Herdubreid, half a mile wide and two or three miles long. It is beautiful: stone serpents coil in and out of each other in endless convolution and patterned cracks break the sinuous streams. One can see it flowing hot over the plain, cooling and cracking as it flows. A wheeled vehicle is grotesquely out of place on its mounds and fissures, but there is no choice. The lava stream is about thirty feet above the level of the river which, at the bottom of the precipice, sprawls widely over quicksand. We climb, traverse, descend the tortuous stone coils, all in low gear, sometimes stopping and backing down, to essay a rock again from a better angle. For three quarters of an hour the Bronco is never on a level, until at last the boundary is reached. There both lava stream and quicksand give way to a long gray-green valley of grass and gravel through which the river, bordered with flowers, meanders in gracious curves. The scene is anomalous. There is not a lava rock in sight. In the bucolic meadow sheep graze, and on the side of a low hill is a human habitation, a stone hut with a turf roof. No one lives here, nor ever did. It is only about eight feet square and four feet high, and was intended as a refuge when the farmer rode out to collect his sheep. The trip took more than a day and he slept here. No one uses it now; the farmer is mechanized and herds his sheep by Land Rover.

At the end of the sheep meadow the rocks begin again, a confusion of torn boulders, the end of another of Herdubreid's lava streams. Sound is with us after the windy silence of the plains, the roar of water where the sleepy river suddenly collects its scattered streams and flings itself over the rocks in a series of splashing cascades. The soft lava rock around the falls is water-carved into near human shapes. One cannot identify limbs or torsos but the curved, generous and serene proportions are those of classical sculpture. It is like a dream of antiquity; no detail is specific but the spirit is archetypal.

345

We climb a hill of sand from the top of which the Odadah-raun is laid out before us. It looks deceptively flat and all gray. Mountains rise singly in the near and far distance, some snow-capped, and farthest away is a tremendous range that spreads whitely over the southern horizon, the peaked heights of Vatnajö-kull. Nearest is the Herdubreid massif, a long lumpy ridge with the heavy 5,520-foot mass of Herdubreid commanding its smaller peaks like a goose with her goslings.

Herdubreid is a volcano which was formed during the Pleisto-cene epoch when all of Iceland was covered by glacier. Its remarkably geometric shape, a perfect cone with its top missing, comes from the same kind of elemental battle that produced Surt-sey. Where Surtsey was born of the conflict between fire and water, the dominant force in Herdubreid's formation was ice. Magma flowed from a volcanic fissure below the ice. The pressure of the surrounding element kept it from erupting above the surface and it cooled into pillow lava. As more molten rock came out of the earth, the glacier melted from underneath and the pile of pillow lava rose into an inverted ice dome full of water, like clay formed into shape in a mold. At last the thinning ice gave way at the top, the volcanic gases, having accumulated under the tremendous pressure, exploded violently, and the magma burst out of the ice into the open air. The result of sudden explosion and rapid cooling is not lava but tephra, volcanic ash. The fountains of tephra settled around the vent, piling on top of the dome of pillow lava to form a high circular collar, the beginning of the mountain. But the bat-tle was not over. If the eruption had stopped there the tephra would have been scattered by wind and weather over the ice before it had time for the lengthy process of hardening into palagonite tuff, and the new mountain would have remained a subglacial dome. This time the eruption continued. The tephra collar insulated the vent against the ice, and the fresh magma, able to cool more slowly, erupted in the form of lava, which spilled around the collar in a black necklace. The hardened lava sealed the mountain's form and the battle was won; a permanent, perfect table mountain stood above the ice.

The progress of these events is clear on Herdubreid. The gradual incline of pillow lava at the bottom gives way to the steep sides of the collar of congealed tephra, glassy palagonite tuff, which in turn is capped by a ring of black cliffs, the final lava flows. The mountain is streaked with black where lava has run down to stream in rough rivers across the plains, and that is what we have been driving over. New snow touches the crenellated rocks of the upper rim and a big gray cloud rests in the immense crater. It is a forbidding mountain, monotoned like the desert around it, geometric, lifeless and very old.

In its shadow is one of two refuge huts for campers, the other being at the foot of Askja, wooden A-frame buildings that can sleep twenty-four. This one is named Herdubreidarlindur, Herdubreid Spring, and in front of it is one of those oases which are the more touching for existing in such desolate surroundings. A brook murmurs over rocks, to spill its minor waterfall into a clear pool edged with swamp cotton and cow parsnip. Here we eat lunch, the cold hunched mass of Herdubreid above us, the song of a snow bunting floating up from the sedges below.

Not far from the refuge, hidden around a curve of the mountain, the brook widens into a pond called Swan Lake and there are appropriately two swans and three ash-colored cygnets. They are not part of the flock that swings in over Myvatn every afternoon, because swans become solitary and silent at breeding time, each pair seeking nesting places on lonely bogs, moors or islets. There the pair shares the labor of brooding and raising the young. While the cygnets are growing their flight feathers, the adults are losing theirs. During the dangerous time, when the whole family is flightless, they are safer in their secluded retreats, where the adults can hide or run and the young melt into the surroundings, than they would be, huge and obvious, on populous Myvatn. After the molt, in August, the swan families come together again and the proud voices are raised once more as they form their long wavering chevrons for the flight south to the slightly warmer climate of continental Europe.

The track continues south alongside Herdubreidartögl, Herdubreid's Horsetails, a series of escarpments six miles long, product of a postglacial fissure eruption. At its southern end we make a right angle turn, leaving the river at last, to head straight through a long valley at the end of which is the vast spread of the Dyngjufjöll-

Askja massif. The valley, ringed with smaller volcanic peaks, is composed entirely of pumice; when you run it feels as if you were running over bottle corks. A piece thrown in the air does not fall at once but blows away. Scattered over the tan-colored pumice are dark lava bombs that look like deformed tombstones and seem, as one nears them, to have been burned all the way through, so broken and porous are they. The country is without life. No plant can root for long in the ever-shifting pumice, and the fresh lava streams have not yet collected the yellowish tufts of *Rhacomitrium lanuginosum*, the moss which is the first plant to colonize volcanic deserts. The colors are grays and browns, bitter-chocolate brown of the newest lava, khaki-colored pumice, dark gray cliffs of Askja's nearest peak, pale gray of last winter's snow above them. The sky reflects the somber shades: strings of dark mist fly across a light gray cloud cover.

Dyngjufjöll and Askja are not single mountains but a great complex of peaks and precipices, products of titanic postglacial volcanic upheavals, in a rough circle around a central *caldera* of more than twenty square miles. The Dyngjufjöll group lies on the northern side of the *caldera* and Askja surrounds the rest. A *caldera* is the center of a collapsed volcano. Repeated lava eruptions form a cone volcano; later a particularly violent one blows out the top of the cone, leaving a wide depression, the *caldera*, surrounded by a ring of hills. Though this combination of explosion and dissolution generally signifies the extinction of a volcano, molten rock is still seething beneath Askja's arc of peaks. Every few years an eruption adds a new crater to the chain surrounding the sunken basin. The most recent one was in 1961, a winter outpouring of black basalt lava over the snow-covered plains. Before that, in 1875, a huge explosive eruption (explosive means tephra; effusive means lava) spread ash as far east as Leningrad, 1,500 miles away. All the arable country to the north and east of the Odadahraun was scorched and poisoned by deep deposits of ash.

Askja's 1961 eruption broke a new hole in the rim of the *caldera*, sending a viscous stream ten feet thick and about five-hundred yards wide between two foothills down into the valley of pumice. The block lava, exactly resembling a stream of monstrous cinders, is piled neatly, its edges straight, and it stops short

348

without tapering off at all. Grettir's giant might have been shoveling ashes out of a furnace, careful not to scatter them. We parallel the flow, following it straight into the middle of the mountain. The road rounds the corner of a cliff and comes to a sudden end in a snowfield. The rest of our journey has to be on foot. We stand for a minute to get used to the enormous loneliness. Askja's foothills enclose us; the valley behind has disappeared and we are ringed with rock and snow. Before us the mountain's great flanks rise unevenly, without visible end, into the clouded sky. It is not quiet. Waterfalls crash onto the disheveled lava, streams growl under the snow. In spite of the live hot earth at her roots Askja is very cold. Wind, funneled between the towers of ancient eruptions, tears over the snow, whipping wet fog into our faces. The snowfield rises steeply between two old lava flows to the floor of the *caldera*, a long oval bowl full of snow, tipped gently upward to its far end, where a rock buttress stops it off. Surrounding the basin, which is about five miles long and four wide, are hills, the products of old and new eruptions, the older ones snow-covered mounds, the late ones black pinnacles. We go up the first, that of the 1961 eruption. Its crater is cold and empty now but the several lava streams spilling over its rim are sharply red and black, as if they were still hot. About a mile up the *caldera* is the crater of 1875. It is still live: far down slab-sided walls stained pink and yellow and green is a milk-colored pool with steam rising from it, strongly sulphurous. The water quivers, whether touched by the wind reaching even into that deep hole or agitated by a force underneath one cannot tell.

Up to this point we have walked in deep spring snow, soft and clinging, crusted with a thin frozen layer which sometimes supports the feet, sometimes gives way. On the last third of the *caldera*, which ascends in a bolder slant, we note with relief that the snow has washed off under rain, wind and sun, and the ground shows through in patches. But the cleared earth is far worse than the snow. It is thick mud that sucks our feet in to the ankles and, when we have pulled loose, closes glutinously over our footprints.

The final climb is the rock buttress at the head of the *caldera*, a lava-strewn peak that is part of the rim of the mountain's biggest remaining crater, a prehistoric lake, Öskjuvatn, Lake of Askja. The lake, roughly a mile and a half in diameter, is a great eye sunk deep in its surrounding rock girdle, its ice shining, its free water darkly rippled. Around it the edges of the rim rise and fall and rise again to Askja's tallest point, 4,956 feet, a checkered black and white hill falling off slowly at first, precipitately at its base to the water 1,800 feet below.

We stand on the lip of this ancient blowhole, cold as eternity, lifeless as the moon, and wonder at what time, an hour from now, next year or next millennium, the earth will breathe again. Below us is the hot spot, the heart of the plume out of which our ever-living planet is pushing a mountain range, broadening the ocean, pulling back into itself the old, tired, familiar boundaries of our world — like Iceland's human history, creative and destructive at the same time.

For, paralleling her geological, her mortal chronicle follows an unevenly rising line. From the formation of her audacious farmers' republic, as new to the world as Surtsey, to her self-destruction through exaggeration of her proud individualism; from the long sad years of quiescence to the present uplift of spiritual and physical vitality, Iceland's history has had a turbulent gallantry that could have come out of one of the family sagas. Everything about her speaks of a young country with a young people.

In Iceland, so new under the stars, lives a simplicity and a hope that echo the freshness of her creation.

Chronology

Lutheran Reformation and death of Jon Arason, last Catholic bishop of Iceland	1550
Establishment of commercial monopoly by Danish royal house	1602
Eruption of Laki and Haze Famine	1783–1787
Lifting of Danish monopoly	1787
Jon Sigurdsson, father of Iceland's liberation	1811–1879
Reinstitution of the *Althing* as a consultative assembly	1843
Restoration of freedom of trade	1854
Constitution and control of finances granted by Denmark	1874
Home Rule for Iceland	1904
Establishment of the University of Iceland	1911
Iceland gains sovereignty though still in union with Denmark	1918
Military occupation of Iceland by the British	1940
United States forces take over defense of Iceland	1941
Reestablishment of Iceland as an independent republic	1944
Iceland joins NATO	1949
Birth of Surtsey	1963
Beginning of return of Icelandic manuscripts from Copenhagen	1971
Extension of fishing limit to fifty miles	1972
Volcanic eruption on Heimaey	1973
Celebration of 1100th anniversary of the first settlement	1974
Extension of fishing limit to two hundred miles	1975

Index

As Icelanders rarely have family names, both men and woman using their father's given name as their second name, it is the common usage to list people alphabetically by first names. The index follows this usage except in the few cases where a family name or *nom de plume* exists.